THE QUEEN

THE QUEEN

70 CHAPTERS IN THE LIFE OF ELIZABETH II

IAN LLOYD

DEDICATION

To Stephanie Tattersall, Anthony, William, Alex,
Oliver and Michelle with much love.

First published 2022

The History Press
97 St George's Place, Cheltenham,
Gloucestershire, GL50 3QB
www.thehistorypress.co.uk

British Library Cataloguing in Publication Data.
A catalogue record for this book is available from the British Library.

ISBN 978 0 7509 9856 7

Typesetting and origination by The History Press
Printed and bound in Great Britain by TJ Books Limited, Padstow, Cornwall.

CONTENTS

FOREWORD

Forty years into the longest reign in British history; the Queen reflected, 'I find that's one of the sad things – that people don't take on jobs for life'. Hers has been more than a job. It has been a true vocation in which she has been sustained by her belief in duty, the support of the Duke of Edinburgh and latterly by three generations of her family, and above all by her religious faith.

She became head of state six and a half years after the end of the Second World War and at the age of only 25, the same age as the first Elizabeth. The prime minister at the time, Winston Churchill, had fought at the Battle of Omdurman in 1898. Harry S. Truman was President of the United States, Chiang Kai-shek ruled China and Joseph Stalin still governed the Soviet Union. All four men were born before Elizabeth's parents.

In 2007, she became the longest-lived monarch in British history, as well as the first to celebrate a diamond wedding anniversary. Eight years later, in September 2015, she surpassed Queen Victoria's record to become the longest-reigning British monarch, and with the retirement of Robert Mugabe in November 2017, Elizabeth succeeded him as the oldest serving head of state. Should she live to be 98 years and 36 days, she will, on 26 May 2024, break an even more impressive record held until then by Louis XIV of France and become the longest-reigning monarch of any sovereign state.

Like the late Duke of Edinburgh, she has never been impressed by achieving landmark anniversaries and had to be cajoled into celebrating her 80th and 90th birthdays with massive public walkabouts. The most famous woman in the world has happily remained one of its most private ones, resolutely inscrutable, never giving an interview or writing a memoir. She has poured her thoughts into a journal she has kept daily since being a child, although she conceded, 'It's not really a diary like Queen Victoria's' and her entries may possibly offer more facts than emotion.

Those who know the Queen best – her friends and family – have always earned her trust by remaining frustratingly discreet. I am grateful to one or two members of the inner circle who have allowed me to interview them over the years – principally, the late Mrs Margaret Rhodes, her cousin and close confidante, whose dry sense of humour and willingness to share some of her memories of growing up with the woman she only ever knew as 'Lilibet' was a delight on several occasions. I would also like to thank Prince Philip's cousin Lady Pamela Hicks for allowing me to interview her (on and off the record) on six occasions since 2004. She too has been unsparing in her co-operation as well as being an entertaining raconteur.

I am also thankful to the following people for help and advice: Ivon Asquith, Gerald Bodmer, Pierre Brassard (for recalling his hoax call to Her Majesty), Margaret Clancy, Gilbert Clayton (the Queen Mother's great-nephew, for answering questions on the Bowes-Lyon family), James Crawford-Smith (for sharing his detailed knowledge of royal fashion), Gordon Findlay, Nigel Fulton, Genevieve James, Joe Little (managing editor of *Majesty Magazine*), Paul Mailer, Darren Royston and Sam Taylor.

This book is not a straightforward biography of the Queen but aims to highlight various themes, from her sense of humour to her religious faith. It could not have been written without the invaluable help of published sources from approved biographers. Robert Lacey remains the doyen of royal biographers, whose 1977 *Majesty* still stands the test of time as the acclaimed work on the first twenty-five years of her reign. Ben Pimlott's *The Queen: Elizabeth II and the Monarchy* is as near to a definitive history of the monarch's life as we have. Sally Bedell Smith's *Elizabeth, The Queen* is another detailed and well-researched account of Elizabeth's life. Finally, Gyles Brandreth's *Elizabeth and Philip* gives a valuable insight into the married life of the Queen and Duke. A full list of other sources consulted is available in the bibliography.

Lastly, I am indebted to Simon Wright, commissioning editor at the History Press, for agreeing to publish the book and for stretching the agreed deadline way beyond its elastic limit.

Ian Lloyd,
Oxford,
January 2022

1

MAYFAIR BABY

Elizabeth Alexandra Mary Windsor arrived in this world at 2.40 a.m. on Wednesday, 21 April 1926. She had been expected at the end of the month and her mother, the Duchess of York, was out and about enjoying the first night of a West End play the previous week. It had been decided the baby should be induced and, as the difficult labour progressed, the doctors in attendance – Sir Henry Simson, Dr Walter Jagger and Sir George Blacker – decided a caesarean section would be advisable. In the first bulletin released after the birth, the Palace coyly referred to the operation: 'a certain line of treatment was successfully adopted.'

Also present, in an adjacent room, was the Home Secretary, Sir William Joynson-Hicks. The convention of having a senior minister present to witness the birth was established after the birth of James Stuart in the summer of 1688. When Mary of Modena, queen to the unpopular James II, gave birth to this Roman Catholic heir, pamphleteers declared the baby to be an imposter, smuggled into the queen's bedchamber in a warming pan. The practice was abandoned in 1948 prior to the birth of Prince Charles.

In retrospect, it seems a peculiarly British practice for the Home Secretary of the day to stay up until the middle of the night for such arcane reasons. After all, with the escalating dispute between the coalmine owners who wanted to reduce their employees' wages and the General Council of the Trades Union Congress (TUC) who supported the miners, Joynson-Hicks and his colleagues had their hands full. Two weeks after

Marriage to Lady Elizabeth Bowes-Lyon gave the shy and insecure Prince Albert, Duke of York, the security he craved. The birth of their daughter Elizabeth was the icing on the cake. 'We always wanted a child to make our happiness complete,' he wrote to his mother, '& now that it has happened it seems so wonderful & strange.'
(© Classic Image/Alamy)

the Princess's birth, the TUC called a general strike and some 1.5 million workers came out in support of the miners.

Born third in line to the throne, Elizabeth's arrival was global news. The *Dundee Courier* subheading 'World-Wide Chorus of Congratulation' was typical of the media coverage. The *Daily Sketch* pointed out presciently, 'A possible Queen of England was born yesterday.' It went on to explain that the last Queen regnant, Victoria, was the daughter of the King's fourth son, so 'it cannot be forgotten that our new Princess is a possible Queen-Empress'.

Elizabeth II is the only British monarch to have been born in a private house – and one with a door number to boot. No. 17 Bruton Street, London was no ordinary house, but a substantial mansion leased by her grandfather, the 14th Earl of Strathmore, from late 1921 until the end of the decade. It has had an eventful history as the residence of several earls, an occasional base for charities and latterly as the site of various businesses.

In 1859 Ivo Bligh, later the 8th Earl of Darnley, was born at the house. He is best remembered as the captain of the victorious English cricket eleven on the 1882–83 tour of Australia. A group of women in Melbourne presented him with a small terracotta urn reputedly containing the ashes of a bail, symbolising 'the ashes of English cricket' following the team's defeat by the Aussies at the Oval earlier in 1882. The cricket-mad aristocrat gave the ashes to the Marylebone Cricket Club, where it remains in its museum at Lord's. Bligh and his teammates are referenced in a poem etched on to the urn:

When Ivo goes back with the urn, the urn;
Studds, Steel, Read and Tylecote return, return;

From the 1860s, No. 17 Bruton Street was the London residence of Hallyburton Campbell, the 3rd Baron Stratheden of Cupar and Campbell of St Andrews. Following his death in 1918, it was the temporary address for the Liberty League, a liberal political organisation whose founder members included the writers Rudyard Kipling and H. Rider Haggard. The aim of the short-lived league was to combat the threat of Bolshevism spreading from revolutionary Russia and instead to promote classical liberal ideas throughout Britain and its empire.

No. 17 was the focus of attention on 23 April 1923 when Lady Elizabeth Bowes Lyon left here with her father for her wedding to Prince Albert, Duke of York, at Westminster Abbey. Three years later, still searching for a permanent London home, Elizabeth and 'Bertie' moved back to the Strathmores' residence on 6 April 1926 to await the birth of their baby, which arrived at 2.40 a.m. on the 21st. Huge crowds gathered in Bruton Street throughout the day as various visitors, including the King and Queen and their daughter Princess Mary, came and went.

After the Strathmores left, the lease was taken by the Canadian Pacific Railway Company (CPR). The house was transformed into offices, though the room Elizabeth was born in was kept intact and, according to the CPR, would be open to reasonable public access.

A new eight-floor office building called Berkeley Square House, which included No. 17, was completed on the site in 1939 and leased to the UK Government. We next hear of it in 1944 when it was bought for £1.25 million by Queen Anne's Bounty, which administered the fund for helping poor clergymen.

In the 1970s, No. 17 Bruton Street was the offices for the finance company Lombard North Central Ltd, a subsidiary of National Westminster Bank. Today it is the home of Hakkasan, a Cantonese restaurant. The venue boasts two plaques marking the birthplace of Elizabeth II, one unveiled in the Silver Jubilee year of 1977 and the other to mark the Diamond Jubilee in 2012. The Queen is unlikely to be impressed with these tributes, since in 1953 she gave her approval for a similar plaque to be added to Berkeley Square House but asked that it should be removed following her coronation on 2 June of that year. The reason is unclear but perhaps she felt it was *lesè-majesté* to be permanently associated with an office block.

2

'MY BELOVED PAPA'

'You can do a lot if you are trained and I hope I have been,' declared the Queen, forty years into her reign. Her training was largely at the hands of her father, Prince Albert, Duke of York, who acceded to the throne as George VI following his brother's abdication, and had no experience in the duties of kingship.

In preparing Elizabeth for her eventual destiny, he also forged a close bond with his eldest daughter. She, in return, idolised her father, admiring what she called his 'steadfastness'. 'She and the King were very close,' said Lady Pamela Hicks, *née* Mountbatten, who was with Elizabeth when she became Queen in 1952. 'They were "we four" with Queen Elizabeth (later the Queen Mother) and Princess Margaret.'

The abdication catapulted Elizabeth's father onto the world's stage from a life of relative obscurity, but happy domesticity. He was a man of limited intelligence – his biographer Sarah Bradford considers his academic record as a naval cadet 'disastrous' and he came bottom out of a class of sixty-eight at the Royal Naval College, Osborne. Nevertheless, as King, he strove hard to learn the essential skills that would enable him to emulate his own father, George V.

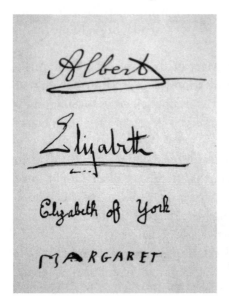

'We four', as the King referred to his family, were a tight-knit group. For the first ten years of her life, Elizabeth II was a Princess of York, as we see in her signature from a visitors' book of the early 1930s. (Author's collection)

The assiduous way Elizabeth has tackled her daily government boxes, helped by her ability to skim-read as well as her keenness to learn facts, has been likened to her father's approach to paperwork. Both were in marked contrast to Edward VIII, who left unread documents on his desk for all to see and returned some with stains from spilled cocktails on them.

The King found confidence and happiness in marriage and fatherhood. Historian Robert Lacey noted, 'He had been brought up in an environment where the human emotion was suppressed, where raw love, anger, pain or exultation were not regarded as topics of polite conversation.'

George was certainly more hands on with his children than his own parents had been with theirs. He took part in bath time with the girls and later on in pillow fights in their bedrooms. He and Queen Elizabeth played card games with the girls – Snap, Happy Families, Racing Demon, Rummy – as well joining in charades, word games and family jokes. The enforced lockdown of life at Windsor during the Second World War, where the princesses spent the duration while many of their cousins went to the safety of the USA or Canada, brought the family even closer.

After the war, Queen Mary's lady-in-waiting, Lady Airlie, recalled the relaxed family atmosphere at Sandringham with the princesses and their friends doing jigsaws together in the hall while 'the radio, worked by Princess Elizabeth, blared incessantly'.

When it came to lessons for his daughters, the King made sure, first and foremost, that they should be taught in an environment conducive to learning. He visited his old schoolroom at the top of Buckingham Palace with Marion Crawford, the royal governess, and declared, 'That won't do', and found a larger room with better light. He passed on his copy of *Punch* to Elizabeth as a way of making her aware of political issues and drew her attention to articles in *The Times*, which he was given specially printed on rag (a copy went to the monarch as well as the copyright libraries). He also arranged for Elizabeth to have lessons in constitutional history from the vice provost of Eton, Henry Marten, a bashful and eccentric figure who nervously addressed the Princess as 'gentlemen', the usual way he addressed a classroom of boys.

Elizabeth and her father had much in common. Both remained fundamentally shy. The Princess's cousin, Margaret Rhodes (*née* Elphinstone), told the author in 2006, 'It was always very difficult sitting next to him at dinner, as he so obviously wanted to talk, but found it awkward, so I used to get round by having some questions ready to ask him, and that worked.' Elizabeth's first private secretary, John Colville, noted, 'Princess Elizabeth has the sweetest of characters, but she is not easy to talk to.' This shyness was something that strongly concerned the King.

Quite often, of course, it depended upon who she was talking to, with both the Princess and her father very confident within the family group. Artist Rex Whistler recorded his impressions of sitting next to Princess Elizabeth, aged 17, at a Windsor Castle dinner. He found her 'gentle and a little demure from shyness but not *too* shy, and a delicious way of gazing – very serious and solemn – into your eyes while talking, but all breaking up into enchanting laughter if we came to anything funny'.

Elizabeth, like her father, is conscientious and dogged in her approach to her role. She admired the way her father dealt with the challenge of public speaking despite his stammer. Princess Margaret recalled, 'It was a worry when he made a speech. I had vicarious nerves for him.' The tension was one of several reasons for his 'gnashes', outbursts of temper that Queen Elizabeth could jolly him out of. Princess Elizabeth had a temper in her schoolroom days, once pouring a bottle of ink over herself, but was successful in masking the trait later on.

Elizabeth was a more confident speaker. When she performed her first solo duty, opening a dock, during the royal tour of South Africa in 1947, the King listened to the broadcast on the radio aboard the White Train and had tears of pride pouring down his cheeks.

She inherited her love of the outdoors from her parents. She enjoyed riding with her father in Windsor Great Park at the weekend and they also took long walks during which he gave her advice on politics and government.

Both of them had a straightforward and sincere faith, nothing like the questioning approach to religion that Prince Philip developed. Each morning, the King listened to *Lift up Your Hearts*, an uncomplicated mixture of Bible readings and hymns on the BBC's Home Service, and would test his daughters' knowledge by querying, 'What were the Ten Commandments?', and so on. Queen Victoria did the same with her children and grandchildren. Clambering out of her carriage she once barked, 'What were the Epistles?' to Princess Victoria Eugénie of Battenberg. The terrified girl squeaked, 'Were they the wives of the apostles?' Even in old age, she could recall the breeze moving Victoria's veil and the look of incredulity on her face!

King George was a possessive father. Initially, he refused to allow Elizabeth to do some form of war work, unlike Margaret Rhodes, who was a secretary with MI6, and Lady Mary Cambridge, another cousin, who was a volunteer nurse. It was a source of friction until Elizabeth was allowed to join the Auxiliary Territorial Service (ATS) in the closing months of the war.

He was also reluctant to see her leave the family unit to marry Prince Philip of Greece and insisted she didn't make any formal announcement of a betrothal until the royal family had returned from their tour of South Africa. Partly, it was to ensure Elizabeth was committed to her relationship but also because he couldn't face losing her.

When Elizabeth did marry in November 1947 it was, according to the King's authorised biographer, 'a day of mixed emotions'. Mingled with his pleasure for her was 'a deep sorrow

Princess Elizabeth taking out the plugs of a car while training as a second subaltern in the Auxiliary Territorial Army (ATS). (© Pump Park Vintage Photography/Alamy)

at losing her from his own home'. In a poignant letter, he wrote to her, 'I was so proud and thrilled at having you by my side on our long walk through Westminster Abbey but when I handed your hand to the Archbishop I felt that I had lost something very precious.'

The final few years of the King's life saw him dogged by ill health. Decades of heavy smoking caused him to develop arteriosclerosis (a potentially serious condition where arteries become clogged with fatty substances) and lung cancer. Elizabeth was forced to deputise for her father, taking the salute at the Trooping the Colour, laying a wreath at the Cenotaph on Remembrance Day and carrying out a tour of Canada (with a brief stop-over in Washington) in October 1951. This was also useful preparation for the role she would take on at only 25.

When she became Queen, Elizabeth was keen to follow the example of King George in as many ways as possible. She frequently asked her private secretary, 'What would my father have done?' One of her approved biographers, Ben Pimlott, noted, 'Despite the politician-talk of renewal and a dawning age, the most striking feature of the succession was a sense of continuity from one reign to the other.'

In October 1955, Elizabeth unveiled a statue of George VI in the Mall. Her speech was, for her, surprisingly personal:

> Much was asked of my father in personal sacrifice and endeavour, often in the face of illness; his courage in overcoming it endeared him to everybody. He shirked no task, however difficult, and to the end he never faltered in his duty to his peoples.

Not only was it a daughter honouring a much-loved father but a monarch honouring another monarch, who had been her guide and mentor.

3

ELIZABETH AND A FLYING ACE

Few celebrities can claim to have patted the Queen's cheek, but one global superstar managed to do so as he was leaving Buckingham Palace.

The date was 31 May 1927 and the American aviator Charles Lindbergh had just had an audience with baby Elizabeth's grandfather and been personally invested with the Air Force Cross.

Ten days earlier, 25-year-old Captain Lindbergh had entered the record books by becoming the first person to fly solo across the Atlantic from New York to Paris. (In 1919, the British aviators John Alcock and Arthur Brown had flown a shorter route from Newfoundland to the west coast of Ireland where the duo ignominiously nosedived into Derrygimlagh Bog near Clifden.)

Lindbergh became an instant legend. When he landed his single engine monoplane, *The Spirit of St Louis*, at Le Bourget after his thirty-three-and-a-half-hour flight, tens of thousands of people gathered to see the landing, including two future Indian prime ministers, Jawaharlal Nehru and his daughter, Indira Gandhi. After a celebratory welcome in Paris, he left for Belgium. On the way, he performed a quick aerial display along the Champs-Élysées, added two loops of the Eiffel Tower and dropped a tricolour, weighted with a sandbag, bearing the message, 'Goodbye Dear Paris. Ten thousand thanks for your kindness to me. Charles A. Lindbergh.'

The aviator expected a more muted welcome from the normally emotionally repressed British and was startled to find Croydon Airport engulfed by an estimated 100,000 well-wishers near the landing site and lining the streets outside. According to his biographer, 'women fainted, silk hats were crushed and umbrellas went flying, while twelve hundred bobbies hopelessly blew their whistles'.

The third day of his stay was given over to royalty. At 10 a.m., he joined Prime Minister Stanley Baldwin to watch the Prince of Wales take the salute at a Trooping the Colour rehearsal on Horse Guards Parade. Later in the day, the aviator met the Prince at York House. A press photo was taken outside and captioned, 'The two most popular young men in the world'. At 10.45, he was driven through cheering crowds to Buckingham Palace, where he had a twenty-minute audience with George V. 'I was flattered to find his questions showed he had read a great deal about [my flight] and understood it perfectly,' Lindbergh wrote (or had written for him) in the *New York Times*. Leaning forward, conspiratorially, George 'asked the question about transatlantic travel that interested everyone else. "Now tell me, Captain Lindbergh. There is one thing I long to know. How did you pee?"'.

After ten minutes, Queen Mary joined them to witness the King award Lindbergh the Air Force Cross, the highest military honour that could, at the time, be given to a civilian for a great flying achievement that didn't involve operations against the enemy.

His arrival inside Buckingham Palace was witnessed by 13-month-old Princess Elizabeth in the arms of her nanny, Clara Knight. They stayed in the vestibule until the aviator left. Courtiers watched as he bent down, shook her hand and patted her cheek. After signing autographs for members of the household he went back to the Princess and took her hand in farewell.

Lindbergh's relaxed warmth on meeting baby Elizabeth has a certain poignancy since, five years later, his own 20-month-old baby, Charles Lindbergh Jr, was abducted from his crib in the aviator's New Jersey home. The nation was gripped by the sensational story, dubbed 'The biggest story since the Resurrection' by the American journalist H.L. Mencken. Despite the ransom demand of $50,000 dollars being paid, the child was not returned and was found murdered by the side of the road some 7km south of the family home.

4

GRANDPAPA ENGLAND

The royal governess Marion Crawford claimed that 'Grandpapa England' was young Elizabeth's name for her beloved grandfather, King George V. Princess Margaret refuted this, claiming, 'We were much too frightened to call him anything but Grandpapa.'

George V, like his son George VI, was a second son and never expected to be king. In his case, his elder brother, Prince Albert Victor, contracted influenza in January 1892, which developed into fatal pneumonia. George not only inherited his brother's place in the line of succession but also his fiancée, since the intended bride, Princess Mary of Teck, was considered by Queen Victoria to be far too worthy a choice to be sent packing. George and May (as she was known, thanks to her birth month) dutifully complied with the arranged marriage but did eventually fall in love. Both were emotionally repressed and found it easier to confess their adoration for each other in letters.

George V succeeded to the throne in May 1910 and reigned for just over a quarter of a century, a period that witnessed the First World War, the post-war social upheaval, the roaring twenties and the Great Depression. The King and Queen, both imbued with a strong sense of duty and formidably regal in appearance, commanded respect and, in their later years, affection from the public.

George was a gruff former naval officer, who ruled his sons with a rod of iron. His widely quoted comment to the Earl of Derby (though possibly apocryphal) is often used to illustrate this, 'My father was frightened of his mother, I was frightened of my father, and I am damned well going to see to it that my children are frightened of me.'

Without doubt, he adored his eldest granddaughter, Princess Elizabeth, and she in turn venerated him. In the spring of 1927, Elizabeth's parents went on an extended tour of Australia and New Zealand, leaving the baby in the care of both sets of grandparents. In March, George V wrote to tell the Duchess of York, 'Your sweet little daughter has four teeth now, which is quite good at eleven months.' The following spring, the King and

Queen asked Bertie and Elizabeth if their baby could stay on at Sandringham as they wanted more time with her. When she eventually returned to London with her nanny, the King wrote to his son, 'I miss your sweet baby more than I can say, breakfast and tea are quite different without her'. He thought the Norfolk air must have agreed with her as 'she has come on a lot'.

In the autumn of 1928, George developed septicaemia and came close to death. The following spring, his doctors prescribed sea air and he and the Queen went to Bognor to recuperate. Baby Elizabeth arrived, in the words of biographer Harold Nicolson, as 'an emollient for jaded nerves'. She would walk next to his wheelchair along the seafront and make sand pies in the garden. One day, the Archbishop of Canterbury arrived to find the King, on all fours, on the carpet playing horses with his granddaughter, who was leading him along by his beard.

George was less interested in Elizabeth's education than the Queen was, but he did have one request of Marion Crawford. He said to her, 'Teach Margaret and Lilibet to write a decent hand. That is all I ask of you. None of my children can write properly'.

George V died three months before Elizabeth's 10th birthday. It was her father who familiarised her with the duties of a constitutional monarch. In doing so, he educated her on the social and political issues of her grandfather's reign. There are certainly more than passing similarities between George V and Elizabeth in how she regards her role and how she has handled specific situations.

In both reigns, the monarchy became more accessible to the people. Over the years, George and Mary visited the industrial heartlands of the North, the Midlands and Wales. 'Away days' and longer tours have been a main ingredient of Elizabeth II's reign. She once said, 'I have to be seen to be believed', and she has criss-crossed the United Kingdom more than any previous monarch. The 'walkabout' became a regular feature of Elizabeth's public engagements from her first one in the UK (in

Coventry in 1970) and allowed her to be seen at close hand by people from all walks of life.

George was willing to adapt the monarchy to suit changing times, but his main consideration was whether any initiative would enhance or damage the monarchy. Preserving the dynasty was, then and now, a number-one priority. George only had to look at his contemporaries to see how quickly a regime could fall. By the end of the First World War, the three great European monarchies of Germany, Russia and Austria–Hungary had all collapsed.

George V was a first cousin of Emperor Wilhelm II of Germany and Tsar Nicholas II of Russia, as well as of the German-born Tsarina Alexandra of Russia. After the overthrow of the Romanov family, George could have offered them asylum in Britain but was mindful of the hysterical anti-German feeling in his country (which prompted him to change the name of the royal house from Saxe-Coburg-Gotha to Windsor). After the British Government, under David Lloyd George, approved plans for the Russian royal family to be evacuated to the United Kingdom, George backtracked. His private secretary Lord Stamfordham urged the government to rescind the offer, writing that the presence of the Imperial family in this country 'will be very hard on the King and arouse much public comment if not resentment'. While republicanism wasn't a serious threat at the time, the King had been informed, said Stamfordham, 'how much the matter is being discussed, not only in clubs, but by working men, and that Labour Members in the House of Commons are expressing adverse opinions to the proposal'.

Neither George nor his advisors could have foreseen the massacres of Nicholas and Alexandra and their five children at the hands of their Bolshevik captors in July 1918. In choosing to save his own dynasty, George had undoubtedly sealed the fate of his Russian cousins. As George V's biographer Kenneth Rose noted, 'The first principle of an hereditary monarchy is to survive, and never was King George V obliged to tread the path of self-preservation more cautiously than in 1917.'

Elizabeth II has, on occasions, had to follow her own path of self-preservation, notably after the '*annus horribilis*' of 1992 and the death of the Princess of Wales five years later. These were two periods when the monarchy was roundly criticised, particularity by the tabloid press, reflecting the feeling of many that the monarchy was out of touch.

More recently, the Queen proved a tough negotiator when the Duke and Duchess of Sussex opted to leave their life as full-time working royals and become private members of the family. This no doubt raised the spectre of the Duke and Duchess of Windsor, who very much wanted to return to the royal fold despite the Duke having renounced the throne. The Queen wouldn't countenance a half-in, half-out option and made it clear in her statement of January 2020 that, if the Sussexes wished to pursue their own ambitions, they would have to do so without many of the perquisites of their royal status. Henceforth, they would not be allowed to use the style of His/Her Royal Highness, and they would lose their official military appointments (something close to Harry's heart), as well as their public funding and publicly financed security.

George V proved adept at working with all political parties. Two years before Elizabeth's birth, he appointed the first Labour Government, commenting at the time, 'My grandfather would have hated it, my father could hardly have tolerated it, but I move with the times.' Not only that, but he found, to his surprise, that he got on remarkably well with some of the ministers.

His favourite was J.H. Thomas ('Jim', to the King) who was Secretary of State for the Colonies. According to Kenneth Rose, Thomas was 'a man of coarse speech and coarser wit' and the King loved it. He once asked Thomas about the state of the economy and was told, 'If I were you, King, I'd put the colonies in the wife's name.' Lamenting the fact that his sons never seemed to want to visit Sandringham, George asked Thomas if he could think why, and was told in no uncertain terms, 'I do not wonder at all – it's a dull house. You ought to get out more.' History has it that when the King was recovering from surgery on a lung abscess in 1928, Thomas made him laugh so much with one of his filthy jokes that the stitches over George's wound split open.

Elizabeth II had a particularly good working relationship with Labour Prime Minister Harold Wilson and his successor, Jim Callaghan. During one of their audiences, Wilson asked the Queen if she had seen the story in the evening papers about President Giscard-d'Estaing driving all over France with some ladies of doubtful virtue in the car. The Queen was delighted with the story and laughingly said, 'Ho-ho, Mr Wilson!' A few days later, Wilson visited Paris and had a private dinner with the president. Her Majesty couldn't wait to hear how he'd got on and at their next meeting asked, 'Well, how did it go?' the moment the PM walked into the room.

Wilson gave a breakdown of all the points he had discussed, until the Queen leaned forward and asked, 'Ho-ho, Mr Wilson?'

'Ma'am,' replied the Labour Leader, 'there was no ho-ho; everyone went to bed early.'

Both George V and Elizabeth II had happy marriages and preferred spending leisure time with the family and, preferably, outdoors. In George's case, it made for a dull, if virtuous, life-style. His official biographer, Harold Nicolson, lamented that 'for seventeen years he did nothing at all but kill animals and stick in stamps'.

Neither of them are known for their fondness for the arts. Unlike Princess Margaret, the Queen has rarely attended the opera and ballet privately, and her circle of friends has never included the artists, writers and musicians who have delighted her mother and eldest son. She has, however, been more diplomatic than her grandfather. 'Went to Covent Garden and saw

Fidelio and damned dull it was' was a typical reference in the King's journal. He told the conductor Sir Thomas Beecham that his favourite opera was *La Bohème*. Beecham was fascinated to know why the King liked this particular work and was told 'because it's the shortest'.

Faced with a stunning work by Cézanne at the opening of the Tate Gallery extension, he called over to the Queen, 'Here's something to make you laugh, May!' Like his granddaughter, he wasn't an avid reader, declaring, 'People who write books ought to be shut up.' Having said that, he did keep a handwritten list of books he had read since 1890. Among the royal biographies, military histories and sports books, he had included *Lady Chatterley's Lover* – the unexpurgated version.

Elizabeth II, like her grandfather, has regarded herself as a trustee of the monarchy, both keen to see its survival after their own times. By the time of his death in January 1936, George was already concerned about his successor, Edward VIII. He knew his eldest son was infatuated by the divorced American socialite Wallis Simpson. 'After I am dead,' he said prophetically, 'the boy will ruin himself in twelve months.' Another alleged comment from the King-Emperor is even more prescient, 'I pray to God that my eldest son will never marry and that nothing will come between Bertie and Lilibet and the throne.'

5

A TERRIFYING GRANDMAMA

From her distinctive, unchanging hairstyle to her brilliant blue eyes which can dazzle with warmth or freeze anyone who oversteps the mark, Elizabeth II has more than a passing resemblance to her grandmother, Queen Mary. Despite only ever reaching a height of 5ft 4in, the Queen has always had tremendous presence.

Her grandmother, a few inches taller, seemed statuesque in her toques and heels, so much so that Princess Margaret recalled with mock fear that 'she had such an image'. The diarist Sir Henry 'Chips' Channon felt her appearance was 'formidable, her manner – well it was like talking to St Paul's Cathedral'. (Her similarity to monumental edifices once confused the short-sighted writer E.M. Forster. He was a guest at the wedding of Queen Mary's grandson, George Lascelles, Earl of Harewood, in 1949 and bowed to the multi-tiered wedding cake thinking it was the royal matriarch.)

Queen Mary's impact was due in part to her personality, which was as well-frosted as the cake, but was also due to her fashion, which remained resolutely Edwardian until her death. She was forever shrouded in three-quarter-length coats, often fur-trimmed, and floor-length dresses.

Occasionally, these could be a hazard, as George Harewood recalled in his memoirs. In 1933, the King and Queen visited Leeds to open the Civic Hall. During the visit, Queen Mary, normally renowned for her cast-iron bladder, was taken short and was escorted to the Lady Mayoress's parlour. Unfortunately, the lavatory, with its inward opening door, wasn't spacious enough to cope with the Queen's voluminous skirts and she was obliged to stand on the seat to open the door and let herself out.

Her granddaughter has been far more adventurous with her designs over the years, though she has tended to avoid the extremes of fashion, unlike her sister, who tried every image from Dior's 'New Look' in the 1940s to the mini, midi and maxi in the late 1960s.

In later life, Princess Margaret remembered her grandmother as 'absolutely terrifying'. Both she and the Queen could still recall 'the hollow empty feeling' they had in the pit of their stomachs when Queen Mary sent for them. They were taught to perform a deep curtsey before kissing her on either cheek, in recognition of the fact that she was strictly a Queen Consort first and a grandmother second.

Beneath the chilling exterior, Queen Mary felt tremendous pride in the young Elizabeth and told her friend and lady-in-waiting Lady Airlie that her granddaughter 'would always know her own mind. There's something very steadfast and determined about her.' She felt that Elizabeth was developing the right sort of personality and outlook for her later role in life. She herself contributed to this development by personally supervising Elizabeth's education, instructing the royal governess, Marion Crawford, to provide more history ('very valuable to her future career'), more geography ('especially the dominions and India'), more poetry ('wonderful memory training'), but less arithmetic ('she will never have to add up her own accounts'). She devised 'instructive amusements' for her granddaughters, accompanying them on trips to the Law Courts, the Tower of London, the Bank of England, the Royal Mint, and an endless stream of art galleries and museums.

She also taught Elizabeth how to behave regally and with dignity, as well as knocking her down to size if she thought the Princess was getting complacent. Noticing that her granddaughter was getting restless at a concert, she suggested she should go home. 'Oh no, Granny,' came the reply, 'think of all the people who'll be waiting to see us outside.' Mary promptly ordered her lady-in-waiting to take the precocious child ignominiously out of the back door straight home.

Queen Mary taught Elizabeth how to be stoical and unemotional in public – something we recently witnessed at the funeral of Prince Philip, as well as two decades earlier when her mother and sister died. By the time of her death, Mary had not only outlived her husband but three of her sons.

Above all, Elizabeth's grandmother instilled in her, by example, a belief in the importance of duty as well as the sanctity of the monarchy. At no time was this more apparent than in 1936, when her eldest son, Edward VIII, abdicated to marry divorcée Wallis Simpson. Later, he would recall, 'To my mother, the monarchy was something very sacred and the sovereign a personage apart. The word "duty" fell between us.'

From Queen Mary's point of view, a sovereign anointed by God should never be willing to sacrifice the position for any frail desire – a lesson that Elizabeth would never forget. When Queen Wilhelmina of the Netherlands abdicated in 1948 at the age of 68 in favour of her daughter Juliana, Mary sniffed, 'that is no age to give up your job.' When Juliana herself abdicated in 1980 and was succeeded by her daughter Beatrix, an equally unimpressed Elizabeth II was heard to murmur, 'Well, that's the Dutch for you!'

Such comments suggest an honesty bordering on bluntness, and indeed, both Mary and Elizabeth had in common a distinctly deadpan approach to many issues. Seeing the newborn Elizabeth of York for the first time, her grandmother peered into the cot and said, rather flatly, 'I wish you were more like your little mother!' Some fifty-six years later, the remark was bettered when Elizabeth looked at the newborn Prince William and exclaimed, 'Thank goodness he doesn't have his father's ears!'

It is a well-known fact that the Queen has a delicious sense of humour which, surprisingly, so did her grandmother. In private, Queen Mary delighted in the odd risqué joke. When the comedian George Formby visited her at Marlborough House, he sang, at her request, the uncensored version of 'When I'm Cleaning Windows'. She also liked her moments of family fun. Earl Mountbatten's wife, Edwina, was part of the house party at Sandringham in January 1951 and noted, 'All in good but "childish spirits", the youngest of the party being Queen Mary ... who was kicking Charles' balloons around the room last night.'

Queen Mary died on 24 March 1953, exactly nine weeks before her granddaughter's coronation at Westminster Abbey (a curious parallel with the Queen Mother, who was to die nine weeks before Elizabeth's Golden Jubilee celebration weekend). The previous year, following the death of George VI, the 25-year-old Elizabeth broke off her visit to Kenya and returned to London as Queen Elizabeth II. There to greet her at Clarence House was her grandmother, who had declared, 'Her old Granny and subject must be the first to kiss her hand.' The frail 84-year-old matriarch dropped into a curtsey, just as she had taught Elizabeth herself to do all those years earlier. As she did so, she proclaimed in ringing tones, 'God save the Queen!'

6

A BEST FRIEND

It all began in 1930 when, aged just 4, Princess Elizabeth of York bumped into Sonia Graham-Hodgson while out playing in Hamilton Gardens, behind the York family's London home, No. 145 Piccadilly, a stone's throw from Hyde Park. The meeting was significant because, as Elizabeth's governess, Marion Crawford recorded, 'Sonia was the one friend whom the Queen chose for herself'. The Princess's existing circle of friends consisted of cousins – near and distant, from both sides of the family – and the selected offspring of aristocrats and courtiers.

While Sonia wasn't from the highest echelons of society, she was certainly from a comfortable background. Not only was she a neighbour of the Yorks but also her father, Dr Harold Graham-Hodgson, was one of the country's leading authorities on the diagnostic use of X-rays.

In November 1928, King George V fell dangerously ill with a streptococcal infection of the chest. Graham-Hodgson was called in to corroborate the diagnosis. He brought his cumbersome equipment to Buckingham Palace on a lorry, fed the cables through a window and took his plates as the King lay in bed. It was the first time X-rays had been taken of a patient outside a main hospital, and after his recovery, the grateful monarch made the specialist a Commander of the Royal Victorian Order, which was later upgraded to a knighthood by Elizabeth's father.

Two years later, the King-Emperor's granddaughter came up to the X-ray man's child and said, 'Will you come and play with me?' Later, when in her eighties, Sonia recalled, 'We played French cricket. She was wearing a pink and white check dress. I was wearing a blue coat.' Although she conceded that seven decades later, when they occasionally met, 'We always argue over what we were wearing'.

After playing for an hour in Hamilton Gardens, they left to have tea and the Princess said, 'Goodbye. See you tomorrow.' They would go on to see each other nearly every day after that, apart from family holidays, until Elizabeth moved to Buckingham Palace seven years later.

Looking back, Sonia recalled the Princess as 'a thoughtful and sensitive child, and naturally well-behaved. She never seemed aware of her position and paid no attention to the people who stood by the railings to watch her play.'

The girls were usually accompanied by their nannies, and occasionally left the seclusion of their private garden to play in other London parks. A charming press photo of the time shows the girls, walking hand in hand through Hyde Park, with Sonia a good 5 or 6 inches taller than the Princess, despite being only eight months her senior.

The two learned to skip, played hopscotch and took dancing lessons together. 'I suppose I was the bossy one,' Sonia conceded in a 2006 interview, 'I think it was usually me who decided what games we should play.' Sometimes Elizabeth's father joined in, particularly relishing the hide-and-seek game of Sardines. 'I remember my starchy nanny saying that she found it very undignified having to hide in a bush with him.'

She also had the rare distinction of having the future Queen write a short story for her in her own hand. Entitled 'The Happy Farm', Lilibet dedicated it 'To Sonia, My dear little friend and lover of horses'.

At first Sonia had had no idea her friend was a princess, although it was soon made clear. 'I had to curtsey to the Duke and Duchess of York and to Queen Mary,' though she was allowed to call Elizabeth by her pet name of 'Lilibet'. This changed in 1936 when, with the abdication of Edward VIII, Elizabeth's parents became King and Queen, and Sonia's 10-year-old friend became Heiress Presumptive. 'And so, things became more formal,' Sonia remembered. 'We called her Princess, we curtsied to her. She grew up a lot. She became, well, more serious.'

The royal family moved out of No. 145 Piccadilly and into first-floor apartments at Buckingham Palace. Elizabeth's thirty toy horses went with her, apart from a favourite one called Ben, which she gave to Sonia. The Princess was concerned that he 'would not like being packed away in a removal van and put in storage. So she asked me to look after him.' A couple of weeks later, Elizabeth wrote and asked Sonia to come round to Buckingham Palace and to bring Ben with her.

During the war, Elizabeth was sent firstly to Birkhall and then to Windsor and the two girls didn't see each other for the duration. The friends were reunited in 1946 when Elizabeth took her fiancé, Lieutenant Philip Mountbatten, with her to Sonia's 21st birthday. 'He was very good looking and I could tell the Queen was very fond of him,' Sonia remembered. The following year,

'I was there at their wedding in Westminster Abbey and had a marvellous seat up near the front. It was all terribly impressive; and the Queen looked so happy.'

The two friends continued to meet from time to time at Sonia's house for tea or dinner parties, even after Elizabeth became Queen in 1952. 'She used to say how nice it was to get out of Buckingham Palace' and 'once she had arrived, she was completely at ease'.

In October 1953 Sonia married Anthony Berry, who had proposed to her outside Buckingham Palace on coronation day. With the newly crowned Elizabeth's permission, the ceremony took place at the Queen's Chapel, St James's Palace and the Dean of Windsor officiated.

Berry was a director of the prestigious London wine firm Berry Bros and Rudd, based at No. 3 St James's Street, which has supplied the British royal family since the reign of George III. He and Sonia had two children, a daughter, Victoria, and a son, Simon. The latter is now chairman of the family firm and, in 2007, to the delight of his parents, became Clerk of the Royal Cellars, responsible for drawing up the royal wine list and selecting wines and spirits for the Queen's cellar at Buckingham Palace and other official residences.

The Berrys retired to a spacious apartment in a Georgian crescent in Bath, where signed photos of the young Elizabeth were a reminder of her special royal friendship.

Sonia was occasionally invited to royal parties and in March 2004 was at the Ritz Hotel when the Queen hosted a gathering of friends and family to mark the fiftieth anniversary of her coronation the previous summer. The two also exchanged letters and cards and in 2006 Sonia sent the Queen an 80th birthday greeting and a silk scarf as a present.

In an interview that year she paid tribute to her friend and monarch:

She has taken the job tremendously seriously and made a great success of it. The Queen was determined that she would work hard; not just enjoy the privileges. She has wonderful dedication.

The Queen is absolutely steadfast and she sets an example to other people. Perhaps at one point she was a little too remote – out of shyness – but that has changed, too. I feel terribly privileged to have been her friend for so long. I am very lucky.

Sonia Berry died peacefully at home on 16 March 2012, at the age of 86, two years after the death of her husband. They left two children, five grandchildren and one great-grandchild. She also left many memories for the Queen of a special relationship that began on a summer's day over eight decades earlier when a 4-year-old princess, isolated in that rarefied world of pre-war royalty, just needed someone to play with.

7

GRANNY AND GRANDPA, NON-ROYAL

As a child, Princess Elizabeth spent several weeks of each summer at Glamis Castle, near Dundee, the official residence of her maternal grandparents, the 14th Earl and Countess of Strathmore. For Elizabeth and Margaret, there was relatively little formality, in contrast to their visits to the King and Queen at Windsor, Balmoral and Sandringham.

There was also a sizeable contingent of non-royal cousins, the children of the Queen Mother's nine brothers and sisters. The

The Earl and Countess of Strathmore celebrate their Golden Wedding with their extensive brood in 1931. Elizabeth is on the front row (third from the right). Her mother is on the second row (fourth from the left), with Princess Margaret on her knee. The Duke of York stands (fifth from the left) behind his wife and her father. (© World History Archive/Alamy)

princesses had twenty-three maternal cousins, of which only two – Simon and Albemarle Bowes Lyon – survive at the time of writing. Elizabeth was closest to Diana Bowes Lyon, three years her senior, and Margaret Elphinstone (later Rhodes), born in 1925. 'The Queen and I were fascinated by our grandfather's bushy moustache which he would solemnly part before drinking his tea,' Mrs Rhodes recalled. These two were lifelong friends of the Queen and were bridesmaids at her wedding in 1947.

Photographs in the Glamis archive show Elizabeth constantly laughing as she was snapped skipping, playing tug of war or simply running around the gardens and vast lawns. Occasionally, Elizabeth's father would load the car with buckets and spades, picnic gear and several of the cousins, and would head to the beaches on Scotland's east coast.

Royal biographer Robert Lacey claimed Elizabeth's visits to Glamis '[were] to shape her as significantly as the more obvious influence of her royal grandfather'. Many of the Queen's character traits were evident in the personalities of her grandparents.

Her grandfather, Lord Strathmore, was, according to another biographer, Dorothy Laird, 'a quiet, courteous, religious man, conscientious to a degree', which could obviously apply to Elizabeth II. Like his granddaughter, he loved the outdoors and spent hours each day on the estate, leading shooting parties or pollarding the trees for kindling. His favourite pastime was cricket and each year he would host a competition for various teams including the Eton Ramblers.

He was an undeniably eccentric figure. His great-grandson Gilbert Clayton told the author, 'He often wore an old mackintosh tied around with string when he was outdoors and was delighted when, more often than not, he was mistaken for his own estate workers.' A strict Sabbatarian minister, spotting a figure engaged in manual work on the holy day, wrote to the Earl of Strathmore to complain about such blasphemy and received a contrite letter back saying it wouldn't happen again. It's not clear if he revealed that he himself was the culprit.

Elizabeth II likes to fool unsuspecting tourists who are hoping to spot the Queen. Former protection officer Richard Griffin shared the memorable story of walking with the Queen at Balmoral, in her country casuals of a headscarf and tweed coat. When a group of American tourists asked her if she'd ever met the Queen, the monarch replied, 'No, but he has', pointing at the police officer.

The Earl had a reputation for being loyal to his staff, never laying them off or sacking the incompetent ones. The Countess was also supportive of the staff and turned a blind eye when her butler regularly overindulged in alcohol – he was known to spill wine down the back of dinner guests. Her daughter, the Queen Mother, was similarly indulgent. Towards the end of her life, she coped well when her loyal steward, William Tallon, was occasionally 'tired and emotional' after a liquid lunch.

Once, Princess Margaret arrived at the Royal Lodge, her mother's country retreat in Windsor Great Park, to find the Queen Mother stoically sitting without her afternoon tea, as her butler and two elderly maids were having a nap upstairs. Margaret herself could be a hard taskmaster, but she and the Queen commanded loyalty from their own staff, unlike some of the younger royals who have had a much higher turnover of employees.

According to the Queen Mother's official biographer, William Shawcross, Cecilia 'inculcated in them [her children] a sense of history and romance, a love of tradition and a sense of duty'. This was certainly passed down through the female line to Elizabeth II. The Queen Mother instructed her children that duty always came first and, said her granddaughter Lady Mary Clayton, taught them 'to be in control of their temper and moods, and to never allow their moods to dominate', something which is again reflected in the Queen's personality.

Elizabeth certainly isn't a carbon copy of her maternal grandmother. Cecilia was a competent gardener, laying out the Italian Garden to the east of the castle, following a design by Arthur Castings. The Queen has limited her green-fingered adventures to deadheading a few roses when out walking the corgis. She can play the piano – though not as well as Princess Margaret could – whereas Cecilia played the harmonium for the family services in the chapel each Sunday. She was also a competent embroiderer, especially in crewel work, whereas Elizabeth tried her hand at knitting during the war and stopped at that.

The Queen, like her mother, has never been someone her children and grandchildren turned to for emotional support. On the other hand, Cecilia was happy to listen to the young pour out their troubles or ask for advice. Lady Mary Clayton recalled her grandmother's 'delicious laugh' and the Strathmores were a fun-loving, close-knit unit, who enjoyed post-dinner party games and singsongs round the piano.

It this positive family aura that attracted Albert, Duke of York, and made his wooing of Elizabeth Bowes-Lyon such an enjoyable task. Family life at Glamis certainly had its attractions after the rigid formality of Balmoral and 'Bertie' angled for an invitation as much as possible. The well-mannered, polite Prince was approved of by the Earl and Countess, who had no illusions about his family. 'Some people have to be fed royalty like sea lions with fish' was Cecilia's withering comment on fashionable society. Claude agreed, saying, 'If there is one thing I have determined for my children, it is that they shall never have any post about the Court.' Neither were enamoured by stories of the court of Edward VII 'the Caresser', or the fast set surrounding Edward, Prince of Wales, but would certainly have approved that their granddaughter has always managed to be both fun-loving and respectable.

8

PILGRIM'S PROGRESS

A key function of the Queen's role is to be a comforting figurehead at times of national crisis. It was a lesson she learned as a child of 8 when she accompanied her grandparents to a special service at Westminster Abbey to inaugurate the Cathedral Pilgrimage in aid of the unemployed during the Great Depression of the early 1930s.

Britain's economic collapse was part of the global fallout from the Wall Street Crash of 1929 when shares on New York Stock Exchange plummeted. The effects of the crash were felt throughout Europe. In Britain, production of coal, iron and steel as well as shipbuilding and textiles were drastically reduced, bringing widespread unemployment to the industrial communities of northern England, south Wales, Scotland and Northern Ireland. At its peak in 1933, some 2.5 million people – 25 per cent of the workforce – had lost their jobs.

The idea of a Cathedral Pilgrimage to raise money for those in desperate need originated with social workers. The Archbishop of Canterbury sponsored the project and by the time George V and Queen Mary offered their support, some fifty cathedrals had agreed to take part. Tickets cost half a crown or a shilling for children and, in return, pilgrims were invited to special services, an opportunity to meet senior clergy, a tour of the building and so on.

The King and Queen spearheaded the campaign by purchasing several tickets before attending an inaugural service at Westminster Abbey on 1 July 1934. Young Elizabeth accompanied them to the event, her first official event at the abbey. Like her grandparents, she wore a white metal pilgrim badge.

Besides being an example of duty for Lilibet, it was an early indication for her of how the media covers royal events. Reporters were fascinated that, instead of sitting on the backless stool placed between two great oak chairs for the King and Queen, Queen Mary ushered Elizabeth on to one of the thrones while she sat on the stool. It was speculated that protocol dictated that she should be seated next to the King and not her granddaughter, while others suggested she wanted to give the Princess an elevated view of proceedings. Either way, Elizabeth ended up perched on a throne-like seat with her feet barely able to touch the floor.

She watched, fascinated, as gold-tasselled cushions were laid in front of her grandparents for them to put their collection money on. She would have seen how the pilgrim tickets were ceremonially carried to the high altar in a Renaissance casket, and she would have slid down from her perch to sing 'Jerusalem' and 'To Be A Pilgrim'.

Photos of the Princess leaving the abbey show a poised, serious child, far older than her 8 years. Coverage of her visit apparently inspired other children to attend services and buy pilgrim tickets. So, leading by example was another of those royal communication skills she learned at an early age, although this time it wasn't at her grandmother's knee.

9

VIC'S CHICKS

In 1880, Queen Victoria's youngest son, Prince Leopold, visited the United States with his sister, Princess Louise. The irreverent American press reported the royal visit under the headline 'Vic's Chicks'. It so happened that Leopold had, just as irreverently, named his fox terrier 'Vic'. Their mother, none the wiser, wrote to Leopold, 'How strange they should mention your dog'.

Elizabeth II met three of 'Vic's chicks' many times as a child: Princess Louise, Duchess of Argyll (1848–1939), Prince Arthur, Duke of Connaught (1850–1942) and Princess Beatrice (1857–1944). Louise and Beatrice lived in vast apartments at Kensington Palace, dubbed 'the aunt heap' by the future Edward VIII due to the array of Victorian princesses that resided there.

The Duke of Connaught was one of Elizabeth II's godparents. His own godfather was the Duke of Wellington, the victor of Waterloo after whom he was named and with whom he shared the birthday of 1 May. Connaught lived in Clarence House. Following his death in 1942, it was used by the Red Cross during the war, before being refurnished for Princess Elizabeth and the Duke of Edinburgh to use as a London residence. In one further link, he was Colonel of the Grenadier Guards, a role that Elizabeth took over at the age of only 16, a few months after the death of this great-great-uncle.

Each summer, the Duke of Connaught inspected the King's Bodyguard of the Yeoman of the Guard in the garden of Clarence House. Princess Elizabeth attended this colourful ceremony three times in the early 1930s, watching the march past of the yeomen, dressed in their distinctive Tudor uniforms of red, white and yellow. In 1931, she was joined under the portico of Clarence House by her mother and Princess Louise.

Victoria's three surviving children were present, sitting behind the King and Queen, at the wedding of Prince Henry, Duke of Gloucester, to Lady Alice Montagu Douglas Scott. Princesses Elizabeth and Margaret were bridesmaids. The ceremony in November 1935 was low key and held in the private chapel at Buckingham Palace, since the bride's father, the Duke of Buccleuch, had died shortly before.

The Princesses would have also seen Princess Louise at the baptism of the present Duke of Kent, which was also held in the private chapel in November 1935, as well as at the christening of his sister Princess Alexandra in February 1937.

In May 1937, Elizabeth and Margaret were present with their great-great-aunts Louise and Beatrice at the 70th birthday lunch for Queen Mary held at Marlborough House.

The curtain finally fell on that Victorian generation when Princess Beatrice, Victoria's ninth and youngest child, died at the age of 87. The senior mourners at her funeral in St George's Chapel were the King and Queen; Beatrice's daughter, Queen Victoria Eugénie of Spain; the Kings of Norway and Greece; and 18-year-old Princess Elizabeth.

The Queen must have inherited her longevity from her mother, who died at the age of 101, but, on her father's side, both Princess Louise and the Duke of Connaught lived to a remarkable age. In fact, the brother and sister both lived to be 91 years and 260 days. The record for the longest-lived member of the British royal family is held by Princess Alice, Duchess of Gloucester, whose wedding all of the above attended. She died on 29 October 2004 at the age of 102 years and 309 days.

10

'THE MOST FAMOUS LITTLE GIRL IN THE WORLD'

She was born third in line to the throne, but Princess Elizabeth was the elder daughter of George V's second son, the Duke of York. Her equivalent today is another Princess of York, Princess Beatrice. The assumption was that Edward, Prince of Wales, aged only 31 when Elizabeth was born, would marry and have his own family. Nevertheless, she attracted global interest from the moment of her birth, which surprised even her mother, who wrote to Queen Mary in 1928: 'It almost frightens me that the people should love her so much'.

May 1926: A new rose was named after her at Chelsea Flower Show. In August 1927, another 'Princess Elizabeth' rose, a red and gold bloom grown from the Queen Alexandra stock, was grown by Wheatcrofts of Nottingham.
November 1926: Seven-month-old Elizabeth was named one of the founders of the International Hall of Residence for University Women at Crosby Hall, once the home of Richard III.

June 1927: The Duke and Duchess of York returned from their five-month tour of Australia and New Zealand with over 3 tons of gifts, from a silver doll's tea set from the children of Cobar, New South Wales, to hundreds of dolls handed to the Duchess of York by well-wishers.

29 April 1929: Elizabeth was on the cover of *Time* magazine to celebrate her 3rd birthday. The feature opened with the ominous warning that 'if death should come soon and suddenly to three men' – the King, the Prince of Wales and the Duke of York – 'England would have another Virgin Queen'. For those who missed the point, it hammered home the message, 'She is but three removed from the Throne'. It also advertised 'Princess Elizabeth prams' at $250 each.

December 1930: Two trees in Cherry Ave on the Kingston bypass were named after Princesses Elizabeth and Margaret.

9 February 1931: The British Australian and New Zealand Antarctic Research Expedition under Sir Douglas Mawson discovered the territory they named Princess Elizabeth Land, in the area claimed by the Australian Government. In 2012, to mark the Diamond Jubilee, an area of the British Antarctic Territory was named Queen Elizabeth Land.

June 1931: Sir Edward Elgar conducted his 'Nursery Suite', dedicated to Elizabeth and Margaret, in front of the Duke and Duchess of York at the Kingsway Hall, Holborn.

December 1931: a 6 cent, dark-blue stamp from Newfoundland was the first to feature the image of Elizabeth. It was part of a royal set that included the King, Queen and Prince of Wales.

December 1932: Elizabeth was presented with the first chocolate ever made from ingredients entirely produced in Britain, by the Rowntree Cocoa and Chocolate Works in York, which had grown cocoa trees from seeds in their tropical plant house.

November 1933: The LMS engine No. 6201 was named *Princess Elizabeth*. It was the second of its class built at Crewe for the Anglo-Scot Express. The first was named the *Princess Royal*, after her aunt. For those keen to have their own generic loco-motive, for 300 BDV cigarette coupons it was possible to own a Bassett-Lowke clockwork, scale model loco called *Princess Elizabeth*. It featured an automatic gear for stopping, starting and reversing.

11

BOBO

For over six decades, the Queen's right-hand member of staff was a no-nonsense Scotswoman she always knew as 'Bobo'. She was nursery maid and later a dresser, but she was also personal assistant, advisor, critic and, above all, a friend.

Margaret MacDonald was born on the Black Isle in Ross-shire in 1904. Her father was a coachman-gardener who later became a railway surface worker.

It is interesting that the Queen Mother, as Duchess of York, was able to headhunt her staff from friends and family, simply because of the deference shown to the royal family, even by those closest to them. The royal nanny, Clara Knight, worked for the Duchess's sister, Lady Elphinstone, whose daughter, Margaret Rhodes, joked to the author, 'She was my nanny, but she was clearly destined for higher things!' Elizabeth's governess, Marion Crawford, was working for the Duchess's other sister, Rose, before leaving her high and dry to move to London.

Margaret MacDonald was a nursery cleaner for the Marchioness of Linlithgow, who Lady Rose thought ideal for the York household, and she too headed down south at the age of 22.

All three women were called by variants of their name coined by their royal charges. Clara, who was also nanny to Elizabeth's mother, was named 'Allah' by the Bowes-Lyon children, who couldn't say her name. Thanks to Princess Elizabeth, Marion Crawford became 'Crawfie' and Margaret for some reason ended up as 'Bobo'.

The first we hear of the nurserymaid was in 1937 when 11-year-old Princess Elizabeth wrote an account of her father's coronation. Part of it tells how she was woken by the noise of the crowd outside at 5 a.m. 'I leapt out of bed and so did Bobo. We put on dressing gowns and shoes and Bobo made me put on an eiderdown as it was cold, and we crouched by the window ...'

It was clear from this account that Bobo shared Elizabeth's room during her childhood, starting in 1930 with the birth of Princess Margaret. Allah had to concentrate on the new baby and Bobo was given sole charge of Elizabeth. By now, she was one of the few to call the Princess 'Lilibet', which she did for the rest of her life, though only in private. In front of other members of the household, she sometimes referred to the Queen as 'my little lady', though mostly as 'Her Majesty'.

Bobo remained close to Lilibet even after her marriage. Philip's cousin, Lady Pamela Hicks, explained that this had its drawbacks. 'Bobo was always around. If, for instance, the Princess was having a bath, it was impossible for Prince Philip to sit in the bathroom and chat to her because of Bobo. It was frustrating for him at times and reminiscent of Lehzen, who was the same with Queen Victoria.' Lehzen was the governess and, later, companion to the young Victoria until Prince Albert orchestrated her dismissal.

Bobo accompanied Elizabeth and Philip on over forty tours and was with them at Sagana Lodge in Kenya in 1952, when Elizabeth was told that the King had died and she was now the Queen. She was always a stickler for protocol. Philip's valet, John Dean, who was also with the royal party in Kenya, recalled introducing himself to her as 'John', only to be told, 'Well, to me you will always be Mr Dean. We have to keep up a certain standard in the house.'

Sometimes she was the main standard bearer, as on one occasion when Lilibet and Philip spent the weekend with his cousin Patricia Knatchbull (later Countess Mountbatten) and her husband, John. Patricia remembered, 'We were in a small house in Kent, not the one we lived in for most of our marriage. As the royal car turned into the drive the Queen was amused to hear Bobo's shocked voice: "Och this won't do, this won't do". The Queen wasn't in the least bit bothered!'

Bobo remained one of the few people who could tell the Queen what she thought of her TV appearances, when other people close to the monarch, including the Queen Mother, tended to be flattering. John Dean recalled her as 'a rather peremptory Scotswoman', but it was her directness that appealed to the Queen.

In the 1970s, a cost-cutting exercise at Buckingham Palace forbade members of the household to be given meals in their rooms. Bobo promptly took to her bed with a cold, which went on and on, forcing assistants to bring in her meals three times a day. She stuck to her guns and remained exempt from the room service ban.

It was Bobo who brought the Queen her morning tea in her room, apart from each 4 July, Bobo's birthday, when the monarch brought a cup of tea to her much-loved friend.

After half a century of service, Bobo was given a brooch of diamonds set in gold, made by the royal jewellers, Garrard. In 1986, she was also made a Lieutenant of the Royal Victorian Order.

Bobo even resembled the Queen, thanks to the fact they shared a hairdresser. After Charles Martin tended to the Queen's hair in her Buckingham Palace suite, he would pop upstairs to Miss MacDonald's rooms on the floor above and produce the same hairstyle for her too.

In her final years, Bobo suffered a series of falls, breaking a leg in 1986 and her hip four years later. After this last one, she was admitted to the King Edward VII Hospital for Officers. She returned to Buckingham Palace, and it was there that she died in September 1993. The Queen attended her funeral at the Queen's Chapel near Marlborough House, where she gave thanks to the memory of the woman who gave sixty-seven years of faithful service and never once let her 'little lady' down.

12

CRAWFIE

In 1949, two well-connected American journalists approached Buckingham Palace about producing a series of articles on the education of Princess Elizabeth. What sounded like an innocent project would snowball out of control, turning into a major conflict between the King and Queen and their daughter's governess, Marion Crawford.

'Crawfie', as she was known to Elizabeth and Margaret, was born in Scotland in 1909. She emigrated to New Zealand as a baby but, when her father was killed in an industrial accident when she was 2 years of age, she returned with her mother to live in Dunfermline.

She was educated at Edinburgh's Moray House, whose later alumni included author J.K. Rowling, Olympic gold-medal winning cyclist Chris Hoy and actor Robbie Coltrane. Marion's report card put her among the top students, and she planned a career in child psychology. She clearly had a change of heart because, in 1932, she accepted a job in an aristocratic household, tutoring the future Earl of Elgin. She moved on to educate the two children of Lady Rose Leveson-Gower. Here, she came to the notice of Rose's sister, the Duchess of York, who was impressed by Crawford's stamina and love of walking as much as her competence as a tutor.

Crawford moved to No. 145 Piccadilly in 1932, when Elizabeth was 6 and Margaret 2, and would stay with the family for the next sixteen years, including the war years at Windsor Castle. In her written account of her time as the royal governess, she suggests the Duchess of York was not particularly interested in her daughters' tutoring. Certainly, in her later years, Princess Margaret voiced her regret at the limitations of her education.

Marion Crawford (far right) accompanies the Princesses and their mother's lady-in-waiting Lady Helen Graham when they took a ride on the London Underground. (© World History Archive/Alamy)

Queen Mary had concerns about her granddaughters' lessons and, according to Crawfie, she was a 'rock of strength and wisdom', offering suggestions and monitoring the girls' progress.

The governess lived with her charges and, in doing so, she put her own life on hold. She had a long-term, long-distance engagement with George Buthlay, an Aberdeen banker. They only married in the summer of 1947, shortly before Princess Elizabeth's wedding. Even then, by her own account, she came under considerable pressure from her employers to stay in her post to act as companion and governess to 17-year-old Margaret now that Elizabeth was about to leave home. 'You must see, Crawfie, that it would not be at all convenient just now,' Queen Elizabeth explained. 'A change at this stage for Margaret is not at all desirable.' Queen Mary was more forceful in her reaction, 'My dear, you can't leave them … I don't think they could spare you just now.'

When she did eventually retire from her duties, she did so with a modest pension, the award of a Commander of the Royal Victoria Order (CVO) and, most impressively, a grace-and-favour home: Nottingham Cottage, a detached house designed by Christopher Wren, in the Kensington Palace complex. It would later become newsworthy as the first London home of Prince William and Catherine Middleton, and later of Prince Harry and Meghan Markle.

George Buthlay was a determined and ambitious man and he convinced Marion she had been short-changed by the royal family. He made her believe she should have had a better pension and been made a dame rather than a Commander of the Royal Victoria Order. It's also claimed she nursed the ambition of becoming Elizabeth's lady-in-waiting, something her working-class origins wouldn't have entitled her to be at the time.

Meanwhile, the American journalists Bruce and Beatrice Gould, of the *Ladies' Home Journal*, proposed a series of articles on the younger years of Princess Elizabeth. Queen Elizabeth was cautiously supportive of the project, providing it would be penned by the historian Dermot Morrah, the author of several Palace-approved hagiographies. It was expected that Crawfie would be one of the main sources for the project.

Instead, in February 1949, backed by the ruthless Buthlay, she approached Queen Elizabeth about writing her own account of her years of service. The Goulds, hearing of Crawfie's dissatisfaction about her retirement settlement, jumped ship and sidelined the dry-as-dust Morrah for the chance of working with the gullible governess. In March, Princess Margaret wrote to her former tutor to inform her that there was widespread dismay at the Palace about the idea. When the Buthlays appeared undeterred, the Queen herself penned a strong-worded letter to Marion, urging her to be 'utterly oyster' – her favourite phrase for tight-lipped. She included the firm suggestion, 'I do hope you will put all the American temptations aside very firmly'.

Crawford ignored the Queen's feelings, signed a contract and began work on her memoirs, still naively hoping her former employers would approve it. A copy was sent to the Queen by former politician Nancy Astor, who had acted as go-between with the publishers. The Queen wrote to Astor, 'Our late and completely trusted governess has gone off her head', having, the Queen said, promised not to write her memoirs. Thirteen items the Queen felt strongly about were removed and the articles appeared in the *Ladies' Home Journal* in the United States before being serialised in the UK in *Woman's Own*. Later, in 1950, the memoirs appeared in book form as *The Little Princesses*.

According to the Queen Mother's official biographer, Princess Elizabeth 'was as horrified as her mother' by Crawfie's treachery. She still sent her former governess a Christmas card and gift that year, but her parents cut the Buthlays off straight away. They still had her pension and Nottingham Cottage, but as the entire court froze them out – 'she snaked', a retired member of the household told biographer Ben Pimlott – the couple presumably felt uncomfortable living in their enclave at Kensington Palace and returned to Scotland.

Crawfie suffered a further, more public, fall from grace five years later. She had by then produced several anodyne books on the royal family and earned a comfortable income writing for women's magazines. In 1955, a tight deadline meant that she was forced to write features on that year's Trooping the Colour ceremony and Royal Ascot meeting ahead of the events. Unfortunately for her, both events were cancelled at short notice due to a national train strike and, as it was too late to pull the pieces from the magazines, they appeared on the news-stands. Crawfie ended up with egg on her face.

She retired with her husband to Aberdeen, where they bought a house on the road that links the city with Balmoral, which meant that from time to time over the summer months a royal car or two would pass her home. Rather late in the day, she developed an aversion to the press and would never comment on royal events. When asked about Prince Andrew's wedding to Sarah Ferguson in 1986, she rebuffed the journalist with, 'I'm not interested. I have no comment to make on anything.'

Sadly, she attempted suicide more than once, finally passing away in an Aberdeenshire care home at the age of 78. Although she had been victim to the ambitions of her husband and the two publishers, the royal family never forgave her treachery. 'Doing a Crawfie' became Palace speak for anyone who betrays the trust of the family and sells their story.

Nevertheless, there was an interesting coda to the governess and the princess she tutored more than eighty years ago. In the 2016 documentary, *Elizabeth at 90: A Family Documentary*, to mark the monarch's 90th birthday, the Queen and Prince Charles are shown watching old family movies. In one scene, the princesses are shown dancing the Lambeth Walk on board the royal yacht. The Queen identifies the fourth member of the group as 'Miss Crawford'. It is about as near to the latter's reputation being restored as she will ever get. There was no explanation or comment other than those words. The Queen as always remained tight-lipped, unlike poor Crawfie.

13

HEIR AND SPARE

One of the key dates in the Queen's life was 11 December 1936. In the early afternoon, the Royal Assent was given to Edward VIII's Instrument of Abdication. As next in line to the throne, Elizabeth's father succeeded as King George VI and she became the Heiress Presumptive.

Quite when she was told that her Uncle David was renouncing the throne in order to marry Wallis Simpson – and the implications it would have for her family and her future – is still unclear, and only her official biographer might, one day, be able to shed some light on it.

The principal source, as always, regarding the Queen's youth is Marion Crawford's memoir, *The Little Princesses*. Crawford, however, wrote some thirteen years after the events of December 1936 and is unreliable when it comes to a timeframe.

According to Crawfie's account, the Duchess of York, who was ill in bed with influenza, received Queen Mary, 'suddenly old and tired', in her bedroom before telling the governess, 'I'm afraid there are going to be great changes in our lives, Crawfie'. The governess wrote, 'When I told Margaret and Elizabeth that they were going to live at Buckingham Palace they looked at me with horror. "What!" said Lilibet. "You mean forever?"'

Queen Mary visited the Duchess on 10 December, hours after Edward had signed the Instrument of Abdication.

Crawfie then jumped to 12 December, the morning the King attended his Accession Council at St James's Palace. She claimed she 'had to explain to them [the princesses] that when Papa came home to lunch at one o'clock he would be King of England and they would have to curtsey to him'. He had, in fact, been King since the previous afternoon.

Another eyewitness was Lady Cynthia Asquith, a trusted biographer of the princesses and their parents. She recorded visiting the two girls and their governess on Friday, 11 December. She recounted Margaret telling her, 'Isn't all this a bore. We've got to leave our nice house now', while Elizabeth noticed a letter on the hall table addressed to Her Majesty the Queen and said, 'That's Mummie now, isn't it?'

The Queen Mother's official biographer, William Shawcross, wrote that 'their parents had protected them from the drama, and they had been told nothing of it until it was over'. More likely, as historian Ben Pimlott notes, it had all 'been absorbed by Princess Elizabeth gradually'. Princess Margaret told Pimlott that the princesses knew about the change in status but did not discuss it. 'When our father became king,' she recalled, 'I said to her [Elizabeth] "Does that mean you're going to be Queen?" She replied, "Yes I suppose it does." She didn't mention it again.'

Abdication Timeline

16 November: Edward VIII dines with his mother, Queen Mary, and his sister, the Princess Royal, and breaks the news to them that he intends to marry Wallis Simpson. At some point after this, he informs his three brothers – the Dukes of York, Gloucester and Kent.

10 December: Shortly after 10 a.m., Edward signs the Instrument of Abdication, witnessed by his three brothers. During the afternoon, Queen Mary visits the Duchess of York at No. 145 Piccadilly.

11 December: The Royal Assent is given to the Instrument of Abdication at 1.52 p.m. and the Duke of York succeeds to the throne as George VI. Later the same day, Lady Cynthia Asquith takes tea with the princesses and Marion Crawford.

12 December: George VI attends his Accession Council at 11.25 a.m. At 3.00 p.m. Heralds of the College of Arms proclaim the accession of George VI from the Friary Court balcony of St James's Palace. According to *The Times*, the ceremony is watched from a window at Marlborough House by the new King, the two princesses and Queen Mary.

13 December: George VI, together with Princesses Elizabeth and Margaret, attend Divine Service in Marlborough House

Five months after the abdication, Elizabeth attended her father's coronation. Her gown (far left, with her gold coronet), together with those of her mother and sister, are shown on display at Glamis Castle in 2017. (© Ian Lloyd)

Chapel, during which prayers are said for the new King and Princess Elizabeth, as they are at church services throughout the land.

14

MANNERS MAKETH THE MONARCH

In 1970, the American actor Mia Farrow was at a dinner party at No. 10 Downing Street hosted by Prime Minister Edward Heath. The guest of honour, the Queen Mother, asked Farrow how her twin baby boys were getting along. The actress said they were fine and, to fill a long silence, asked the Queen Mum, 'What in your view is the most important thing I can teach them?'

The royal matriarch replied, 'I think it's … *manners*', adding, 'I believe that manners can get you through *anything*.'

The Queen Mother had perfect manners and it is a characteristic that was inherited by the Queen (although perhaps not so wholeheartedly by Princess Margaret). We have always seen it in the perfect way she appears in public – one of her designers told me, 'The Queen is perpetually dressed for a wedding.' We've seen it in many less-significant ways, such as the fact she has never been photographed nodding off or yawning, never been seen looking at her watch or turning her back on a dinner guest. We've also seen it at Buckingham Palace investitures when the lollipop lady receiving an MBE is given the same amount of time and the same number of questions as Elton John getting a knighthood.

It is a particularly useful characteristic when she has had to exchange diplomatic niceties with other heads of state, something she has become *the* past master at. A fine example of this occurred in May 2011, during President Barack Obama's state visit. At the official banquet, he was in the middle of proposing a toast when things went slightly awry. He put down his notes, raised his glass and declared, 'To Her Majesty the Queen.' The string orchestra of the Scots Guards, believing this was the end of his speech, took it as the cue to play the national anthem.

While the Queen and her guests stood solemnly to attention for the anthem, Obama carried on speaking and, as the music swelled, turned to her and said, 'To the Queen.' She left him and his glass hanging, so to speak, but she did smile and say, 'Very kind', before turning back for the end of the music. Had she not talked over it too, and reassured him, it would have been a noticeable faux pas.

There was another show of regal good manners during the state visit of one of her favourite leaders, Nelson Mandela. After

Take your partners: the Queen and Prince Philip arrive for a lunch hosted by Nelson Mandela at the Dorchester Hotel during his state visit to Britain in July 1996. (© Ian Lloyd)

a lunch at the Dorchester Hotel, the two heads of state attended a charity 'Two Nations Celebrate' concert at the Royal Albert Hall. One of the highlights was the rousing Ladysmith Black Mambazo singing group, who encouraged everyone to get up. Mandela was on his feet straight away, swaying back and forth to the music. He was swiftly followed by his daughter and the Prince of Wales when, to everyone's surprise, the Queen got up and joined them. One jaw-dropped official in an adjacent box was heard to say, 'My God, the Queen's dancing!'

One of the oddest examples of the Queen as the master of soft power occurred at a private dinner at Windsor Castle on her 47th birthday in April 1973. Her guest that night was the Australian Prime Minister Gough Whitlam and his wife, Margaret, dubbed 'Big Marge' by courtiers. Whitlam had come into power the previous year and had already announced that he wanted to replace 'God Save the Queen' as the national anthem. He would quite like to have replaced the Queen as well as her anthem, and so a major charm offensive was needed.

The Queen put the Whitlams up in a suite overlooking the Long Walk and no effort was too great to make them feel at home. When they went down to dinner, they took with them their present – a deep-piled, cream sheepskin rug. An Aussie rug wouldn't normally have been at the top of the Queen's must-have list, but she reacted as if it was the best gift anyone had ever given her. Prince Philip had already taken his shoes off and was treading on it in his stockinged feet. After several glasses of champagne had been drunk, the Queen sprang into action. 'That evening she was quite determined to catch her man', as her private secretary, Martin Charteris, told royal biographer Graham Turner:

A lot of her sexuality has been suppressed, but that night, she used it like a weapon. She wrapped Gough Whitlam round her little finger, knocked him sideways. She sat on that rug in front of him, stroked it and said how lovely it was. It was an arrant use of sexuality. I was absolutely flabbergasted.

Then she got Princess Margaret to join her and the two women lay on the rug pulling it round them and thoroughly relishing it.

An impressed Whitlam said to Charteris afterwards, 'Well, if she's like that, it's all right by me!'

The upshot was that, although the British national anthem did bite the dust down under, almost half a century on the British monarch is still head of state. There remains just one puzzle: nobody seems to know what happened to the sheepskin rug.

15

PHONEY TIMES

'The children could not go without me, I could not possibly leave the King, and the King would never go.'

This oft-quoted remark of the Queen Mother was in response to the suggestion that, with Britain at war, the Princesses Elizabeth and Margaret should be evacuated to Canada or the United States as so many of their friends and relations had been. We now know that, instead, they spent over five years confined to the family fortress of Windsor Castle where, according to Princess Margaret, 'rather flimsy barbed wire wouldn't have kept the Germans out, but certainly kept us in'.

It is less well known that it was the King and Queen's original plan to keep the two girls at Balmoral Castle for the duration, and in fact, they spent the first four months of hostilities – a period known as 'the Phoney War' – on their Aberdeenshire estate. Until Germany surrendered, there would be a news blackout on their whereabouts, and the public only ever knew the princesses were at 'a house in the country'.

The royal family arrived at Balmoral on 1 August 1939, but the growing threat of war meant the King was obliged to leave for London on 23 August, followed five days later by Queen Elizabeth. 'Who is this Hitler, spoiling everything?' sulked Margaret, who had been looking forward to another six or seven weeks of holiday. The girls had little idea they would not now see their parents until Christmas.

Elizabeth and Margaret were left in the care of their nanny, Clara Knight, and their mother's lady-in-waiting, the Hon. Lettice Bowlby. Their cousin, Margaret Elphinstone (later the Hon. Margaret Rhodes), was sent to keep them company.

In a 2009 telephone call with the author, Mrs Rhodes recalled the day war was declared, 3 September 1939:

> I went to Crathie Kirk with the princesses. The service is always at 11.30 so we missed Neville Chamberlain's speech on the wireless, but I do recall the minister, Dr Lamb, preaching a very doom-laden sermon, and ending it with a dramatic 'and now we are at war!'
>
> I don't think we were at the age when we quite knew what that meant. As children we practically thought of it as knights on horseback, but we now knew there was a war on. I can still remember that.

The girls were moved to Birkhall, now the Deeside home of Prince Charles, where they were joined by Crawfie, who taught them lessons in the morning followed by walks on the deserted grouse moors or rides on their ponies that had been brought up from Windsor. Mrs Rhodes recalled French lessons from a tutor named Georgina Guerin, who had been sent to Scotland to take some of the pressure off Crawfie.

Naturally, the girls were worried for the safety of their parents. 'Do you think the Germans will come and get them?' an anxious Margaret asked Crawfie. Elizabeth, ever the protective sister, told the household, 'I don't think people should talk about battles and things in front of Margaret. We don't want to upset her.'

The girls did, however, study *Jane's Fighting Ships* to familiarise themselves with the British fleet. When the battleship *Royal Oak* was sunk at Scapa Flow by a German U-boat with the loss of 833 lives, Elizabeth was horrified and jumped up from her chair shouting, 'Crawfie, it can't be! All those nice sailors!'

A useful distraction was the nightly telephone call from the King and Queen, always at 6 p.m. A less-welcome voice was that of 'Lord Haw-Haw', the infamous William Joyce, who broadcast Nazi propaganda to listeners in Britain. His efforts were greeted with peals of laughter from the girls and the occasional book or cushion thrown at the wireless.

A sewing party was organised on Thursday afternoons for the wives of estate workers, local farmers and crofters. The princesses served them tea, sandwiches, drop scones and jam and fruitcake. They also played gramophone records on an old-fashioned horn gramophone – a royal version of 'music while you work'.

The 1939 stay was the longest the Queen has ever spent on Deeside. As winter approached, she and her sister were fascinated by the heavy north-country frosts and early falls of snow. With no central heating at Birkhall, the girls woke to find their drinking water frozen solid and their sponges and flannels rock hard, which, according to Crawfie, 'delighted them immensely'.

The princesses joined a Girl Guide company based in the village hall, and in the evenings, entertainment was occasionally laid on by a local man, who would come to Birkhall with a movie projector to show old Charlie Chaplin and Laurel and Hardy films.

With Christmas nearly upon them, the princesses rehearsed a nativity play and went shopping for presents at Woolworth's in Aberdeen, buying sixpenny china ornaments and brooches for their parents. The girls were familiar with the city, since Elizabeth had paid regular visits to a dentist there to adjust the rubber bands she was obliged to wear to straighten her teeth.

The novel experience of a Highland winter came to an abrupt halt when the cowman on the estate caught diphtheria. Everyone had to be inoculated. The princesses were stopped from going to the Girl Guide meetings and the nativity play in which they had starring roles was cancelled.

Eventually, in late December, their mother telephoned to tell the girls the news that, as the 'Phoney War' looked set to continue, they would be coming south for Christmas. It was several years before they returned to Scotland. In May 1940, the princesses moved to Windsor Castle where they remained until VE Day, five years later.

16

VE AND VJ

For 19-year-old Elizabeth and 14-year-old Margaret, 8 May 1945 was a double celebration. Not only were they joining millions in marking the end of six years of war against the Nazis but they were also allowed to leave the confines of Buckingham Palace

and join the thousands of revellers in the streets of the capital. Margaret Rhodes described it as 'a Cinderella moment in
reverse, in which they could pretend that they were ordinary
and unknown'.

This one-off occurrence on such a historic day was even
the subject of a 2015 film, *A Royal Night Out*, which, like many
others in this royal genre, was only a vague representation of
the truth. The princesses partied in the streets not just once, but
on four nights. As Princess Margaret commented in a 1995 BBC
interview, 'There was VE night and VE night plus one, and VJ
night and VJ night plus one,' adding, 'we got quite good at it in
the end.'

The Queen's sister described those final days of the war as 'a
terrible fizzle. We waited, waited and waited and nobody quite
knew whether the war was over or not because the message did
not arrive or no one was quite certain.' She went on to recall
loudspeakers being erected in Buckingham Palace's forecourt
so the crowds could hear Winston Churchill's speech at 3 p.m.
Later in the day, he memorably appeared on Buckingham
Palace balcony with the King and Queen and their daughters.
Margaret remembered him putting out one of his famous cigars
in an ashtray before stepping outside.

The noise was deafening as the mood of euphoria swept
through the people outside Buckingham Palace. The Queen
recorded her memories for the 1985 BBC Radio 4 programme
The Way We Were, marking the fortieth anniversary of VE Day.
'My sister and I realised we couldn't see what the crowds were
enjoying. My mother had put her tiara on for the occasion, so
we asked my parents if we could go out and see for ourselves.'

Margaret agreed that it 'was my parents' idea' to go out,
though elsewhere she claimed it had been planned by her maternal uncle, David Bowes Lyon. He was part of the group of about
sixteen people who joined the Princess in slipping out to join the
throng. The others included Margaret Elphinstone; her brother

John Elphinstone (who arrived at Buckingham Palace the previous day with the King's nephew, George, Viscount Lascelles, having both been released from POW camps in Germany); Jean Gibbs (lady-in-waiting to Elizabeth, who would marry John and Margaret's brother, Andrew Elphinstone); Peter Townsend (the King's equerry, who Princess Margaret would sensationally fall in love with several years later); Lord Porchester (later the Queen's racing manager); Marion Crawford (the royal governess); and Vicomtesse de Bellaigue (known as 'Toni', who taught the princesses French).

The group linked arms and caroused along St James's Street and Piccadilly, stopping before the end as the King had drawn the line at going as far as Piccadilly Circus. Elizabeth remembered 'lines of unknown people linking arms and walking down Whitehall, all of us just swept along on a tide of happiness and relief'.

She wore her ATS uniform on the day and recalled how she pulled her cap 'well down over my eyes' to stop herself being recognised. But, she added, she was reprimanded by a fellow officer. 'A Grenadier officer amongst our party of about sixteen people said he refused to be seen in the company of another officer improperly dressed, so I had to put my cap on normally,' she said. Margaret, who was not yet 15, was too young to join the forces and recalled being 'frightfully annoyed' that, unlike her sister, she was in 'civvies' and 'was kept at the back'.

They joined in the 'Hokey Cokey', the 'Lambeth Walk', 'Roll out the Barrel' and so on, before returning to the Buckingham Palace railings to see the King and Queen. The euphoric mood was due to sheer relief and Margaret observed, 'We never saw anyone drunk', perhaps because, as she put it, 'for one thing there was very little liquor'.

The Queen admitted to pulling a few strings. 'We were successful in seeing my parents on the balcony, having cheated slightly because we sent a message into the house to say we were waiting outside.' She also had in interesting brush with the law.

It came to light when she met the author Hammond Innes at a literary party. For some reason, they got on to the topic of police helmets. Innes, taken aback, said, 'How would you know about them, Ma'am?', to which the Queen replied, 'Of course I do. I knocked one off on VE Day.'

Elizabeth later recalled the royal family appearing on the Buckingham Palace balcony, time and again:

> I remember the thrill and relief after the previous day's waiting for the prime minister's announcement of the end of the war in Europe. My parents went out on the balcony in response to the huge crowds outside. I think we went on the balcony nearly every hour, six times.

After cheering the King and Queen, the group sneaked back into Buckingham Palace unobserved. Toni Bellaigue recalled that, in the early hours of the morning, Queen Elizabeth made sandwiches for them all herself.

The princesses went out again the following night, 9 May. This time, the group danced to Trafalgar Square, along Piccadilly and back via Pall Mall. They saw their parents appear at 12.30, carried on partying in the palace and went to bed at 3 a.m.

The war continued in the Far East and when, eventually, the Japanese surrendered, the princesses joined Londoners in celebrating VJ Day. This time, they were recognised twice, including once by a Dutch serviceman who linked arms with the group, spotted who was in the line-up and then quietly slipped away. It was during this night of freedom that the future Queen drank in the Dorchester Hotel and then danced a conga through the Ritz.

The following night, VJ plus one, was the last time the sisters partied in the streets. Elizabeth noted that there were fewer revellers due to the rain, but it failed to deter the royal party, which congaed back through the gates of Buckingham Palace, sang songs until 2 a.m. and went to bed an hour later.

In May 1995, the Queen, the Queen Mother and Princess Margaret appeared on the balcony of Buckingham Palace to celebrate the fiftieth anniversary of VE Day, joining in the community singing led by Cliff Richard and Dame Vera Lynn. Now it is over three-quarters of a century since the end of the war and Elizabeth is the only survivor of the group of sixteen who wildly celebrated victory over the Axis powers. It was, in her own words, 'One of the most memorable nights of my life.'

17

SISTERLY LOVE

I think she's got an aura, a twentieth-century aura.

This was Princess Margaret's opinion of her sister, then aged 43. Fast forward to 2006, and the sisters' cousin, Margaret Rhodes, told the author, 'I think she caused the Queen a great deal of heartache over the years, but she always forgave her.'

Princesses Elizabeth and Margaret were chalk and cheese. Elizabeth was, and would remain, self-controlled, emotionally restrained and dutiful. Margaret, four years her junior, was passionate, mercurial and ill-disciplined. Without a meaningful role in her adult life, Margaret would test the Queen's patience time and again.

She was often frustrated with the constraints of royal protocol and relished her occasional forays outside the Buckingham Palace walls, especially in the 1960s. On the other hand, she would never have abandoned her privileged position in the way Edward VIII or Prince Harry did. She relished being the daughter of the last King-Emperor and, in public at least, she venerated her sister.

This sister was given her first glimpse of Margaret just a few hours after her birth on 21 August 1930 at Glamis Castle and several times the following day. Accounts of her reaction suggest 4-year-old Lilibet was happy with the arrival. 'I have a new little baby sister,' she told a tenant farmer on the Glamis estate, adding, 'She is so lovely and I am very, very happy.' She had raided her own toy cupboard for gifts for her sister, including a blue velvet frog, dancing dolls and a couple of picture books.

The young Margaret would grow up to be a natural entertainer. Her grandmother, Queen Mary, not renowned for her sense of humour, told a friend her granddaughter was 'so outrageously amusing that one can't help encouraging her'. The royal governess, Marion Crawford, noted, 'Though Lilibet, with the rest of us, laughed at Margaret's antics – and indeed it was impossible not to – I think they often made her uneasy and filled with foreboding.'

Stories emerged of Margaret's entertaining and wilful behaviour. Like her great-nephew, Prince Harry, the Princess blamed Fleet Street rather than herself. 'When my sister and I were growing up she was made out to be the goody-goody one,' she told biographer Andrew Duncan in 1969. 'That was boring, so the press tried to make out I was as wicked as hell.'

In fact, she *was* as 'wicked as hell' from time to time. The sisters squabbled and fought, as sisters do, with Margaret known to bite and Lilibet to lash out with her fists – apparently, a left hook was her speciality. A common complaint from Elizabeth was that 'Margaret always wants what I want'.

The solution for their parents was to treat the girls as equals. Despite their age gap, they were dressed identically and had identical hair styles – short with some curls. At the 1937 coronation of George VI, they wore the same style of white-laced dress with short socks, but when it emerged that Elizabeth would be given a longer ermine-trimmed purple mantle, Margaret had a major tantrum. Throwing herself on the floor, she screamed that it wasn't fair, until it was explained to her that given their 4in height difference, the trains had to be designed in proportion.

The fact that she could twist her father round her little finger was no hindrance to Margaret's cause. 'She was thoroughly spoiled,' recalled Margaret Rhodes, 'and knew how to bring out her father's personality.' It has often been said that while Elizabeth was George VI's pride, Margaret was his joy. Although the order of succession dictated Princess Elizabeth's status, in private he treated his daughters as equals. 'I've never suffered from second daughter-itis,' Margaret explained to her biographer, Christopher Warwick, 'I never minded being referred to as the younger daughter. But I do mind being referred to as the younger sister.'

When her sister married and started a family, Princess Margaret remained, initially, in the nursery with Crawfie, until she began to undertake solo engagements. Occasionally, she appeared to outrank her sister. At thanksgiving services for the King and Queen's silver wedding anniversary in 1948 and for the Festival of Britain three years later, the Princess travelled to St Paul's Cathedral in the first carriage with her parents while the Edinburghs followed in the second carriage. Such pre-eminence would only last during the King's lifetime and ended abruptly with his death in February 1952 when Margaret was only 21.

His passing affected her greatly, and more than a year later, at Elizabeth's coronation, one of the maids of honour, her good friend, Lady Anne Coke, noticed the Princess's eyes appeared

red-rimmed after the service. Margaret explained the reason for
her sadness, 'I've lost my father and I've lost my sister. She will
be so busy. Our lives will change.'

One thing that changed their lives dramatically and may
well have been the real reason for Margaret's distress was her
love affair with her father's equerry, Group Captain Peter
Townsend, which was already well under way by the time of the
coronation. The problem for the Queen was that Townsend had
recently been divorced – and was, in terms of the royal family,
a pariah, because at the time, divorced people were not allowed
at Buckingham Palace garden parties or inside royal palaces.
Moreover, as Supreme Governor of the Church of England,
which wouldn't recognise the marriage of a divorced person, it
put her in a deeply awkward situation.

She did, however, show sympathy to her sister and to
Townsend. The latter recalled a dinner party hosted by Elizabeth
and Philip. It left him with one 'unforgettable impression … the
Queen's movingly simple and sympathetic acceptance of the
disturbing fact of her sister's love for me'.

Others were far from sympathetic. Elizabeth's private secretary, Alan Lascelles, told Townsend bluntly, 'You must be either
mad or bad.'

The old guard rallied to protect the Queen and the monarchy
rather than indulging the Princess. Prime Minister Winston
Churchill agreed that Townsend should be posted as Air
Attaché in Brussels. The appointment was such a swift one that
the British Ambassador, Sir Christopher Warner, knew nothing
until he read about it in the newspapers during a visit to the
Belgian Congo.

Churchill insisted Townsend should leave for Belgium two
days before Margaret and her mother flew back from a tour of
Rhodesia. The Princess later told Christopher Warwick that
she returned 'utterly lost and lonely'. If so, she had calmed
down considerably, because she had exploded with rage on

hearing the news during the tour and took to her room with 'a heavy cold'.

Before Townsend left, the Queen thoughtfully included him in the royal party as her equerry for a visit to Northern Ireland. It was a shrewd move, giving the impression that she bore the couple no ill will. Like her mother, dubbed 'the imperial ostrich' by courtiers for her fondness for burying her head in the sand when faced with anything disagreeable, Elizabeth naively hoped that time would be a great healer.

Press interest – 'a journalistic orgy', according to Noël Coward – reached fever pitch during the summer and autumn of 1955. Under the Royal Marriages Act of 1772, when the Princess reached the age of 25 on 21 August that year, she could marry whomever she chose without the consent of the Queen. Although it would protect the monarch from direct involvement in the decision making, Margaret would still need the permission of Parliament and, almost certainly, lose her place in the order of succession and her Civil List allowance.

Elizabeth and Philip, with the Queen Mother, had a final discussion with Margaret about the situation at Windsor on Sunday, 23 October. Afterwards, the Princess rang Townsend in 'great distress'. He would later recall, 'We had reached the end of the road, our feelings for one another were unchanged, but they had incurred for us a burden so great that we decided together to lay it down.' The Princess returned to London feeling 'thoroughly drained, thoroughly demoralised'.

The couple had a final meeting at Clarence House on 31 October, before the Princess released a statement later that day announcing, 'I would like it to be known that I have decided not to marry Group Captain Peter Townsend'. Ironically, the statement was the first official confirmation from the Palace that Margaret and Townsend were in a relationship.

Margaret spent the rest of the 1950s at Clarence House, cooped up and increasingly frustrated as her friends in 'the Margaret Set' gradually married and settled down, one by one. She took out her frustration on her mother, on one occasion throwing a book at her head, and also on her sister. When Elizabeth and Philip hosted a party at Buckingham Palace in 1957 to mark their tenth wedding anniversary, the Princess deliberately arrived an hour before it ended. Prime Minister Harold MacMillan witnessed Margaret's unedifying behaviour when he was in a private audience with the Queen. The Princess walked in wearing a dressing gown and said, 'No one would talk to you if you were not the Queen.'

There was an improvement in the Princess's behaviour and her relationship with her family when, in 1960, she married the society photographer, Antony Armstrong-Jones. Initially, it was a highly passionate relationship in more ways than one. They were tremendously physically attracted to each other, and the dynamic young snapper was able to introduce the Princess to aspects of Bohemian London she could only have dreamed of.

The Queen was relieved that her sister was clearly happy to have found love. Other royal relations greeted the news with dismay. When Noël Coward visited the Queen's aunt, the Duchess of Kent, and her daughter Alexandra, he noted 'a distinct *froideur*' when he mentioned the couple's engagement, adding, 'they are not pleased'. European royals stayed away in droves, with the only significant guest being Margaret's godmother, Queen Ingrid of Denmark, who felt duty bound to attend.

The Queen was very fond of Armstrong-Jones, whom she ennobled as Earl of Snowdon in 1961, shortly before the birth of Viscount Linley. In letters to him, she addressed him as 'Tony' and signed herself 'Lilibet', though he was scrupulously deferential in return and always addressed her and her mother as 'Your Majesty' and 'Ma'am'.

Both Elizabeths remained fond of Snowdon during the eventual collapse of his marriage to Margaret, and afterwards. When he wrote to the Queen to tell her the union with his sister had spiralled out of control, she wrote back that she found his letter 'devastating'. Like her mother, she knew that the highly strung Margaret could be hell to live with and much of their sympathy was given to her soon-to-be ex-husband. Others were less fulsome in their praise for Snowdon. 'He pulled the wool over their eyes,' recalled Margaret's lady-in-waiting, Anne Glenconner.

Although Margaret and Tony both had extra-marital flings during the later years of their marriage, it was her romance with Roddy Llewellyn, seventeen years her junior, that was the straw that broke the camel's back. When a Sunday newspaper cropped a group photo to show just Margaret and her toy-boy lover in swimwear on Mustique, it caused a sensation. The Princess flew home alone and, after consultation with her sister, announced her separation from her husband. It was, of course, ironic that divorce had prevented her from marrying Townsend, but in 1978, the Princess became the most senior royal to divorce since Henry VIII and Anne of Cleves in 1540.

According to Margaret Rhodes, the Queen found her sister 'a total enigma'. To the author, Mrs Rhodes added, 'Princess Margaret had terrible taste in men.' A former private secretary revealed the Queen had once spoken to him about the Princess's 'guttersnipe life'.

Certainly, the Queen was no fan of Roddy Llewellyn, and refused to have him as a guest in any of her homes. When they did meet, it wasn't in the best of circumstances. Roddy was staying at the Royal Lodge and wandered into a room in his shirt and underpants searching for the Snowdon children's Nanny Sumner to sew a button on his trousers. Bumping into the Queen, he spluttered, 'Please forgive me, Ma'am, I look so awful', to which the Queen, making the best of a bad situation, joked, 'Don't worry, I don't look very good myself.'

When Princess Margaret celebrated her 50th birthday at the Ritz Hotel in November 1980, there was a row between the sisters, because the Queen refused to have Roddy present during the dinner. Following the Princess's funeral in February 2002, the Queen did, however, thank Anne Glenconner for introducing her sister to Roddy because 'he made her really happy'.

The two sisters grew closer during the 1980s and 1990s and spoke on the telephone most days. When the Queen was on a tour of California in 1983, she rang Margaret full of excitement at what she had seen and done. When she flew on Concorde for the first time she was asked if she would like to make a phone call and promptly rang her sister.

The Princess occasionally wrote to Elizabeth, too. During the dismal summer of 1992, when the failed marriages of the Prince and Princess of Wales and the Duke and Duchess of York dominated tabloid headlines time and again, Margaret penned a letter to her sister, telling her she had found 'great comfort' being with her at Balmoral. Writing from Italy, she was clearly trying to boost the Queen's flagging morale when she told her, 'Everyone loves you all over the place, I was so pleased for you', ending by adding she hoped her sister was encouraged by this.

Such fulsome praise wasn't new. In 1969, she had discussed the Queen with author Andrew Duncan and enthused, 'I get enormously impressed when she walks into a room. It's a kind of magic.'

The Queen continued her role of protector to her younger sister, on and off, throughout their seventy-one years together. When Margaret had what many consider to be a breakdown, due to the collapse of her marriage and the uncertainty of her romance with Llewellyn, the Queen went to Kensington Palace and took her sister away to Windsor for the weekend. The

The Queen and Princess Margaret weathered many storms in their relationship but remained the best of friends. Here they attend a celebratory lunch to mark their mother's 95th birthday. (© Ian Lloyd)

monarch joked, 'I feel exactly like the night nurse taking over from the day nurse.'

In the final years, when Margaret suffered a series of strokes and had scalded her feet in an accident while staying in Mustique, the Queen asked her private secretary to organise a Concorde flight to bring her sister home. She was naturally devastated when Margaret had a final stroke in early 2002, passing away on 9 February.

After the Princess's funeral, six days later, the Queen stood alongside Margaret's children watching as the hearse prepared to take her sister's body to Slough Crematorium. It was half a century to the day since their father's funeral at St George's Chapel. Much had happened between the sisters in the intervening five decades, but no matter how far the Princess had strayed from the path of royal duty and self-sacrifice, she ultimately retained an abiding faith and affection for her country and her Queen.

18

DANCING QUEEN

Elizabeth II has been known to bop to the famous Abba track during dress fittings with her fun-loving personal assistant, Angela Kelly. Dancing has been a regular pursuit ever since childhood, when she and her sister took lessons from Betty Vacani and her aunt Marguerite. The princesses were in the audience at a gala at the London Hippodrome in 1935 and would have seen another Vacani pupil, the 3-year-old Elizabeth Taylor. The future Hollywood icon was so taken with her starring role that it took a great deal of persuading to stop the precocious child from performing.

On VE Day, when his daughters memorably danced the night away in the streets with thousands of other revellers, George VI noted in his journal, 'Poor darlings, they have never had any fun yet'. The recently published diaries of their wartime friend Alathea Fitzalan Howard paints another picture. There are several references to dances at Windsor Castle, with the Guards officers protecting the royal family, during the Second World War. One, on 23 July 1941, in which Elizabeth, aged 15, took part with gusto, went on until 3.15 a.m., and Princess Margaret, aged 10, had been allowed to stay up for the duration.

The King and Queen were careful not to hold dances if the Allied forces had suffered any setbacks. Queen Elizabeth was very aware of how such frivolity would look to the general public. A dance scheduled for December 1941 was called off at the last minute when the Japanese bombed Pearl Harbor.

With clothing rationed from 1941, the Queen was careful that her daughters should follow the 'make do and mend' policy, with the girls appearing at one dance in their mother's old Hartnell gowns, suitably altered. For a year they wore the same dress at every castle dance.

As the conflict came to an end, Elizabeth and her friends were able to sample the London nightlife. She and Prince Philip danced at Ciro's and Quaglino's. One night they were chased by a photographer, which she hated. Inevitably she drew attention whenever she dined or partied in public, so she tended to prefer private parties.

She often danced with groups of friends at Coppins, the Buckinghamshire home of her widowed aunt, the Duchess of Kent. In February 1946, she attended a party at the London home of the banker Arthur Grenfell, whose daughter, Frances Campbell-Preston became a lady-in-waiting to the Queen Mother. The Princess danced all evening, apart from 'brief and skimpy intervals' when she 'ate merrily' before racing back to dance. In her memoirs, Frances recalls her dancing several Paul

Joneses (a mixer dance that involves changing partners several times), reels, a palais glide, Boomps-a-Daisy and the Lambeth Walk. Shortly before leaving at 2.30 a.m., Elizabeth led the guests on a conga through the ground-floor rooms, her partner clinging to her waist behind her. The conga was a royal tradition, since George VI usually led one through the state apartments at the end of parties. The King was renowned as a fabulous waltzer and Frances records seeing him 'dancing away for all he was worth' at a Buckingham Palace dance that same month.

Contemporaries recall Elizabeth dancing with tremendous energy, joining in nearly all the dances, partly so as not to disappoint the young men who vied to partner her. The diarist Henry 'Chips' Channon recalls seeing Elizabeth, pregnant with Charles, at a fancy-dress party at Coppins. The Princess was dressed as a Spanish Infanta, in a black-lace dress complete with mantilla and comb in her hair. He noted with amazement that she danced until nearly 5 a.m.

Other eyewitnesses testify to Elizabeth's love of music. The late Jean Woodruffe was a lady-in-waiting to the Princess in the post-war years and recalls that they whiled away the time between engagements by singing popular tunes in the royal limousine. The Queen is adept at following the rhythm and is regularly spotted tapping her foot to the beat when a military band plays. Once, during the royal tour of Luxembourg in 1976, after several glasses of champagne had been quaffed, the Queen even took to the drums, hitting them in time and shaking her head to the beat.

Occasionally she has danced in public during royal tours. In Canada, in 1951, she attended a square dance at which Philip wore blue jeans so new that they still had the price tag on. Bobo was sent out to buy Elizabeth a flared cotton skirt.

A more official dance was filmed at the White House during the 1976 state visit to the United States to mark the bicentenary of American independence. The Queen, looking regal in a yellow gown and fringe tiara, was whirled around the dance floor in a foxtrot with President Gerald Ford, while the band played, somewhat incongruously, 'The Lady is a Tramp'.

Meanwhile, the private dances continued, with staff balls each Christmas at Buckingham Palace and Windsor, and a Ghillies' Ball at Balmoral every September. The band leader Joe Loss played at many of the parties and recalled those in his band who were new to playing for royalty always doing a double take when they saw the Queen being whirled around the dance floor.

There were certainly wide eyes in the American band that played at Claridge's on the evening of Charles and Diana's wedding in July 1981. The Queen and Duke hosted the party, with a television in the corner playing highlights of the wedding. When it came to the exchange of vows when Diana fluffed her lines and married 'Philip Charles Arthur George' instead of 'Charles Philip Arthur George', Prince Andrew apparently joked, 'She's married my father.' Philip, wearing a Charles and Diana straw boater, squired his wife around the dance floor. When they left at 1.30 a.m., the Queen told her cousin Elizabeth Anson, who had organised the party, 'I'd love to stay and dance all night.'

She was less exuberant at the 21st birthday bash she hosted for Prince Andrew at Windsor Castle that same year. Elton John was among the guests. He performed 'Your Song', dedicating it to the Queen and did a quick Charleston with Diana. It was when the DJ came on that things got a bit surreal, since it was the quietest disco the singer said he'd ever been to. Princess Anne asked him to dance to Elvis singing 'Hound Dog' and they were awkwardly shuffling from one foot to the other, hearing every step above the 'ridiculously low' music, when the Queen came over. 'May we join you?' she asked and joined in the slow-shoe shuffle, this time to 'Rock Around the Clock'. All the time she still had her black handbag over her arm.

Usually she is the star attraction, but confusion can reign when other royal ladies take to the dance floor. The Queen Mother was once partnered by a young subaltern at Windsor when, unexpectedly, she was called to the telephone. When she returned, he was nowhere to be seen, so her equerry found her another plus one. As she glided round the room she noticed her first partner dancing with the Queen so, steering her own subaltern towards them, she tapped the young man on the shoulder and whispered in his ear, 'Snob!'

19

HANDBAGS AND GLADRAGS

Like many sisters of the 1930s and 1940s, the young Elizabeth and Margaret were dressed in identically matching coats and dresses with white knee-length socks and buttoned shoes. For many years, Lilibet lost her own identity, as her governess Marion Crawford recorded, 'The Princess was always conservative about her dress and content to wear whatever was laid before her.'

She was happy to follow her mother's advice and have Norman Hartnell design many of her clothes. Inevitably, some of them were matronly, but Hartnell came into his own with meticulously embroidered gowns. He made Elizabeth's ivory duchesse satin wedding dress in 1947, embellished with 10,000 American seed pearls and a 15ft train of ivory silk tulle.

The coronation gown was another Hartnell tour de force. Made of white satin, it was encrusted with seed pearls and crystals to create a lattice effect. Following the fashion of the time, it was tight-bodiced, with a full skirt. It also carried symbolic patterns made out of the emblems of all the Commonwealth countries, from the rose of England to the lotus flowers of India and Ceylon.

By the 1950s the two main designers were Hartnell, who continued to make the lavishly embroidered gowns, and Hardy Amies, who made some of the Queen's finest suits and coats. Hartnell's assistant, Ian Thomas, eventually set up his own studio and designed for the Queen until his untimely death, aged 64, in 1993.

The job of the designers was made easier by the Queen's stunning appearance. Aged 25 at the time of her accession, she could have easily rivalled the looks of the world's most beautiful actresses, from Audrey Hepburn to Elizabeth Taylor. She was dark haired, slightly buxom and with a perfect peaches-and-cream complexion – all of which were in vogue at the time. At 5ft 4in, she was petite, though her mother and sister were both 2in shorter.

Bobo established a relationship between the Queen and her designers, and those ground rules still apply today. The designers and milliners come to the Queen, rather than the other way round. They will have already submitted a few ideas, patterns and swatches of material and when the final selection has been made, they are given an appointment to see the Queen – either at Buckingham Palace or, latterly, Windsor Castle, though she has been known to pay for them to fly to Scotland and see her at Balmoral.

The Queen's dressing room at Buckingham Palace is part of her suite of rooms on the first floor of the north side, over-looking Green Park. At one time, a fitting session could take anything up to three hours and occasionally involved a milliner being present to make sure a new hat matched the outfit being designed. Only women assistants and the Queen's dresser are present when the Queen is getting ready. The designer waits in an anteroom before being admitted to make any necessary adjustments to the clothes.

It has always been essential that the dress or coat is comfort-able and made of a material than doesn't crease too much. If it is designed for a tour, it has to be suitable for the weather in that part of the world and, if possible, the clothes should diplo-matically flatter the host nation with a particular colour or pattern, for example, the colour of the national flag or a symbol, such as the dress of Californian poppies she wore when she met President Reagan, a former Governor of California.

The past few years have seen a transformation in the Queen's style. Following the deaths of Hartnell, Amies and Bobo MacDonald, the Queen has had to turn to a younger genera-tion of designers. This period coincided with the appointment of Angela Kelly as the Queen's senior dresser and she is now also her personal assistant.

The Queen regularly wore couture by Karl-Ludwig Rehse, whose studio was in London's Chiltern Street, just a few doors away from that of the late Philip Somerville, one of the Queen's favourite milliners. A recent favourite has been Stewart Parvin, who was only 33 when Angela 'discovered' him and asked him to supply designs. Two early Parvin designs, which the Queen wore several times, are the yellow suit worn at her coronation anniversary service at Westminster Abbey in 2003 and the embroidered pale-blue lace evening dress worn at a Downing Street dinner in 2002 to mark her Golden Jubilee.

Angela Kelly's in-house team are an asset to the Queen, since it cuts down on the time she has to spend on fittings and, more importantly, saves money. Ms Kelly also designs some of the matching hats, while others are made by Rachel Trevor-Morgan, based near St James's Palace.

So successful is her recent look that the Queen has won over some of the harshest critics in the world – the clothes designers themselves. During her tour of Italy in 2000, Gianfranco Ferre gushed, 'She is always so nice, she is fantastic. You should be so proud of her.' Miuccia Prada was even more effusive, 'Everybody is very impressed … I always was a big fan. She is one of the most elegant women in the world.' A year later, Dior's fashion designer, John Galliano, enthused, 'I think the Queen's sublime. She has created a style of her own. I have fantasised about designing for her, but I don't think I could take that job on.'

Even in her mid-nineties the Queen has proved she still has a style that can wow fashion critics and designers as well as the general public.

Accessorising the Monarch

As with her designers, the Queen has, for decades, kept to the same tried and trusted firms to supply her bags, shoes, gloves and even her umbrellas.

Handbags
The Queen has been a devotee of Launer bags since her mother gave her one as a present and the Walsall-based company was awarded the royal warrant for supplying the monarch with them in 1968.

Only the Queen knows the answer to that perennial question: 'What does the Queen keep in her handbag?' This particular design is called 'Sofia'. (© Ian Lloyd)

According to Gerald Bodmer, Launer's chief executive officer:

We supply the Queen with patent leather bags – with a mirror finish – in black or white or beige for day use and occasionally gold or silver for evening wear. Occasionally she will request them in black calf.

Each one takes 5 or 6 hours to make at our factory in Walsall, and they are customised for her, so for instance there are usually no divides in the middle unlike our normal range. We sometimes add a purse but there are usually no partitions in the middle unlike the normal design. We also make sure the handles are slightly longer so they don't get caught up when she is greeting people. We use a frame in the middle so she can reach deep inside.

The names of the ones she likes most are the 'Traviata', 'Turandot', 'Royale' and 'Lisa'. The Queen carried a customised 'Lisa' handbag to Prince William's wedding to Catherine Middleton in 2011:

About twenty years ago she opted for a smaller more feminine design and we supplied six in different designs for day and evening use. She knows what she wants and I think she is keen to update her look. Normally we would only supply one or two a year as the Queen isn't over the top about these things.

Such quality bags don't come cheap: the price range is between £1,100 and £2,160. Several of the designs appeared in the Netflix series *The Crown* and Helen Mirren featured a 'Traviata' in the Broadway play *The Audience*, both of which led to an increase in sales for the company.

Shoes
The Queen's shoes are manufactured by Rayne. The company was originally founded in 1885 by Henry and Mary Rayne and gained its first royal warrant in 1936 from Queen Mary. The Queen Mother bought her shoes from the same company and the Queen wore Rayne silk slingback sandals in beige at her wedding (three identical pairs were made in case of disasters). Princesses Margaret and Anne also wore Rayne shoes on their wedding days. Other famous clients include the Duchess of Windsor, the Princess of Wales, Margaret Thatcher (a pair of her black stilettos sold for £150 at auction) and Elizabeth Taylor in her role as Cleopatra.

The company went into liquidation in the 1990s, but the Palace traced one of its employees, David Hyatt, who had moved to Anello & Davide, and he continued to make shoes for the Queen. The new company managed to get the royal and celebrity lasts from the liquidators. Sadly, they were all destroyed in a fire at the company's Park Royal warehouse in 2009.

In an interview with the author in 2006, David commented:

We normally supply the same styles, though in a different material or fabric. The court shoes are calf leather and the main colours are black, beige or navy usually with a 2-¼" heel with the option of another ¼" on the sole for use on grass or when the weather is inclement. There are three different designs for evening shoes – in satin, silver and gold.

It probably takes a couple of days to make a pair of shoes but in addition they remain on the lasts for about a week so the leather shrinks to the shape of the last – which of course is the shape of the foot.

We normally supply one or two pairs a year. We occasionally renew the tops and re-heel them or change the insole. The Queen doesn't waste money. She's no Imelda Marcos.

Today, the royal warrant is once again held by Rayne, under the directorship of the founder's great-grandson, Nigel.

Gloves

The royal warrant for supplying gloves has been held for many years by Cornelia James Ltd. Cornelia was a Jewish refugee who fled Vienna following the rise of Adolf Hitler. Her association with the Queen also began at the time of the royal wedding, when she was recommended by the royal couturier Norman Hartnell to make the gloves for Princess Elizabeth's going-away outfit, and she would go on to make the ones for the coronation.

The Queen's gloves are normally brushed cotton for the daytime, made from double-shrunk cotton in order to hold their shape. They are breathable and help to protect her hands when she is shaking so many others, and of course they are washable. When the Queen undertook overseas tours, the Palace requested a dozen or so pairs.

The company supplies a variety of colours and types. For the evening events, she chooses nylon ones, which she finds lighter to wear, usually in black or white but occasionally in navy or beige, depending on the outfit they need to complement. Her favourite design has two points down the side of the hand and, ever frugal, she has been known to send them back for repair if a stitch or two comes loose.

In Cornelia's day, she supplied gloves for the Queen Mother and most of the royal ladies, including the Princess of Wales – she always said Diana used them to hide her nails, which were quite bitten. Over the years, their best customer has probably been the Princess Royal, who wears gloves at most of her engagements.

The younger royals don't often wear gloves, but the company has supplied merino wool gloves for the Duchess of Cambridge, at whose wedding in 2011 Princesses Beatrice and Eugenie both wore Cornelia James designs.

Umbrellas

The Queen's famous see-through brollies are provided by Fulton Umbrellas. The company was created by Arnold Fulton, a mechanical engineer by trade, in Whitechapel, in the East End of London in 1955. He invented the 'Birdcage' umbrella in the late 1960s, using clear PVC and longer ribs than usual to make the domed shape. It sold very well initially, and then went out of fashion in the late 1970s.

A member of the Queen Mother's household contacted the company to supply ones for her and, like her handbags and gloves, the style was adopted by the Queen, who gave them the royal warrant in 2008.

Liaising with the Queen's senior dresser, the company is able to colour co-ordinate the brollies to exactly match the colour of Her Majesty's coat and hat. The Palace sends a swatch of material and Fulton's printers match it exactly, producing the same shade for the handle, the ferrule (the end of the umbrella) and the tips of each of the eight ribs. The matching-coloured borders, which the Queen recently asked to be thinner, are also ultrasonically welded to the umbrella panels.

In 2009 the Queen and Duke of Edinburgh visited their factory, where they were shown how the umbrellas are produced, including a demonstration by Nigel Fulton of the wind-resistant properties, 'by violently inverting an umbrella … being careful not to injure anyone while I was swinging it around!' The royal couple must have given a favourable report to their family, because William, Kate and Camilla are now also customers.

20

TRADITIONALLY SPEAKING

1 **Bodkins:** Every March, a long roll of paper tied with green ribbon on wooden rollers is presented to the Queen during a Privy Council meeting. It is the list of names of those nominated for the ceremonial position of High Sheriff for each county. Instead of signing the document, the Queen uses a brass-handled 'bodkin', with a 3in spike, which she uses to 'prick' the name of each Sheriff designate. The tradition dates

back to the time of Elizabeth I who, according to legend, was outside sewing in the garden and, having no pen and ink handy, pricked the names with her bodkin.

2 Swan upping: The ceremony dates back to the twelfth century. The swans on the Thames are owned by the Queen, or by the Worshipful Company of Vintners and the Worshipful Company of Dyers. Each July, the Queen's Swan Keeper and representatives of the two companies sail in skiffs along the Thames, usually from Sonning on Thames to Abingdon on Thames. They check on the health and well-being of the swans and mark cygnets with a ring attached to the leg. In 2009, the Queen sailed down the Thames with the three crews, the first time a monarch had witnessed swan upping in centuries.

3 Feast of the Epiphany: On 6 January, a service is held in the Chapel Royal, St James's Palace, during which an offering of gold, frankincense and myrrh is made on behalf of the Queen, representing the gifts the wise men gave to the infant Jesus. The gold is in the form of new sovereigns, while the frankincense and myrrh are prepared by the apothecary to the Queen. Monarchs no longer attend in person.

4 Entering the City of London: When the Queen is taking part in a ceremony of state, her procession stops at Temple Bar where the City of Westminster ends and the City of London begins. The Lord Mayor of London hands her the Pearl Sword, which was a gift to the City from Elizabeth I in 1571, and the Queen touches it. This symbolises both her respect for the freedom of the City and, as the Lord Mayor has offered the sword in the first place, it shows his acceptance of the authority of the Crown.

5 State Opening of Parliament: Before the State Opening, Yeomen of the Guard traditionally search the cellars underneath the Palace of Westminster for explosives. This dates back to 1605 when Catholic conspirators including Guy Fawkes were foiled in trying to blow up the Protestant King James I and his government.

6 Hostage taking: Another unseen part of the State Opening ceremony, dating back to the reign of Charles I, is the holding 'hostage' of a member of the House of Commons at Buckingham Palace to ensure the safe return of the monarch. (Prince Philip once referred to it as 'a poor swap'.) Today, it is usually the Vice Chamberlain of the Household – who is also an MP and a junior whip for the government.

7 Maundy Service: Held on the Thursday before Good Friday, it commemorates Jesus washing the feet of his disciples. These days, it takes the form of a distribution of specially minted Maundy money in two small purses to pensioners who have served the diocese where the service is taking place. The number of recipients of each gender is equal to the monarch's age, so, as the Queen was in her twenty-sixth year at her first Maundy, she gave them to twenty-six men and twenty-six women. She attended the 1935 service with her mother at Westminster Abbey. As monarch, she has only missed four of the services in her reign.

The Queen in the procession of Garter Knights before the annual service at St George's Chapel, Windsor. She once said of the elaborate robes: 'They couldn't have been practical even in the days when someone wore clothes like this. It's certainly warm on a June day plodding [downhill].' (© Ian Lloyd)

8 Order of the Garter: Founded in 1348 by Edward III, this is the country's oldest order of chivalry. An annual Garter Service has been held at St George's Chapel nearly every year since 1948, with the Queen and the garter knights walking or driving from the State Apartments down to the Lower Ward of the castle. Prince Philip described processing in medieval style robes as 'a nice piece of pageantry … *Rationally*, it's *lunatic*, but in practice, everyone enjoys it, I think.'

9 Ceremony of the Keys: This has been held each evening at the Tower of London in one form or another for 700 years. The Chief Yeoman Warder carries a lantern and the Queen's keys, and locks the outer West Gate and two inner ones. The Queen herself once revealed she hadn't seen the ceremony, so Princess Margaret organised a dinner for some of her friends and her sister. They ate in the cell where Elizabeth I had been held prisoner, before going out at 10 p.m. to watch the ceremony performed in the name of Elizabeth II.

21

FIRST MEETING

The first time that Elizabeth and Philip recalled meeting each other was on 23 July 1939. The King and Queen and the two princesses were taking their final holiday before the declaration of war and had embarked on the royal yacht *Victoria and Albert*.

On 22 July, the yacht moored in the estuary of the River Dart in preparation for a visit to the Royal Naval College at Dartmouth, which is where the King had served as a cadet before the First World War. Also on board was Philip's uncle, Lord Louis 'Dickie' Mountbatten, who noted in his diary that

'Philip accompanied us and dined on board'. It was perfectly reasonable for Philip to have been invited as he was not only related to Mountbatten but, distantly, to the King, whose grandmother, Queen Alexandra, was the sister of Philip's grandfather, King George I of Greece.

But was there another reason for the invitation? Was the wily Lord Louis already planning a possible union with the future Queen? After all, Mountbatten's ambition was limitless and, after allying himself strongly with Edward VIII, both as Prince and King, he promptly jumped ship following the abdication and nailed his colours to the mast of the new regime, hence his presence on the yacht. The equally canny Queen Mother always had her suspicions about Mountbatten, and once claimed, 'We always treated Dickie with a pinch of salt.' Mountbatten's official biographer, Philip Ziegler, said, 'It is hard to believe no thought crossed his mind that an admirable husband for the future Queen Elizabeth might not be readily available.'

Elizabeth and Philip met on the second day of the royal visit to Dartmouth. As luck would have it for Mountbatten's scheme (if we go along with this theory), there was an outbreak of mumps on the campus and the college doctor recommended the princesses should not attend chapel with their parents but stay at the captain's house. Philip was sent to entertain them, which is odd in itself, since one would have expected him to have been kept at a distance like the other young men.

The 18-year-old cadet knelt and played trains with the princesses, sipped lemonade and ate ginger crackers. He must have been bored playing with these two sweet little girls in their matching pastel dresses and ankle socks, so he suggested, according to Marion Crawford, 'Let's go to the tennis courts and have some real fun jumping the nets.' Crawfie felt 'he showed off a good deal', but she noted the girls 'were much impressed'. Elizabeth enthused, 'How good he is, Crawfie. How high he can jump.'

The governess noted, 'She never took her eyes off him the whole time.' He, on the other hand, 'was quite polite to her but did not pay her any special attention'.

Afterwards, he was invited to the yacht yet again and Mountbatten wrote, 'Philip came back aboard V & A for tea and he was a great success with the children'.

Proof of the impact on Elizabeth came nineteen years later. In the official biography of George VI, which was read and approved by his daughter, John Wheeler Bennett wrote of Prince Philip of Greece, 'This was the man with whom Princess Elizabeth had been in love from their first meeting'. The die had been cast.

22

COURTING COUSINS

For Elizabeth it was said to be love at first sight when she met Philip at Dartmouth Naval College. The romance started innocently, with the exchange of cousinly letters and a schoolgirl crush on the Princess's part. It wasn't an exclusive relationship. He dated Canadian-born socialite Osla Benning, while the Princess had crushes on some of the Grenadier Guards protecting Windsor Castle, including Hugh Euston, later Duke of Grafton.

Philip spent occasional shore leave with the royal family at Windsor and by the end of the war they were clearly in love. By 1946, the press had cottoned onto the relationship and predicted a royal marriage.

22 July 1939: Elizabeth, aged 13, becomes infatuated with Philip during the royal visit to Dartmouth Naval College.

Jan–Apr 1940: Philip spends four months serving as a midshipman on HMS *Ramillies*. His captain, Vice Admiral Harold Tom Baillie-Grohman, noted a conversation he had with the Prince during their time at sea:

> Philip said, 'My Uncle Dickie has ideas for me; he thinks I could marry Princess Elizabeth.' I was a bit taken aback, and, after a hesitation asked him: 'Are you really fond of her?'
>
> 'Oh yes, very,' was the reply and 'I write to her every week.'
>
> At the time Philip was 18 and Elizabeth 14 in April.

Christmas 1940: Philip sends Elizabeth a Christmas card from Athens.

21 January 1941: Diarist Henry 'Chips' Channon notes, after talking to Philip's aunt, Princess Nicholas of Greece, 'He is to be our Prince Consort, and that is why he is serving in our navy'. Philip's response when quizzed about Channon's comment in 1971:

> It had been mentioned, presumably, that 'he is eligible, he's the sort of person she might marry.' I mean after all … how many obviously eligible young men, other than people living in this country, were available? Inevitably I must have been on the list …

3 April 1941: Elizabeth confides in her friend Alathea Fitzalan Howard that Philip is her 'boy'. That she does so in front of her French tutor, Mrs Montaudon-Smith, suggests it is banter, as the girls talk about 'beaus' and 'boys' in front of adults.

June 1941: In Cape Town, Philip's cousin, Alexandra, disturbs him writing a letter to Princess Elizabeth and teases him, 'But she's only a baby.' She thinks he is angling for invitations to stay with her family.

23 October 1941: The angling worked, because Elizabeth tells Alathea that her beau Philip had stayed at Windsor the previous weekend …

30 November 1941: … and again this weekend.

21 December 1941: … and yet again.

1943: Elizabeth sends her cousin Margaret Elphinstone a letter which says, 'It's so exciting. Mummy says that Philip can come and stay when he gets leave.'

18 December 1943: Philip attends the pantomime *Aladdin* at Windsor Castle. He stays the weekend and returns to spend Christmas with the royal family. It was during these two visits that the couple fell in love, as Queen Mary explained to her lady-in-waiting, Mabell, Countess of Airlie, at Sandringham in January 1946: 'They have been in love for the last eighteen months. In fact longer, I think. I believe she fell in love with him the first time he went down to Windsor.'

8 July 1944: Philip stays at Windsor with the royal family. They watch the Noël Coward film *This Happy Breed*, and Philip laughs loudly during it.

Early August 1944: Mountbatten meets George VI to discuss Philip taking British citizenship and his possible marriage to Elizabeth.

10 August 1944: George VI writes to Mountbatten, 'I have come to the conclusion that we are going too fast', and asks

Mountbatten to limit discussions to the question of citizenship only.

27 October 1944: Diarist 'Chips' Channon visits Princess Marina of Kent at Coppins. 'As I signed the visitors' book I noticed "Philip" written constantly. It is at Coppins that he sees Princess Elizabeth. I think she will marry him.'

Christmas 1944: Philip sends Elizabeth a photograph of himself and she dances round the room with it. She later places it on the mantelpiece in her room.

1945: Philip's cousin, Queen Alexandra of Yugoslavia is living near Windsor in this year with her husband, exiled King Peter II, and later recalled they 'used to see them holding hands, disengaging themselves sometimes until we came closer and they could see it was only us'.

1 April 1946: Philip is among a party of six accompanying Elizabeth to see *The Hasty Heart* at the Aldwych Theatre, London.

Late April 1946: Philip tells his younger sister Sophie, 'He was thinking about getting engaged' and that 'Uncle Dickie was being helpful'.

29 May 1946: Elizabeth and Philip were photographed together following the wedding of Elizabeth's cousin Andrew Elphinstone to Jean Hambro, though the newspapers didn't speculate on the relationship.

1946: John Dean, valet to Lord Mountbatten, 'had only one piece of evidence to go on' that an engagement was in the pipeline. 'Whenever Prince Philip brought a week-end bag, and I unpacked it, I always found a small photograph in a battered frame – a photograph of Princess Elizabeth.'

Spring 1946: George VI gives Philip a lift from London to Windsor for his reunion with Elizabeth on his return from the Far East.

12 June 1946: Philip apologises to Queen Elizabeth for his 'monumental cheek' in inviting himself to Buckingham Palace. He tells her a voice inside his head said, '"nothing ventured, nothing gained" – well I did venture and I gained a wonderful time.'

Thursday, 5 September 1946: Philip is part of the royal party accompanying the King, Queen and two Princesses to the Braemar Games. It is the gathering in memory and an audience of 20,000 receives a thorough soaking in the open stands.

Sunday, 8 September 1946: The King, Queen and Princess Margaret drive to Crathie Church. Princess Elizabeth is confined to her apartments with 'a slight cold' while Prince Philip walks the half a mile route to the kirk with Queen Elizabeth's brother, Michael Bowes-Lyon, past waiting crowds of onlookers and photographers.

Monday, 9 September 1946: A rumour of an impending engagement between Elizabeth and Philip has been circulating in London, fuelled by a piece suggesting it in the *London Star*. Monday's newspapers report that the King's private secretary, Alan Lascelles, has announced from Buckingham Palace, 'Princess Elizabeth is not engaged to be married. The report published is not true.'

Then, as now, an official Palace denial of an engagement is usually concrete proof that one is on the cards, although the world and many outside the immediate family had no idea.

September 1946: The couple become unofficially engaged at Balmoral.

Friday, 13 September 1946: Philip leaves Balmoral Castle after a three-week stay.

26 October 1946: 'It was my wedding which really put the cat amongst the pigeons,' recalled Patricia, Countess Mountbatten, to the author:

> The Princess was a bridesmaid, and Philip was an usher. The newsreel cameras captured him helping her to take off her coat and although none of us thought anything of it on the day, it was the first intimation that there might be something interesting between the two of them.

23 May 1947: Mountbatten notes in his diary, 'Saw [Queen] Elizabeth re Philip'. The following day, he wrote, 'Philip and I talked about Lilibet.'

9 July 1947: The engagement of Elizabeth and Philip is announced.

23

TOUR DE FORCE

While Prince William and Harry, and now their own children, criss-crossed the globe in their nappies, earlier generations of royal children were later developers. Princess Elizabeth was 20 when she left British shores for the first time. In the spring of 1947, she accompanied her parents and sister on a mammoth tour of the Union of South Africa. The twin objectives behind the visit were firstly to thank the union for its participation in the Second World War and to strengthen ties with the British Crown in the face of increasing nationalism. Secondly, to restore the health of the King, who was exhausted after leading the nation through six years of war. Neither aim was achieved. A year after the visit, Jan Smuts' pro-British United Party was defeated in the 1948 election by the National Party. That same year, King George was diagnosed with severe arteriosclerosis brought on by years of heavy smoking.

On the positive side, it was to be the only time the King and the Queen and the two princesses were able to undertake an overseas tour together. Given that it was almost certain that Princess Elizabeth would marry Prince Philip on their return, it was an opportunity for 'we four' to enjoy a final four-month sabbatical together.

The family set sail from Southampton on 1 February 1947 on HMS *Vanguard*, the battleship Lilibet had launched on Clydebank just over two years earlier. Half a century later, when she returned to South Africa at the invitation of President Mandela, she recalled how seasick the family had been, especially in the Bay of Biscay. When they reached calmer waters and the southern climate, they relaxed more and played deck tennis and tag with the crew.

For Elizabeth, it was a rare opportunity to mix with members of the opposite sex who were neither aristocrats nor courtiers. 'The officers are charming,' she wrote to Marion Crawford, 'and we have had great fun with them ... There are one or two real smashers, and I bet you'd have had a WONDERFUL time if you were here.'

The men were part of *Vanguard*'s company of 1,900. Many of them dined with the twenty-nine members of the royal party and one or two of them were invited to watch films with the King and Queen or to gather round the piano for postprandial community singing.

The winter of 1947 was one of the harshest in living memory. Large drifts of snow blocked roads and rail lines and coal couldn't be transported to the power stations. Many were forced to close, meaning electricity had to be rationed. When the snow started to thaw at the end of February, there was widespread flooding affecting an estimated 100,000 homes. George VI wrote to his mother that he'd rather be back at home with his people, 'having borne so many trials with them'.

Elizabeth also wrote to Queen Mary, telling her grandmother she felt 'rather guilty to be right away from it all'. Being separated from Philip for four months was another trial for her, as was the detailed and daunting official programme. 'My heart rather sinks when I think what is ahead,' she wrote to a relation, adding, 'It is absolutely staggering how much they expect us to do and go on for such a long stretch. I hope we shall survive, that's all.'

Elizabeth's mood was certainly positive when *Vanguard* entered the Port of Cape Town on 17 February. Before her lay the spectacular backdrop of Table Mountain. 'I could hardly believe that anything could be so beautiful,' she enthused to Queen Mary.

After five days in the capital, during which the King formally opened Parliament, speaking briefly in Afrikaans, the royal family left for an extended tour of 7,000 miles across South Africa, the Protectorates and Southern Rhodesia. Their base for thirty-five nights was the White Train, an ivory-and-gold 'palace on wheels' made up of fourteen carriages stretching a third of a mile (730m). Besides the royal family, it was home to all those in attendance, including dressers, valets, secretaries, footmen, speech-writers, the king's hairdresser and so on.

Both princesses were struck by the impact of the wide-open spaces and the vastness of the country. Having never travelled abroad before, it was a heady experience seeing the majestic Victoria Falls, watching the wildlife in the Kruger National Park

The royal sisters pose for a photograph in front of the White Train. At various points along the route the Princesses' horses were made available for them to take a morning ride. While Elizabeth grins for the camera, 16-year-old Margaret's sultry gaze reminds us she would soon become one of the great beauties of the 1940s and '50s. (Author's collection)

and, Margaret's favourite memory, walking in the Drakensberg Mountains at the Natal National Park.

A highlight for the sisters was their first flight, in separate aircraft for security reasons, which took them to the old European settlement of Eshowe. Here, the royal party was greeted by thousands of Zulus doing an impromptu war dance. 'It was an impressive sight,' Princess Elizabeth wrote to her grandmother, 'with 5,000 warriors singing and stamping their feet, ending up with a terrific charge to the edge of the dais where we were. This they were allowed to do only because Mummy begged them to be allowed to come nearer.'

Another memorable moment was when the four of them climbed one of the granite Matobo hills in Southern Rhodesia to visit the grave of the Victorian imperialist Cecil Rhodes, who founded the colonies of Southern and Northern Rhodesia. Queen Elizabeth, wearing her usual teetering and impractical shoes, broke a heel. Lilibet, who had the same-sized feet, handed over her own snazzy two-toned flatties to her mother and completed the walk in her stockinged feet. She commented ruefully, 'so like Mummy to set out in those shoes.'

It wasn't Queen Elizabeth's only error on the tour. In driving through the town of Benoni, a man holding something in his hand grabbed the side of the open-top royal car. The Queen instinctively hit him several times with her parasol, breaking it in half. Later, she found out it was a loyal local man, clutching a 10-shilling note to give to Princess Elizabeth for her forthcoming 21st birthday.

Besides not climbing a mountain in high heels, 'Mummy' taught Elizabeth several other valuable lessons during the tour, especially in public relations. South Africa's ostrich farmers had been badly hit by a downturn in international trade during the war. The Queen and the princesses therefore incorporated ostrich feathers in their coats and dresses. During a visit to a farm outside Oudtshoorn, all three royal ladies tried their hands at clipping the tail feathers from some of the birds.

The tour generated a huge amount of public interest and crowds gathered at various points along the rail route to catch a glimpse of the White Train. The Queen ordered the driver to make dozens of unscheduled stops along the route and would wave at the onlookers from a window or occasionally descend on to the platform. On one occasion, the princesses had retired for the night and were wearing dressing gowns. Their mother encouraged them to wear jewellery to look as if they were in evening dresses as they dutifully waved to the appreciative crowd. Princess Elizabeth took such lessons to heart and would make similar impromptu appearances during her tours of Canada and the United States in 1951 and the great Commonwealth tour of 1953–54. Princess Margaret was usually less obliging.

Apartheid had yet to be enforced in South Africa, but time and again the crowds of schoolchildren and other groups were divided into black, white and 'coloureds'. On one occasion, the three royal ladies were given bouquets by three children of English, Dutch and Bantu extraction. One of the lasting memories for Elizabeth was an awareness of the racial tension of a predominantly black country ruled by a white minority of people of British and Dutch descent.

According to Alan Lascelles, Princess Elizabeth was one of the successes of the tour, 'She has come on in the most surprising way, and all in the right direction. She has got … solid and endearing qualities plus a perfectly natural power of enjoying herself without any trace of shyness.' He also felt she had her mother's knack of taking on 'all the old bores' and had 'an astonishing solicitude for other people's comfort'.

Three days before the end of the tour, on 21 April, Elizabeth celebrated her 21st birthday in Cape Town. Prime Minister Jan

Smuts had declared it a national holiday. It wasn't a holiday for the Princess, since she spent a busy day reviewing armed forces, veterans and cadets, attending a youth rally for all races before changing for a reception at the City Hall and a ball. The prime minister gave her a twenty-one-stone diamond necklace and a gold key to the city.

During the day, a six-minute speech by the Princess was broadcast throughout the Commonwealth. It was drafted by the historian Dermot Morrah, who was covering the tour for *The Times*, as well as being a speech-writer for the King. In it, Elizabeth dedicated herself to a lifetime of duty: 'I declare before you all that my whole life, whether it be long or short, shall be devoted to your service and the service of our great Imperial Commonwealth.'

It was a vow she would uphold for the rest of her life.

24

ELIZABETH'S AUSTERITY WEDDING

Winston Churchill memorably called it 'a flash of colour on the hard road we have to travel'. It was only two years since the end of the war. Rationing was widespread and King George VI feared a backlash of public anger if the royal family was seen to enjoy a lavish spectacle in the middle of a period of austerity.

Clement Attlee, the rather dour prime minister, vetoed a public holiday as 'unwise', and the King agreed there would be no souvenirs produced or stands and decorations along the processional route. The 'flash of colour' came from the

Household Cavalry wearing full ceremonial uniform for the first time since 1939.

Not everyone was happy with this approach. 'Chips' Channon wrote in his diary, 'Someone in the Government apparently advised simplicity, misjudging the English love of pageantry and show. Now it is too late and an opportunity missed.'

One thing that was understandably lavish was the bride's wedding dress, which was designed by Norman Hartnell, although Elizabeth had to use her ration coupons towards paying for the dress. In fact, hundreds of people from across the UK sent her their own coupons but these had to be returned as it would have been illegal to use them.

Hartnell based his design on Botticelli's painting *Primavera*, which symbolises the coming of spring, a suitable metaphor after the dark days of the war. The dress was of a simple cut with fitted bodice, heart-shaped neckline with a low v-pointed waist and a floor-length panelled skirt. In addition, the bride had a 15ft silk tulle, full-court train attached at the shoulders.

Sourcing the materials was a sensitive issue in those 'Buy British' days. Questions were raised in Parliament and Attlee was obliged to write to the King's Private Secretary, Alan Lascelles, seeking clarification about the rumour that foreign silk was involved. Hartnell had to deny that silkworms from the recent Axis partners of Italy or Japan had been used. The only foreign worms used to make silk for the dress itself were politically friendly ones from nationalist-controlled China.

Philip wore his naval uniform. The only embellishment was an ink mark in his naval cap which was several sizes smaller than his best man's one, which would have embarrassingly dropped over the groom's ears if he had picked up the wrong one.

Princess Elizabeth and the Duke of Edinburgh on their wedding day. The dress of ivory duchesse satin was heavily embroidered with symbols inspired by Botticelli's Flora, including ears of corn, roses, starflowers and orange blossom. (© Popperfoto/Getty)

The guests also watched the pennies. 'Anyone fortunate enough to have a new dress drew all eyes,' recalled Queen Mary's lady-in-waiting. Even royalty failed to sparkle, 'I always remember Princess Juliana of the Netherlands looking round at all the jewellery and exclaiming, "but it's all so dirty"', remembered one of the bridesmaids.

Philip's cousin, Countess Mountbatten, recalled having breakfast with Philip on the morning of his wedding 'and I always remember him saying: "I'm either being very brave or very foolish!" Naturally I reassured him that he was doing exactly the right thing, as one would.' In another interview she added, 'He was apprehensive. He was uncertain – not about marrying Princess Elizabeth, but about what the marriage would mean for him. He was giving up a great deal … Everything was going to change for him.'

Philip's earlier nervousness was dispelled by the time he reached Westminster Abbey. 'Princess Elizabeth looked well, shy and attractive,' noted the ubiquitous Channon, 'and Prince Philip as if he were thoroughly enjoying himself.'

The ceremony was witnessed by a Who's Who of European royalty. 'It was a tremendous meeting place,' remembered Princess Margaret, adding cheekily, 'People who had been starving in little garrets all over Europe suddenly reappeared' – the kings of Norway, Denmark and Iraq, to name but three. Others had lost their thrones but still kept their place in the pecking order, and one was about to join the exiled royals club. This was King Michael of Romania, who lost his throne on his return, but at least found love in London in the shape of Princess Anne of Bourbon-Parma.

Missing from the guest list were the Duke and Duchess of Windsor, eleven years after his abdication, an omission which so annoyed his sister, the Princess Royal, that she failed to attend the wedding, claiming incapacity through a heavy cold. Philip's side was noticeably depleted, thanks to the absence of his three sisters who were cold-shouldered by the Palace, it being so soon after the war, and were not invited. 'They minded terribly,' recalled their cousin, Lady Pamela Hicks, to the author. 'I mean it's not as if they were stormtroopers!' Their mother, Princess Alice, sent them a twenty-two-page account of the day in a letter, and their cousin, the Duchess of Kent, volunteered to travel to Germany to give them her account of the day.

Philip's side of the abbey was boosted with the presence of his navy pals as well as villagers from Corsham, where he was currently lecturing and also his fellow skittles players from his local, the Methuen Arms.

Afterwards, 150 guests sat down to enjoy an 'austerity' wedding breakfast. Instead of the ten courses that had fed previous bridal parties, Elizabeth and Philip's guests were given fish, partridge shot on the royal estates and ice cream. Thankfully, royal menus were traditionally written in French, which sounded more tempting: 'Filet de Sole Mountbatten, Perdreau en Casserole and Bombe Glacée de Princesse Elizabeth'. With the influx of twenty-eight royal guests staying at Buckingham Palace, the royal household had also applied to Westminster Food Office for extra rations.

Prince Philip's lack of a place to call home was noticeable when it came to decorating the wedding cake. Since it was a four-tiered, 9ft-tall edifice, weighing in at 500lb (226kg), there was plenty of room for the three craftsmen to create the couple's life histories in sugarcraft. The only problem was there was not too much to say about Philip in comparison to Elizabeth. Having iced her various royal homes, it was decided to add Philip's athletic pursuits to make up for the lack of bricks and mortar in his life. He did much better on the third tier where, alongside the bride's various hobbies, they added the groom's war record.

25

WHAT ARE WE GOING TO DO WITH ALL THESE?

Some 2,500 presents were sent to Elizabeth and Philip in the run-up to their wedding, not including those from family and friends or world leaders. Most of them were from ordinary men, women and children, who had never even met the bride and groom but who felt an affinity with the Princess they felt they knew well through books, newspaper photographs and newsreels.

In a remarkable public relations gesture, the bride and groom, backed by the King and Queen, agreed to display them in five of the state rooms at St James's Palace in the weeks after the wedding. A 1-shilling admission charge to the exhibition was donated to charities chosen by the couple and visitor numbers soared when Elizabeth's wedding dress was added to the display. By the time the oak doors had finally closed, a total of 261,832 people had paid to see Elizabeth and Philip's presents.

An accompanying catalogue was published, with gifts, even the frankly bizarre ones, listed numerically rather than according to importance. For example, present '1191 a Sèvres dinner service from the French Government' is given the same importance as '1344 an afternoon tea-cloth of handmade lace from an anonymous Czechoslovak subject'.

Before her wedding, Elizabeth had a relatively small amount of jewellery by royal standards. To mark the occasion, her parents and grandmother bestowed a sizeable tranche of personal jewels on the bride. The King gave her a diamond and sapphire necklace with matching earrings. As a joint present with the Queen, he also gave a ruby and diamond necklace, a pair of diamond drop earrings and two rows of pearls. Queen Mary gave Lilibet her diamond 'Girls of Great Britain and Ireland Tiara', which thereafter became known as 'Granny's Tiara'. Princess Margaret, who once explained that she and her sister exchanged small, useful gifts at Christmas such as lipstick, gave her sister a practical present of a fitted picnic case.

The Pope sent a table set of Dresden porcelain, and Chiang Kai-shek, President of China, sent a 175-piece dinner service, while Burma sent a necklace of ninety-six rubies set in gold.

Not all the diplomatic gifts were as opulent or as well received. At the suggestion of Lord Mountbatten, Mahatma Gandhi sent a 'fringed lacework cloth made out of yarn spun by the donor on his own spinning wheel'. Queen Mary, on a tour of inspection of the presents, mistook the cloth for one of Gandhi's iconic loincloths. After prodding it a few times with her parasol, she declared it 'indelicate!' On another royal tour the following day, Princess Margaret, sensing danger as the matriarch loomed closer, quickly grabbed it and stuffed it behind a handy vase.

The usual strict royal protocol about not receiving gifts from companies or individuals was waived during the run-up to the wedding. Several businesses, therefore, had a handy marketing opportunity. The directors of Hoover, for instance, sent two vacuum cleaners – an upright and a cylinder with various hoses and Kidderminster Carpet Manufacturing Company sent a Wilton carpet. Meanwhile, the British Electrical Development Association sent a television set with a 9in screen.

The royal couple did very well out of the RAF, which sent them a Steinway grand piano and a cheque for £4,000 raised from voluntary subscriptions from all ranks. The Princess used the money to buy a Daimler DE27, complete with the number plate 'HRH 1'.

Perhaps the most touching thing about the wedding gifts were the vast amounts sent in by people from all walks of life at a time of austerity. Elizabeth was inundated with stockings (mostly nylon, but some silk), tablecloths, bibles, paintings and so on. Some of the gifts were handmade. Mrs F. Cave sent a cream wool bed jacket that she had knitted, and Mrs E. Tyner sent a silk hot water bottle.

The fact that many of the presents were so intimate says a great deal about how the public perceived the Princess. To many, she was more than a royal bride; she was someone they felt they had known as a girl and now a young woman. One or two were even preparing for the next phase of married life, especially 'number 2528: two hand-knitted cot covers'.

26

A LONGED-FOR BROTHER

Margaret Rhodes recalled that following the 1936 abdication, which resulted in Elizabeth becoming heiress presumptive, Princess Elizabeth prayed hard for a brother to succeed her in the line of succession. She never, of course, had one, but one man filled this gap in her life and became Elizabeth's best friend, escort, confidant and protector.

Patrick, 7th Baron Plunket, had the credentials to be yet another chinless aristocrat in the royal household, but, as the art historian Roy Strong recalled, 'he was an immensely beguiling man'. Tall and handsome, with a military bearing, he was hugely charismatic and, according to Strong, was 'one of the few who could give her a glimpse of the real world outside which he savoured to the full'. One lady-in-waiting claimed, 'He was the only person who could talk to the Queen on equal terms' and his premature death at the age of only 51 'was the greatest tragedy of the Queen's life'.

Plunket was born in 1923, the son of Irish peer Terence, 6th Baron Plunket, and his wife Dorothé Lewis, who was the illegitimate child of the Hollywood star Fannie Ward (protégé of Cecil B. DeMille and dubbed 'the Eternal Flapper') and the 7th Marquess of Londonderry.

The Queen's parents were close friends of 'Teddy' and Dorothé Plunket during the 1920s and 1930s. In February 1924, the Duchess of York lunched with Dorothé and afterwards wrote, 'I admired her baby'.

The Plunkets were killed in 1938 in a private plane owned by William Randolph Hearst. The newspaper magnate had invited them to a party held in their honour and sent his own aircraft to collect them. It crashed in thick fog over the skies of California. Patrick was only 14 and a pupil at Eton when he heard the news. He and his younger brothers, Robin and Shaun, were brought up by an aunt who fostered Patrick's love for the arts.

Queen Elizabeth was devastated by news of the crash and wrote, 'They both gave so much happiness to so many people … Those dear little boys make one's heart ache.' The King and Queen closely followed the lives of the three brothers and after Patrick had been to Cambridge and served in the Irish Guards, King George made him a temporary equerry in 1948.

As his cousin, Lady Annabel Goldsmith, noted, 'With an immense capacity for fun, combined with instinctive good manners, he quickly became an extremely popular figure at court.' It was at this point that he grew closer to the newly married Princess and the two would go riding together. It has even been suggested that the King hoped Plunket might marry Princess Margaret, though by then, she was already in love with the other royal equerry, Peter Townsend.

Plunket, however, was not the marrying kind. Possibly gay or asexual, his name was never linked to that of any woman or man, and with his terrific sense of humour he would have been amused at occasional suggestions in the press that he and the Queen were more than just good friends.

It's easy to see why rumours persisted because, as Annabel Goldsmith concedes, 'He adored her from the outset. They enjoyed a very special connection. He was the one member of her staff who could talk to her on equal terms. There was an openness and honesty between them based on respect, friendship – and a lot of teasing.' He proved to be a useful counterbalance to the Duke of Edinburgh's more outgoing and less tolerant personality.

Following the death of the King, he continued as equerry until Elizabeth appointed him Deputy Master of the Household, a role he held from 1954 until his untimely death in 1975. A man of great artistic flair, he was responsible for organising some of the finest parties of the Queen's reign. He even designed the flower arrangements and bought the gifts for the Queen to give to distinguished visitors. He had the knack of putting people at ease, which was particularly helpful to the Queen, who has always been fundamentally shy. He was scrupulously polite to his boss, dutifully calling her 'Ma'am' at all times, but was so relaxed at royal engagements that he was occasionally spotted winking at those he knew, even over the Queen's shoulder.

His colleague, Sir Martin Charteris recalled, 'He wasn't a stuffed shirt. He was great fun. He had a wonderful flair for entertaining but he was also very good at human relations.' The events he organised ranged from a lunch for US First Lady, Jackie Kennedy, and her sister, Lee Radziwill, in 1962, to the funeral of the Duke of Windsor in 1972, which the Queen wanted to be dignified but muted. (Plunket said he could always tell when the ex-king was due to call at Buckingham Palace during one of his London visits because of the sudden chill in the atmosphere.)

One of his successes was a ball at Windsor Castle for the 70th birthdays of the Queen Mother, the Duke of Gloucester, Earl Mountbatten and the Duke of Beaufort. Plunket designed cascades of flowers to decorate the state apartments and had the castle illuminated. The Queen, seeing great pyramids of white flowers, joked, 'You must have emptied every greenhouse in Windsor Great Park.'

He replied, 'Very nearly. There's a bit left!'

On one occasion, he even had a complete tree transported inside and was thrilled to see three crowned heads chatting beneath its branches.

Plunket also diversified the normal formal entertainment by prompting the Queen to host a vast party for people from all branches of the arts and other society figures. Held on 24 March 1971, it included the art historian Kenneth Clark, actresses Dame Flora Robson and Nanette Newman, Princess Diana's future stepmother Raine Dartmouth and Lady Diana Cooper, as well as the Queen's main dress designers, Norman Hartnell and Hardy Amies. Next day's court circular simply mentioned that the Queen had hosted a dinner followed by a reception.

Endearingly, Plunket gave the Queen a glimpse of 'normal' life by taking her to the theatre, cinema and restaurants, all with the full blessing of Prince Philip. These trips out were often on Monday evenings and the two friends would discreetly leave Buckingham Palace in the Queen's Rover and head for the Odeon cinema in King's Road, Chelsea, where they would sneak unnoticed into the back of the stalls. Later, they would stroll across to Raffles Club for drinks and a light supper before returning to the palace late at night. Other times, they might go to the ABC cinema on the Fulham Road before walking to San Frediano restaurant or Spot 3 nearby. For the Queen, it was the first time she had led a 'normal' life in London since she had escaped the confines of the palace to mix with revellers on VE Day.

Plunket was the Queen's partner at private dances, especially when the Duke of Edinburgh was away. Annabel Goldsmith recalls him as the Queen's 'great protector'. If a royal reception was proving heavy going, he was the only person who could possibly have gone up to her and said, 'Ma'am, do you think I ought to close this down … I think you are looking tired.'

Sometimes the two shared a simple supper on trays watching television together when the Duke was on tour or carrying out an evening engagement. Then there was the fun side. Both shared an irreverent sense of humour. Occasionally, courtiers were surprised to see the normally self-controlled monarch with tears of laughter streaming down her face at something Patrick had said, such as the time he claimed to have spotted a sticky bun left over from a Buckingham Palace garden party with a complete set of false teeth embedded in it.

He was occasionally her knight in shining armour. Once, shortly before a white-tie dinner, the Queen found that the safe storing her tiaras was locked. No one could find the key, so Patrick raced home, retrieved the Plunket tiara and hot-footed it back to Buckingham Palace. He even urged her to purchase a new one, having spotted an ideal royal headpiece in an exhibition. 'Ma'am, I've found this absolutely wonderful tiara. You ought to buy it,' he announced excitedly, only to receive the flattening reply, 'My dear Patrick, I have thirty-six tiaras already. What am I going to do with thirty-seven?'

He had more luck in advising her on fashion, being one of the few people who could tell her directly to her face what suited her. He once scolded her, 'You can't possibly wear shoes like that!'

The Queen retorted, 'Well, I can't see what's wrong with them,' before adding meekly, 'If you say so. I mustn't say any more.'

Courtiers admired Plunket's ability to be direct with the monarch. 'He was very easy with the Queen and she was very relaxed with him,' recalled Martin Charteris. 'He treated her almost as an equal, certainly as a friend. If you wanted to say something awkward or difficult to Her Majesty you could do it directly through Patrick.' Oddly, she was never annoyed by his manner. His brother Shaun recalled he could be direct but 'often with a smile, and she would smile back'.

Plunket was trustee of the Wallace Collection and the National Art Collection Fund, and he advised the Queen on purchasing works of art. His own art collection included several Rubens. Along with Prince Philip, he was responsible for turning the old royal chapel, bombed during the Second World War, into the present Queen's Gallery to display exhibitions from the Royal Collection to the public. In his will, he left the Queen a seascape by Richard Parkes Bonington that she had admired.

Plunket was close to other members of the royal family, especially Princess Margaret. Along with the Queen, he was asked to be a godparent to the Princess's son, David, Viscount Linley, and they attended his baptism in the Music Room at Buckingham Palace in December 1961.

Patrick developed liver cancer and was eventually admitted to the King Edward VII Hospital for Officers. He chose not to be told that his illness was terminal and believed he might recover. Loyal to the last, one evening, he struggled from his bed and headed for Buckingham Palace, where he changed into formal clothes and stood, as usual, behind the Queen introducing her to guests at a reception. He eventually returned to hospital at 2 a.m. and in the morning found a note on his breakfast tray bearing the message, 'Patrick, I am grateful for what you did last night. Yours sincerely, Elizabeth R'.

Patrick Plunket died ten days later, on 28 May 1975. He was 51. The Queen was said to be devastated and agreed that his funeral should be at the Queen's Chapel. Annabel Goldsmith remembered the service as 'heartbreakingly lovely' and 'caught a look of deep sadness on the Queen's face'. In her memoirs, Annabel summed up the loss the Queen must have felt. 'Not only had she lost one of her closest friends but someone who was almost irreplaceable in the royal household.' It was some consolation to the monarch that she had been able to reward his years of service by making him a Knight of the Royal Victorian Order shortly before his death.

According to his brother, Shaun Plunket, the Queen had a hand in putting together Patrick's obituary in *The Times*. 'She certainly helped. It was quite light.' Much of it was about his service to the House of Windsor, but one paragraph highlights what he himself got back from his association with the Queen and her household. 'In his service to the monarchy, Patrick found fulfilment. The Royal Family, through their love and friendship gave him security and a sense of belonging.'

There was one final tribute from the Queen. She agreed to the construction of a wooden pavilion in the Valley Gardens, part of Windsor Great Park. It would offer a view down an avenue of rhododendron bushes to Virginia Water Lake. It was a place of happy memories for the Queen, for it was here she and Patrick walked many times with the royal corgis.

A few months after his death, a member of the household asked the Queen, 'Have you given some thought to who will replace Patrick Plunket?'

Her reply was straightforward. 'No one will ever replace him.'

27

'YOUR MAJESTY, MUMMY': THE QUEEN AND PRINCE CHARLES

The relationship between the Queen and her eldest son is best summed up as 'complicated'. Margaret Rhodes once said, 'It is not a cosy relationship. It never has been.'

Now, in the last phase of her reign, and with the death of the Duke of Edinburgh, many of the earlier issues have been resolved. Charles has stepped into his father's shoes as a quasi-consort, accompanying his mother at key state events while she is publicly backing him more and more.

Charles Philip Arthur George was born on 14 November 1948, a week before the first anniversary of his parents' wedding. When it came to parenting, Elizabeth and Philip adopted the typical aristocratic attitude of the time. Their baby son was given over to two Scottish nurses. Helen Lightbody was in charge from day to day, assisted by Mabel Anderson. Lightbody was harsh (one ex-courtier remembered her as 'a bitch') and her blatant favouritism of Charles over Anne annoyed Prince Philip, so eventually she had to go. Mabel, on the other hand, remained a lifelong friend of the family. In her retirement, she lived in Frogmore Cottage (in pre-Harry and Meghan days), dined alone with the Queen at Windsor Castle and occasionally joined her on her cruise around the Western Isles in the Royal Yacht *Britannia*.

The Queen's former private secretary, Lord Charteris, told her biographer Graham Turner that Elizabeth:

… really had very little to do with Charles. He had an hour after tea with Mummy when she was in this country, but somehow even those contacts were lacking in warmth. The Queen is not good at showing affection. If I were Prince Charles I'd think my mother had been unfeeling.

Another retired courtier told the same author, 'As children I don't think they could talk to her. She was so strong, so stiff upper lip, so afraid of her emotions.'

In retrospect, it certainly seems strange from today's perspective that Princess Elizabeth extended a stay in Malta with Prince Philip in December 1949, missing Christmas with their son. Then, when she did arrive back in Britain, shortly before New Year, she opted to spend four days catching up on paperwork at Clarence House, with an excursion to Hurst Park to see her horse, 'Monaveen', race, before being reunited with Charles at Sandringham.

Nevertheless, there is evidence the Queen was more caring than she has been given credit for. A letter to her distant cousin, Mary Cambridge, written a couple of weeks after Charles's birth is full of warmth. She wrote that she still couldn't believe she had a baby of her own and that she and Philip were enormously proud of the new arrival, who she said was 'sweet'.

Since Charles and Anne prepared for bed from six o'clock, the Queen asked her first prime minister, Winston Churchill, to put back the time of his weekly audience from 5.30 to 6.30 in order to allow her to take part in the children's bath time before tucking them into bed. It is hardly the behaviour of someone cold and remote.

The Queen's accession at the age of only 25 meant she was preoccupied with affairs of state, from the daily red boxes containing government papers to opening Parliament. Her first tour abroad took her to Jamaica, New Zealand, Australia, Ceylon and Uganda, and she was away from her children for six months. They were reunited in Malta, the children having sailed on *Britannia*'s maiden voyage to the island from Portsmouth. At their reunion, a small incident occurred which has been cited as an example of the Queen's coolness to her eldest son. She was about to greet various dignitaries when Charles, aged 5½, stuck his hand out, as he'd seen the others do, only to be told by his mother, 'No. Not you, dear.'

Again, there is another side to the story. The Queen wrote to tell her mother about the reunion, saying that Charles and Anne were 'somewhat overcome' at meeting their parents again, but that later the ice broke and the two bombarded their parents with questions about the tour and Charles raced around showing his mother the layout of the new yacht, which she had launched the previous year.

While the Queen was head of the country, Prince Philip was very much the head of the family, and, like many fathers, he was determined that Charles should follow in his footsteps when it came to his education. The Prince attended two of his father's former schools: Cheam Preparatory School from the age of 10 to 13 and then Gordonstoun School on Scotland's Morayshire coast.

While Philip thrived on the Spartan regime and he-man tutelage in the pre-war school, the altogether more sensitive Charles hated his father's alma mater, infamously dubbed 'Colditz in kilts'. According to Jonathan Dimbleby, at Gordonstoun the Prince 'was picked on maliciously, cruelly and without respite'. He was punched on the rugby field, had slippers thrown at him while he was in bed, was hit with pillows and occasionally, surreptitiously, punched in the dark. 'Last night was hell, literal hell,' he wrote home, but his father's 'reaction was to write bracing letters of admonition', urging Charles 'to be strong and resourceful'. The Queen seems to have wavered a little after her son revealed how deeply unhappy he was after two terms there. She invited Christopher Trevor-Roberts, a teacher recommended by Martin Charteris, to lunch to discuss the problem, but in the end, she chose not to overrule her husband.

To be fair, the Queen and Duke couldn't really withdraw the Prince from his educational nightmare without causing embarrassment to Gordonstoun and risking the inevitable media circus. The stiff upper lip, grin and bear it, attitude was second nature for the royal parents, but in this case failed to help their sensitive eldest son.

As with his early childhood, there is evidence of a softer side to the mother/son relationship. Barbara Castle, Minister for Overseas Development in Harold Wilson's first Labour Government, recalled a meeting with the Queen at Buckingham Palace. It was on the eve before the Prince would sit his first O level at Gordonstoun, and the Queen interrupted the meeting with Mrs Castle to take a phone call from her son. The minister noted that, on returning to the room, 'The Queen was very relaxed … She chatted on about Charles and said he was very nervous, but she thought he'd get on all right.' The fact that Charles rang his mother for reassurance, rather than another friend or relative, was a sign that their relationship was stronger than they were given credit for, as was her decision to interrupt a meeting with a Cabinet minister.

After studying at Cambridge, Charles followed the traditional path for male royals by serving in the Royal Navy. He undertook a six-week course at the Royal Naval College, Dartmouth, and his six-year career in the navy ended with his command of the minehunter HMS *Bronington*. Like his father before him, he trained to fly helicopters and piloted various types of aircraft.

One curious anecdote suggests the Queen wasn't totally au fait with his plans. A former courtier recalled being at Balmoral when Prince Philip took a telephone call from his eldest son.

Returning to the room, the Duke said, 'He's coming out of the navy next week', to which the Queen replied, 'Oh, I thought he wasn't coming out until next spring.'

Prince Charles left the navy at the age of 28 in 1976, the year he founded the Prince's Trust. He would go on to establish sixteen more charitable organisations, which together are known as the Prince's Charities and raise over £100 million annually. In addition, he has focussed on a wide range of other causes, including architecture, conservation, environmental awareness, alternative medicine and religion. Despite his vast contribution to such worthwhile causes, his parents never particularly went overboard to praise him for it. It was not in their nature. Neither of them ever sought praise for their own efforts and seemed to have taken it for granted that their children and grandchildren should be the same.

There have been times when they surprised Charles by publicly honouring his work. During their Diamond Jubilee tour in 2012, the Queen and Duke asked the Prince to join them on a visit to Burnley, Lancashire, where six of his charities were working together to try to rejuvenate the town. Even then, Prince Philip couldn't resist a jibe at Charles, telling him, 'I can't think why you want to save all these terrible old places.'

Four years later, the royal parents also accompanied Charles and Camilla on a visit to Poundbury, the new town in Dorset built in the architectural style advocated by the Prince. During the visit, the Queen opened the Queen Mother Square. Although neither parent publicly praised the project, as they were about to leave, Philip said, 'Well done,' which must have meant a lot to his son.

Relations between the Queen and the Prince of Wales reached their lowest point in the 1990s, when the monarchy ricocheted from one crisis to another, beginning with the publication of the Andrew Morton biography of Diana, which laid bare the Princess's deep unhappiness at the state of her marriage and told the world about the third person in it: Camilla Parker Bowles.

One of the Prince's confidantes told the biographer Ben Pimlott, 'He felt very let down by his unsympathetic mother and father. When his marriage went wrong, he felt criticised by them.'

It was, however, the publication of another book that deeply upset the Queen. In 1994, Jonathan Dimbleby's biography, *The Prince of Wales: An Intimate Portrait* highlighted the often-volatile relationship between father and son, and portrayed the Queen as a cold and remote mother. The fact the book was authorised by Charles and Dimbleby was given access to the Prince's journals, letters and, crucially, to his inner circle, only made the allegations all the more devastating for the Queen and Prince Philip.

A decade later, Philip's friend and biographer Gyles Brandreth asserted in his 2005 book *Charles and Camilla: Portrait of a Love Affair* that the Queen and Prince Philip were 'appalled' after reading such claims and the Duke of Edinburgh even branded his son 'bloody stupid'.

Relations between Buckingham Palace and Charles's household at St James's Palace deteriorated. According to Ben Pimlott, the Prince found the Palace's attitude 'interfering and patronising', while the Queen's advisors found her son's office 'unpredictable and maverick, and difficult to deal with'.

The Prince only really saw his parents at the usual state occasions and Christmas. The Queen's cousin Margaret Rhodes told the author in 1997, 'They hardly see each other. I wish he would go and stay with them more at Balmoral.' Instead, he preferred to stay with the Queen Mother at nearby Birkhall, which he would eventually take over after her death.

Another blow to the monarch came at the time of the Prince's 50th birthday in November 1998, when his press secretary Mark Bolland leaked to the media that Charles would be 'privately delighted' if his mother were to abdicate. The Prince was forced to apologise to his mother and denied it was true.

The Queen, Prince Philip and Prince Charles attend the opening of the first Welsh Assembly in 1999. (© Ian Lloyd)

The biggest bone of contention between mother and son was over Charles's continued romance with Camilla Parker Bowles, whom he considered a 'non-negotiable' part of his life. The Queen refused to receive Camilla, even after the death of the Princess of Wales, but was coming under increased pressure from some courtiers and her own niece, Lady Sarah Chatto, who realised that there was nothing unusual about Charles and Camilla's relationship in this day and age.

The Queen eventually publicly acknowledged Camilla, albeit briefly, at a party Charles was hosting at Highgrove to mark the 60th birthday of ex-King Constantine II of Greece.

The death of the Queen Mother in 2002 enabled the Queen to adopt her mother's role as royal matriarch and, according to courtiers, it gave her more confidence and allowed her to be more receptive to the eventual marriage of Charles and Camilla. Although she declined to attend the actual ceremony at the Guildhall in Windsor, she was present at the blessing in St George's Chapel later in the day and hosted a reception for the couple in the state apartments. She even made a speech, which was very well received. The wedding coincided with the Grand National race at Aintree. Keeping the mood light, she likened the obstacles the couple had faced to two of the National's most challenging jumps. 'They have overcome Beecher's Brook and the Chair and all kinds of obstacles. They have come through and I'm very proud and wish them well. My son is home and dry with the woman he loves.' The word 'pride' would have meant as much to Charles as the warm reference to Camilla.

Since that day in April 2005, the Queen has grown increasingly close to her daughter-in-law, helped by their shared love of anything horse related. Camilla has joined the Queen at the annual Royal Windsor Horse Show and in 2013, the Queen and her daughter-in-law paid a joint visit to the Ebony Horse Club, of which Camilla is patron, at Brixton. The club helps disadvantaged children, encouraging them to ride and to care for horses.

The retirement of the Duke of Edinburgh in 2017 and his death in 2021 allowed Charles to step into his father's shoes as the Queen's right-hand man. He has accompanied her to the State Opening of Parliament and helped host state visits, including that of Donald Trump in June 2019. Since the Queen's last long-haul flight to Australia in 2011, it has been Charles and Camilla, and, increasingly, the Duke and Duchess of Cambridge, who have flown the flag abroad.

In 2015, at the Commonwealth Heads of Government Meeting in Malta, the Queen took the opportunity to urge leaders to nominate Charles as her successor as head of the Commonwealth, which they duly did. It demonstrated not only her tremendous influence on the world stage, but also her faith in her son and heir.

28

MALTA AND A NORMAL LIFE

In October 1949, Prince Philip resumed active service with the Royal Navy. He was second in command of the destroyer HMS *Chequers*, based at the Mediterranean island of Malta. Between November 1949 and the spring of 1951, Princess Elizabeth spent three lengthy stays on the island, in what amounted to a second honeymoon.

Philip's cousin, Lady Pamela Hicks, told the author about the affection the Queen still holds for the island:

I think the Princess really loved Malta, because she was able to lead a normal life, wander through the town, and do some shopping, and whenever the fleet came in we would rush to the Barrakka [Malta's public gardens on the sea front] to see the whole fleet coming in – which was always a fantastic sight. They were magical days, endless picnics, sunbathing and waterskiing – lovely.

It was the only place of course that she was able to live the life of a naval officer's wife, just like all the other wives, which was wonderful for her and it's why they have such a nostalgia for Malta I think; why they really love it.

Home for the Princess on her four early visits to the island was the Villa Guardamangia, which was leased by the Mountbattens after the war when Lord Louis was made Commander of the First Cruiser Squadron, part of the Mediterranean Fleet:

It was a lovely sandstone house. It had a very nice garden with terraces and orange trees and the house itself had large reception rooms but very few bedrooms, at the most one guest room, so when they came to stay we had to juggle round. The Princess had my mother's room and my mother went into my father's room. We weren't concerned about Prince Philip because he was living on board his ship.

Despite her wish to live a private life on Malta, the protocol of the day and the near reverence for the monarchy meant the visit had elements of formality throughout. Elizabeth flew out for the first visit on 20 November 1949, the couple's second wedding anniversary. She was accompanied by Philip's aunt, Lady Mountbatten. The airport was shut off from the public for her early evening arrival, but she was still formally greeted by the governor of the island, Sir Gerald Creasy, the prime minister and nine other officials.

A crowd of 300 had gathered outside the Villa Guardamangia to see the Princess, who waved to them on her way in and would make a second appearance later when the crowd failed to disperse. Inside the villa, there was a champagne reception and a three-tier anniversary cake for Philip's shipmates, his uncle and aunt and their younger daughter, Lady Pamela.

There was more formality the next morning. Elizabeth breakfasted with Philip at 7 a.m. before he reported to *Chequers* at 7.30. His main duty on that particular morning was to supervise the firing of a royal salute in honour of his wife.

The Princess undertook some duties, including the dedication by the Archbishop of Canterbury of a memorial honouring British servicemen who died on Malta during the war. There were visits to hospitals, a tour of an industrial exhibition, visits to the other ships stationed off the island and a dinner held in her honour by the governor at the San Anton Palace.

Elizabeth's second visit began in late March 1950 and lasted six weeks, until early May. The Princess was pregnant with Princess Anne, who had been conceived on the island during the previous visit.

She celebrated her 24th birthday on the island. Once again, people gathered outside the villa, this time proffering flowers and boxes of chocolates, and once more the fleet was dressed overall and fired a twenty-one-gun salute. The mood of celebration was no doubt helped by the governor declaring the royal anniversary a half-day holiday.

In the afternoon, she presented prizes for a polo tournament. Philip had been sent three polo ponies as a gift and played on the 'Shrimps' team against the 'Optimists'. Earl Mountbatten also played. During her other visits, he gave Elizabeth lessons in riding side-saddle, something she was expected to do at Trooping the Colour, although never in private.

The Princess's final private stay on the island began on 25 November 1950 and lasted eleven weeks, until mid-February. In early December, she and Philip made a private six-day visit to Greece, the land of his birth, as guests of Philip's first cousin, King Paul. As Queen, Elizabeth never made a state visit to Greece, so it was to be her only opportunity to tour Athens and visit the Parthenon and other tourist attractions.

It was the Princess's second Christmas away from home and it seems strange she would want to miss baby Anne's first festive season, though she spoke to her parents by telephone. The UK press reported rumblings of discontent about the Princess's absence from her young children. In early March, it was the lead story in the *Daily Mirror*. 'Stop All This Gossip About the Princess' was the headline, which slyly added fuel to the story it was purporting to denounce. The piece, by the writer 'Cassandra', condemned the anti-Elizabeth feeling, citing an unnamed factory where grumblings ('especially women') were, he said, 'violent and virulent'.

There was no realisation in March 1951 that, a few months later, Philip would have to abandon his naval career to support Elizabeth in her public duties as the King's health deteriorated. Also, less than a year later, she would become Queen and the carefree days when Elizabeth could put personal pleasure above royal duty would never return.

29

PRINCESS ANNE: THE SON THEY NEVER HAD

The Princess Royal is more of her father's daughter than her mother's. Having said that, there are similarities between the monarch and her only daughter, from their strong belief in duty to their interest in everything equestrian.

Anne Elizabeth Alice Louise was born at Clarence House at 11.50 a.m. on 15 August 1950. It was the same day Philip learned he had been promoted to the rank of lieutenant commander in the Royal Navy. In a letter to his grandmother, the Dowager Marchioness of Milford Haven, Philip proudly announced, 'It's the sweetest girl'.

While much has been written about the Queen and Duke's remote parenting skills, particularly with their eldest children, key evidence suggests otherwise. Philip's close friend, and then private secretary, Mike Parker remembered that, no matter how busy the royal parents were, they always set aside time for Charles and Anne.

The Princess herself recalled that Philip, in particular, was always careful to be with the children at bedtime and often read them stories. 'Nanny,' she said, 'was always *Nanny*, never some sort of surrogate parent.' The Queen succeeded to the throne when Anne was just 2½. Inevitably, she was more occupied with royal duties than she had been previously. Nevertheless, she wasn't a remote figure in the way previous monarchs were to their children. 'I've known her longer as a mother than as a Queen,' Anne pointed out a few years ago. 'She has been Queen most of my life but that's not how I think of her – it's the other way round really.'

Like the Queen, she has always accepted her role in the family. The Queen became heiress presumptive at the age of 10 and the sovereign at 25. She never railed against it or complained; it was simply her fate. Anne adopted a similar attitude and 'always accepted the role of being second in everything' (to Prince Charles, and later to her brothers, Andrew and Edward). 'I'm the Queen's daughter and as a daughter I get less involved than the boys.'

Despite being what she called 'a tail-end Charlie', she was more confident than her older brother and picked on him mercilessly as a young child, often forcing the Queen to stop working on her red boxes and go out and intervene. These days, Anne concedes, 'I really don't know how she put up with the noise and aggravation that always seemed unavoidable whenever my brother and I did anything together.'

Anne has never missed an opportunity to praise her father and mother as well as her upbringing. 'Judging by some families, I think we are all on pretty good speaking terms after all this time and that's no mean achievement.'

She has also robustly defended the Queen against claims, such as the ones in the Dimbleby biography, that she was a remote mother. 'It just beggars belief that the Queen was aloof and uncaring,' declared Anne robustly, a few years ago:

> We as children may have not been too demanding, in the sense that we understood what the limitations were in time and the responsibilities placed on her as a monarch in the things she had to do and the travels she had to make; but I don't believe that any of us, for a second, thought she didn't care for us in exactly the same way as any mother did.

Anne was educated by a governess at Buckingham Palace but at the age of 13 went to Benenden School where she gained six GCE O levels and two A levels. The Queen, who was only ever educated at home, felt strongly that Anne should be taught with others. Apart from her time with the Buckingham Palace packs of Guides and Sea Rangers, she herself only had one collective activity which was her short time with the ATS in 1945. As she pointed out to Labour MP Barbara Castle, before that 'one had no idea how one compared with other people'.

Another Labour MP, Denis Healey, recalled being in a meeting with the Queen when Anne tapped at the door and announced that she was off to Sandringham in her car. 'Well darling, do be careful how you drive,' was the reply, which he thought was a typical mother and daughter moment.

After school, Anne began undertaking public engagements in 1968 at the age of almost 18. She and her brother job-shadowed their parents on several overseas tours, including Austria in 1969, Australia and New Zealand in 1970, and Canada later that same year.

Both the Queen and Anne regard their positions as ones of sacred trust. 'Opting out is not an option,' said the Princess, a few years before Harry and Meghan made it seem a doddle. 'It's about serving,' is another Anne observation:

It comes from an example from both my parents' way of working and where they saw their role being ... The queen's has been a lifelong service in a slightly different way [to Prince Philip], but they both have that perspective of service which is about working with people.

Anne usually carries out more than 500 engagements a year and will sometimes pack four or five engagements a day into her itinerary, and not all of them in the same area, but has been known to criss-cross the country in the same twenty-four-hour period.

Mother and daughter have also shown courage when necessary. In 1981, blanks were fired at the Queen as she rode side-saddle on her horse 'Burmese' on her way to the Trooping the Colour ceremony and, once she had reined in the mare, she appeared unruffled. Similarly, Anne showed her mettle when she and her husband Mark Phillips were almost kidnapped at gunpoint by Ian Ball, a fanatical loner, who shot three people during the attack. The Princess typically kept her cool throughout the ordeal and afterwards phoned her parents, who were on a visit to Indonesia. Philip dealt with the phone call at 5 a.m. local time and later proudly remarked, 'If the man had succeeded in abducting Anne, she'd have given him the hell of a time while in captivity.'

Mother and daughter are both famously frugal. Anne is particularly keen on recycling the same outfits time and again, often over decades. She says she does it:

> … because I'm quite mean. I still try and buy materials and have them made up because I just think that's more fun. It also helps to support those who still manufacture in this country. We mustn't forget we've got those skills, and there are still places that do a fantastic job.

Counting the pennies appeals to both of them, as Anne once revealed when talking about her time at Benenden:

> We had £2 a term and as I had been brought up by a careful Scots nanny to appreciate the value of money, I simply didn't spend my allotment. I've always been mean with money and as far as I know I was the only girl in the school who had any left by the end of term.

The two women enjoy time spent outdoors most of all. Both of them have described their ideal holiday as a few weeks at Balmoral.

Anne also goes sailing on the west coast of Scotland with her second husband, Tim Laurence. The love of the water dates back to her childhood when her father took his children sailing on Loch Muick on the Scottish estate.

The family enjoyed other sports too. Anne's former French teacher, Mlle de Roujoux, recalled games of football, 'The Queen was always goalkeeper and Prince Philip, Princess Margaret and the children joined in.'

Of course, their main outdoor hobby has always been horse riding and the Queen taught Anne to ride at an early age. Anne was allowed to pursue her interest in three-day eventing, something the Queen wouldn't have been allowed to do in her youth The Princess has always been grateful that she and her brothers have 'all been allowed to find our own way and we were always encouraged to discuss problems'.

For Anne and her mother, many of these problems have been discussed on horseback. The two were spotted hacking on the Home Park at Windsor following the death of the Queen Mother, and they've used horse riding or country walking as an opportunity to talk about family issues.

Her parents have also supported Anne. They were saddened when her marriage to Mark Phillips ended and they were by her side at Crathie Kirk, on Deeside, when she married Tim Laurence. Biographer Gyles Brandreth claimed the Queen and Duke 'worry about her' and added a 2004 comment from Philip, 'Things aren't easy for Anne'.

The Queen has awarded her daughter with honours over the years, beginning with the title Princess Royal, which Anne was entitled to as far back as 1965 when the last holder of that title, Princess Mary, died. She, however, opted to wait until she felt she deserved it, so it was finally bestowed in June 1987.

Seven years later, she was also made a Lady of the Garter, a rare honour for a royal princess, one that, for instance, Princess Margaret never received.

Then, in 2005, the Queen revised the order of precedence for private occasions with the blood Princesses Anne and Alexandra to become second and third after herself and Camilla fourth. (Though at public events, such as state banquets, Camilla would be second.)

One final similarity between mother and daughter is their attitude to retirement now she is over 70. 'I don't think retirement is quite the same [for me],' she said:

> I think both my father and my mother have, quite rightly, made decisions about, you know, 'I can't spend enough time doing this and we need to find somebody else to do it' because it makes sense. I have to admit they continued being there for a lot longer than I had in mind ... but we'll see.

30

WELL-ENDOWED

In 1956 the Queen received two trumpeter swans, which she sent to Sir Peter Scott's bird sanctuary. However, some gifts are less practical than others, and at least these were more welcome than the brown bear cub that Marshal Bulganin and Nikita Khrushchev gave to 6-year-old Princess Anne. The Queen later said, 'What a ridiculous thing to give to a child!' It was called 'Nikki' and became quite a hit with the public when he ended up in the Regent's Park Zoo.

The ever-practical Elizabeth would no doubt have welcomed the gift from the people of the United States on the birth of Prince Charles – 1½ tons of nappies – which she shared with other new mothers.

In 1958, the Chief of the Kwakiutl, the indigenous peoples of the Pacific north-west coast of Canada, gave the Queen a 100ft totem pole to mark the centenary of British Columbia. It had to sail down the west coast of North America, through the Panama Canal, across the Atlantic and as far up the River Thames as practicable before being taken to Windsor by two lorries to its eventual destination in the Great Park.

During her 1961 tour of Gambia, the villagers of Berending gave the Queen a 2-year-old crocodile in a pierced biscuit tin. Her private secretary, Martin Charteris, was obliged to keep it in his bath in the Royal Yacht *Britannia* for the rest of the tour. In 1962, she received two hippos for Prince Andrew, aged 2, from Liberia.

Six years later, she was given another pair of animals – two jaguars called 'Marquis' and 'Aizita'. Like the hippos and the croc, they ended up in London Zoo, as did an elephant given to her in Cambodia in 1972.

Another gift that must have widened royal eyes was the solid gold chain-mail pinafore that was given to the Queen during her 1979 tour of the oil-rich Gulf States. The countries vied to present their guest with jewellery and golden ornaments. So much so, that one newspaper carried the headline 'The Pearly Queen'. In return, her hosts each received a silver model of the Royal Yacht *Britannia* and a signed photo.

Some gifts really hit the spot. When the Queen attended a gala variety performance at Windsor to mark her Silver Jubilee, instead of the usual bouquet, she was given a silver rose. She was so delighted with it that she kept it on her writing desk.

When President Marcos of the Philippines and his wife Imelda met the Queen, they gave her a painting mounted in a wooden frame, edged with seashells. The Queen put it on display at the royal beach chalet at Holkham, Norfolk. Sadly, both the hut and the painting perished at the hands of an arsonist in 2003.

31

THE SPECIAL RELATIONSHIP

Elizabeth was still a princess when she first set foot on US soil. With Prince Philip by her side, as always, she was a guest of President Harry S. Truman. Both Truman and his successor, Dwight D. Eisenhower, were older than Elizabeth's parents and both men had fought in the First World War.

Elizabeth was the Diana of her day and, according to the British Ambassador, when the 67-year-old President appeared with the 25-year-old Princess in public, he gave 'the impression of a very proud uncle presenting his favourite niece to his friends'. Truman was certainly captivated with his beautiful guest and said, 'When I was a little boy, I read about a fairy princess, and there she is.' Martin Charteris, her future private secretary, put it more succinctly, 'Truman fell in love with her.'

In 1957, President Eisenhower invited the Queen to visit the United States to mark the 350th anniversary of the foundation of Jamestown, the first permanent English settlement in North America. (She would return fifty years later at the invitation of

George W. Bush to mark the settlement's 400th anniversary.) Eisenhower was determined the visit would be an unqualified success and invited the couple to stay in the White House itself. Philip was intrigued to be offered the Lincoln Room, with the four-poster bed once occupied by the legendary president. Elizabeth was given the Rose Room, which was later re-christened the 'Queen's Room'.

She also stayed at the Waldorf Astoria after arriving in New York and receiving a ticker-tape welcome as she drove down Wall Street in Eisenhower's bubble-back limousine. At the hotel, she sat next to Herbert Hoover, the 31st President of the USA, whose single term as head of state was dominated by the Wall Street Crash and the Great Depression. (Hoover lived at the Waldorf after leaving office in 1933 and until his death in 1964.)

Interest in the visit was so great that over 2,000 journalists were accredited to follow the tour. The Queen's formidable press secretary, Richard Colville, ensured they were kept as far away as possible, although at the Waldorf Astoria they were near enough for one to call out, 'Give us some cheesecake, Queen!' as she walked into the dining room. The *Chicago Daily News* also managed to get close enough to note, 'She's a doll, a living doll!'

'The doll' was surprised by the lack of confidence exuded by Eisenhower and his advisors. 'It was as if', she said, 'they all needed a friendly shoulder to lean on.' One biographer commented that Elizabeth 'was surprised and shocked by Eisenhower's anxiety to tell her his problems'.

In 1961, the Queen hosted a dinner for Eisenhower's successor, John F. Kennedy, and his wife, Jackie. The smiling official group shot gives no indication of the tension between host and guests. Jackie later told her distant relation, the writer Gore Vidal, 'I think the Queen resented me', which may have been insecurity on Elizabeth's part. She would have known a comparison between the sensibly dressed and coiffured monarch and the ultra-chic First Lady was inevitable.

Ahead of the Kennedy visit, the Palace had as usual asked the chief guests for a list of people they would like to be invited to the dinner. Top of Jackie's list was her sister, Lee Radziwill, as well as Princess Margaret. The president asked to meet the Queen's aunt, Princess Marina of Kent, whom he'd met in the 1930s when his father Joseph was the US Ambassador. The Queen balked at the idea of the divorced Mrs Radziwill under Buckingham Palace's roof, although she was forced to back down by Prime Minister Harold Macmillan. 'Anyway, the Queen had her revenge,' Jackie recalled. 'No Margaret, no Marina, no one except every Commonwealth minister of agriculture they could find.' Princess Margaret was similarly incensed.

The Queen had a warm relationship with Ronald Reagan, which, according to his wife Nancy, was because 'they both loved horses. That is how they bonded, really.' In 1982, Reagan and the Queen posed on horseback for the cameras at Windsor Castle before enjoying a quiet ride around the Home Park.

Reagan invited her to ride with him on his range near Santa Barbara, and in the following year, she duly obliged on what was termed an 'official' rather than a state visit. Unfortunately, at the time, California was experiencing some of its worst storms, and while the Reagans apologised for the weather, the Queen replied buoyantly, 'Oh no, no, no. This is an adventure.'

She also enjoyed the informal lunch, telling Nancy, 'it was wonderful. No one talked politics!'

The special alliance was strengthened at the time of the First Gulf War by a visit from George Bush and his wife Barbara to Buckingham Palace and the reciprocal visit by the Queen to the United States in May 1991. As always, it is the tiny details that history recalls rather than the bigger picture. As someone had forgotten to pull out a step on the podium for the petite monarch to use while making her speech on the White House lawns, she remained hidden by the lectern and the microphone, and the journalists gleefully noted that they were addressed by 'a talking hat'. Later, addressing a Joint Session of Congress, she opened her speech by saying, 'I do hope you can all see me', which gained her a round of applause before she had even properly begun.

During the visit she had a telling meeting with George Bush Jr, then owner of the Texas Rangers. After a bit of banter, the Queen joked, 'Are you the black sheep of the family?'

Young Bush replied, 'I guess so.'

The Queen agreed, 'All families have them.'

Then, overstepping the mark, he quipped, 'Who's yours?' before his mother hurriedly interjected with 'Don't answer that!' to her guest.

George W. Bush was the first US president to stay at Buckingham Palace when, in November 2003, he and his wife Laura paid an official visit to Britain. He also praised the Queen fully and said that conversations with her 'have kept me on my toes' – not something the other thirteen presidents seemed to have had a problem with.

At a state banquet, the president told the Queen, 'We are grateful for your personal commitment across five decades to the health and vitality of the alliance between our nations.'

Bush Jr's most memorable moment with the Queen came in his welcoming speech during the monarch's last visit to the

United States. Typically gaffe prone, he thanked her for helping to celebrate the Bicentennial in 1776, adding two centuries to her age. He compounded his slip by winking at her and telling the press, 'She gave me the look that only a mother could give a child.' 'Mother' got her own back at the state banquet, opening her speech with the cheeky quip, 'I wondered whether I should start this toast by saying, "When I was here in 1776 …"'.

One of the most memorable moments during a US state visit relates to the First Lady rather than the president. In 2009, Barack and Michelle Obama visited Britain. The Queen remarked on the height difference between the two women and put her arm round Michelle's waist, which prompted Mrs Obama to put her own arm round the Queen's shoulder in response. Rather unfairly, she was blamed for making a faux pas when it was her host who made the first move. Barack Obama has praised the Queen for her dry humour, and during his 2016 visit to the UK said, 'She is truly one of my favourite people.'

Everyone was waiting for Obama's successor, Donald Trump, to knock protocol on the head during his meetings with the Queen. That said, such is his respect for her, inherited from his Scottish-born mother, who was a huge royal fan, that his encounters have been successful, apart from the memorable occasion he walked in front of her while reviewing the Guard at Windsor. Before his 2019 state visit, he praised her in his own unique style. 'If you think of it, for so many years she has represented her country, she has really never made a mistake. You don't see, like, anything embarrassing. She is just an incredible woman.'

What Elizabeth II thought of Trump is another of those many tantalising mysteries she remains diplomatically tight-lipped about.

Fourteen US presidents have held office during the Queen's reign, and she's met thirteen of them, some on several occasions. The only one she never met was Lyndon B. Johnson, who was due to fly to London for Winston Churchill's funeral but was prevented by illness.

She met the latest incumbent, Joe Biden, at the G7 Summit held in Cornwall in 2021, and later for tea at Windsor. As he prepared to leave from Heathrow Airport, Biden told the press corps that he found the Queen 'very gracious' and then broke with protocol to tell them that she asked him about Russian President Vladimir Putin and Chinese President Xi Jinping and that he had invited her to visit the White House.

Then he added, 'I don't think she'll be insulted, but she reminded me of my mother', which was hopefully meant as a compliment.

32

ACCESSION

Queen Victoria died at 6.30 p.m. Her son, Edward VII, passed away at fifteen minutes to midnight and his heir, George V, left this world at five minutes to midnight. We only know that George VI died at some point between midnight on 5 February 1952 and 7.30 the following morning. Therefore, the exact moment when Elizabeth II became Queen is impossible to calculate.

The uncertainty of the timing is just one of many fascinating aspects of Elizabeth's accession. There is also the fact that she was abroad, on a short holiday in Africa, en route to a tour of New Zealand and Australia, the first monarch to succeed *in absentia* since George I in 1714.

The location of her accession is not in doubt. For the entirety of George VI's final night, Princess Elizabeth and Prince Philip were at Treetops, a hotel built among the branches of a giant fig tree at a watering hole in the Aberdare National Park, near the township of Nyeri in Kenya.

Another unusual aspect of the accession was the sheer difficulty of notifying the royal party that the King was dead. In our age of instant communication, the message would reach its destination in seconds. Seventy years ago, the official communiques failed miserably. As Lady Pamela Hicks, lady-in-waiting for the tour, told the author, 'We were almost the last to know about it.' George VI's private secretary, Alan Lascelles, telegraphed his equivalent in Elizabeth's household, Martin Charteris, using the pre-agreed code 'Hyde Park Corner', which would have signified to Charteris that the King had died. The telegram never arrived at Nyeri, and one theory is that the clerk who sent it mistook the message for the address.

Meanwhile, the Palace sent telegrams in cypher to Government House in Nairobi. Unfortunately, the governor had already set off for Mombasa to greet the royal party prior to their departure for Australasia by sea, taking with him the book of codes that could decipher the message.

A sign of the times was Elizabeth's rigid internalisation of emotion on hearing the news of her father's death, which was so typical of her generation. Her first thought was of others, and she sat down to write telegrams apologising for cancelling her visits to Australia and New Zealand. When Lady Pamela consoled her, her reply was, 'I'm so sorry, we've got to go back. I've ruined everyone's trip.'

There was more stoicism boarding the aircraft at Nanyuki en route to Uganda. At the top of the steps, Elizabeth turned and waved as she prepared to leave Kenya. Later, at Entebbe, she had to make polite small talk with the governor and his wife as she waited to board an aircraft to London.

Even in the air, she thought of others. In 1990, the author met a steward who had helped prepare the food on the BOAC Argonaut, who recalls Elizabeth appearing in the galley, still not changed into her mourning clothes, wanting to thank the crew for their care.

One final curious fact is the reaction of the press who were covering the trip. They were staying at Outspan Hotel, a short drive away from Sagana Lodge. Martin Charteris asked them not to photograph or film Elizabeth as she left for the airport. Dutifully, they placed their cameras on the ground and stood silently by the roadside as the royal party departed. This pre-paparazzi reaction wouldn't have been understood by photographers three or four decades later. It, of course, meant that no photos or newsreel footage was taken of Elizabeth on the day she became Queen.

Timeline

1951
23 September, 10 a.m.: The King undergoes a pneumonectomy – the surgical removal of his left lung, which was malignant.

1952
31 January: The King waves goodbye to Elizabeth and Philip as they depart for a tour of Australia and New Zealand, via Kenya.

5 February:
Late PM: At Sandringham, the King spends the afternoon shooting with Princess Diana's grandfather, Lord Fermoy and others. They bag 280 hares.
22.30 UK / 01.30 Kenya: The King retires for the night. Princess Margaret later recalled, 'There were jolly jokes and he went to bed early because he was convalescing. Then he wasn't any more.'
6 February:
00.00 UK / 03.00 Kenya: A nightwatchman hears the King (whose bedroom was on the ground floor) adjusting the latch on his window.
03.28 UK / 06.28 Kenya: (Scheduled time for sunrise over Aberdare National Park) Michael Parker, Philip's old naval chum and by then his private secretary, believed he was with Elizabeth at the moment she became Queen. He had invited her to climb up a ladder to a lookout point above the hotel, which enabled them to see over the forest to the horizon. As they did so, an eagle hovered above them. 'I never thought about it until later,' Parker commented in 1994, 'but that was roughly the time when the King died.'
06.00 UK / 09.00 Kenya: In all probability, the King is dead by now and Elizabeth is Queen. As she breakfasts on bacon and eggs, she laughs as baboons steal the lavatory paper from Treetops and send streamers of it all over the jungle floor.
07.30 UK / 10.30 Kenya: The King's valet, James MacDonald, takes a morning cup of tea to his master and is unable to wake him. In Kenya, Elizabeth and Philip enjoy some trout fishing and Elizabeth teases her husband after she catches the most.
08.30 UK / 11.30 Kenya: Assistant private secretary Edward Ford is telephoned by the King's private secretary, Alan Lascelles, who uses a prearranged signal 'Hyde Park Corner' to inform him of the death of the King.
09.30 UK / 12.30 Kenya: After informing the prime minister, Winston Churchill, in person at No. 10 Downing Street, Ford

travels to Marlborough House and informs Cynthia Colville, lady-in-waiting to 84-year-old Queen Mary. The royal matriarch asks to speak to Ford, who finds her sitting down in a state of shock.

10.45 UK / 13.45 Kenya: The Press Association and Reuters news agency are permitted to release the statement from Buckingham Palace. 'It was announced from Sandringham at 10.45 a.m. today, February 6, 1952, that the King, who retired to rest last night in his usual health, passed peacefully away in his sleep earlier this morning.'

11.00 UK / 14.00 Kenya (approx.): Martin Charteris arrives at Outspan Hotel, once the home of Robert Baden Powell, the founder of the scout movement. A journalist tells him the Reuters wire claims the King is dead.

11.15 UK / 14.15 Kenya: The BBC's John Snagge was chosen to broadcast the news. 'This is London. It is with the greatest sorrow that we make the following announcement ...'

11.30 UK / 14.30 Kenya (approx.): After Charteris has spoken to Mike Parker at Sagana Lodge about the news reports of the King's death, Parker is unwilling to tell Prince Philip until he has received official confirmation. He turns on the radio and hears solemn music and the muffled sounds of Big Ben. Eventually, he hears the broadcaster repeat the announcement. Parker walks round the outside of the building to a veranda where he can see Philip resting inside. He breaks the news. 'He looked as if you'd dropped half the world on him. I never felt so sorry for anyone in all my life.' Philip told Parker it would be 'the most appalling shock'.

11.45 UK / 14.45 Kenya: Philip asks Elizabeth to join him outside. 'He took her up to the garden,' recalled Mike Parker, 'and they walked slowly up and down the lawn while he talked and talked and talked to her.' He also noticed 'she was weeping desperately for the loss of her father'.

14.00 UK / 17.00 Kenya (approx.): The royal party leaves Sagana Lodge for Nanyuki Airport, to catch a flight that will take them to the royal aeroplane in Uganda. Ordinary Kenyans reportedly line the roads, calling, '*Shauri mbaya kabisa!*' ('The very worst has happened!').

16.00 UK / 19.00 Kenya: The DC3 aeroplane takes off from Nanyuki.

17.44 UK / 20.44 Uganda: The royal party arrives in Entebbe.

19.00 UK / 22.00 Uganda: A storm rages over Entebbe, preventing take-off.

20.40 UK / 23.40 Uganda: The Queen, in a borrowed mackintosh, boards the BOAC Argonaut 'Atalanta'.

20.47 UK / 23.47 Uganda: The aircraft leaves Entebbe.

23.06 UK time: The following message from the Queen Mother was received by Atalanta's captain, entered into the log book and then copied out by hand on to a BOAC signal form before being shown to Elizabeth:

> To: Her Majesty The Queen
> All my thoughts and prayers are with you.
> Mummie
> Buckingham Palace

7 February:

06.12 UK / 08.12 Libya: The aircraft lands at El Adem for refuelling and a change of crew.

07.10 UK / 09.10 Libya: The aircraft takes off from El Adem.

16.19 UK: The royal party lands at London Airport. The Queen's uncle, the Duke of Gloucester, and the private secretary, Alan Lascelles, go on board. Looking out of the window, Elizabeth notices the formal Palace cars instead of her own and comments, 'Oh God! They've sent the hearses.'

16.30 UK: The Queen descends from the aircraft onto British soil and is met by Earl Mountbatten, Prime Minister Winston Churchill, Clement Attlee and Anthony Eden.

In step: the Queen and her mother had much more in common than their love of pearls and pastels. They shared a belief in duty and the sanctity of the monarchy, as well as a strong religious faith. Here they leave Sandringham Church after morning worship. (© Ian Lloyd)

33

THE OTHER QUEEN ELIZABETH

The Queen has inherited many of her mother's characteristics, including her sense of humour, youthful spirit, devotion to the monarchy and her religious faith. She also has Queen Elizabeth's belief in homeopathic medicine and her love of horse racing, though her prime interest is in flat racing while her mother enjoyed National Hunt racing with its thrill of the 'jumps'.

Both women tended to avoid unpleasant family issues. The Queen Mother was dubbed 'the imperial ostrich' by some of her aides, due to her ability to bury her head in the sand. An obvious example was her reluctance to directly involve herself in the Margaret/Townsend crisis, preferring to hope the romance fizzled out and the problem went away. Similarly, the Queen avoided involving herself in the breakdown of her children's marriages – until the fallout from Diana's *Panorama* interview forced her to act – believing that they had to be responsible for their own actions.

On the other hand, there were noticeable differences between mother and daughter in several areas. The Queen is notoriously frugal, whereas her mother was extravagant to the nth degree. The Queen Mother was never averse to a bit of mass adulation and continually played to the gallery, which her daughter always thought dishonest. Another major difference was their attitude to tradition. Queen Elizabeth rigidly refused to budge in changing even the smallest of traditions, believing it to be the thin end of the wedge where the mystique of the monarchy was concerned. The Queen has usually been more pragmatic, backed by the progressive attitude of the Duke of Edinburgh, and over the years has adapted and modernised the monarchy, especially in the light of criticism from both press and public.

The Queen Mother, as Duchess of York and Queen, helped create a warm and secure environment for her husband and children to live in, based on the fun-loving and supportive environment she herself grew up in. Prince Charles once said of his grandmother, 'Any house she lives in is a unique haven of cosiness and character.'

She taught her daughters to read, encouraging them to tackle the classics of literature and to keep a diary. Having said that, she was also typical of her age and class in being emotionally contained, something her daughter inherited. 'She's not mumsy in any way,' one of the Queen's longest-serving ladies-in-waiting said of the monarch. 'The Queen Mother was exactly the same. The Royal Family are just not like the rest of us.'

One former courtier felt 'the Queen's picture of her role was derived from her father and very much reinforced by her mother'. While the King familiarised Elizabeth with the political side of her future role, Queen Elizabeth tried to boost the shy Princess's confidence. For instance, she would rehearse various scenarios with her daughter, from how to meet and greet the Archbishop of Canterbury to having tea with a visiting head of state.

She was also, in her own way, preparing Elizabeth to find a suitable future husband. It was no secret at Court that Elizabeth's mother wanted her to marry a British aristocrat. 'We always joked that Queen Elizabeth had produced a cricket eleven of names she hoped the Princess would fall for,' former assistant private secretary Edward Ford told the author in 1997. 'They were all Eton men and most of them were the heirs to dukedoms – Hugh Euston [Grafton], Johnny Dalkeith [Buccleuch], Sonny Blandford [Marlborough] and so on. The only batsman missing off her list was Prince Philip.'

Although he was a Prince of Greece and a descendant of Queen Victoria, he was widely perceived by those close to the King and Queen as Germanic, especially as one of his sisters and three brothers-in-law joined the Nazi Party and another sister held a lunch party for Adolf Hitler. Queen Elizabeth, who had lost a brother, Fergus Bowes Lyon, during the First World War, and who remained vehemently anti-German throughout her long life, was said years later, in private, to have dubbed her son-in-law 'the Hun' and felt he ran the royal estates 'like a Junker'.

He also lacked the royals' distinctive brand of fun. 'Elizabeth found Philip cold and lacking in our kind of sense of humour,' recalled one lady-in-waiting. 'He wasn't able to see the ridiculous things, and that is perhaps rather Germanic. And he didn't set out to charm her.'

He was unafraid to challenge the opinions of his elders and betters. After one such outburst in early December 1946, the 25-year-old wrote to Queen Elizabeth apologising for getting carried away and starting 'a rather heated discussion'. It was on politics, a subject area in which Philip's views were leftist and the Queen Mother's were conservative with both a large and small 'c'.

Just before Elizabeth and Philip's engagement was announced, Queen Elizabeth wrote to a few confidantes to let them know first. Her letters wax lyrical about her daughter's intended, but to the King's private secretary, Alan Lascelles, who shared her misgivings about Philip, she was more downbeat. 'One can only pray,' she wrote, 'that she has made the right decision, I think she has – but he is untried as yet.'

Four and a half years later, the relationship between mother and daughter was to be tested following the death of the King, when Queen Elizabeth lost her power base, and her forthright and opinionated son-in-law took her place as consort.

Three weeks after the accession, the new Queen was talking to her assistant private secretary, Martin Charteris, when her mother's limousine glided into view and the weary Elizabeth said, 'Here comes the problem!' The problem, according to another courtier, was that 'she was no longer the boss'. One of her family blamed astrology, 'She was a Leo and like all Leos she didn't enjoy being number two.' Although she had the added boost of an additional 'queen' in her new title of Queen Elizabeth, the Queen Mother, to differentiate her from her daughter, she also lost a certain amount of status, particularly when she moved to Clarence House, or, as she called it, that 'horrid little house'.

To compensate her mother for the loss of the King and status, and to motivate her to bring her undeniable charisma back onto the royal stage, the Queen ordered a despatch box to be made for her mother to receive at least some royal papers in. She also made her a Counsellor of State, the first dowager queen to hold this office. This meant she was the quasi-monarch during Elizabeth and Philip's early, lengthy overseas visits, including the six-month coronation tour of 1953–54.

Philip, with that 'new-broomish' attitude the courtiers feared, wanted to change anything he thought could do with it. Courtiers and politicians opposed him, left, right and centre, but his chief opponent was his mother-in-law.

The Queen Mother's crisis of confidence following the death of the King was dealt with sympathetically by the prime minister, Winston Churchill, who visited her in Scotland and cajoled her into focussing on the future. Members of her household believe he suggested the young and inexperienced Elizabeth II would need to rely on her mother in the years ahead. At 51, she was too young to retire, although nobody could have foreseen that the older Elizabeth would be carrying out overseas tours until she was almost 90 and was still fulfilling public engagements in her 102nd year.

As a natural performer, she found the public aspect of her role something she relished rather than dreaded, as Sir Edward Ford pointed out to the author in 1997, 'I always felt [the Queen] was slightly in awe of her mother. Queen Elizabeth thrived on meeting people. The Queen is of course used to it, but still finds it a trial at times.'

It was still not all plain sailing between mother and daughter. Maintaining Queen Elizabeth in the Edwardian luxury to which she'd been accustomed didn't come cheap, and while the naturally frugal Philip and Elizabeth privately despaired at the huge bills generated down the Mall at Clarence House, the Queen readily paid off a vast number of them. Whether it was settling the invoices for her mother's ever-expanding wardrobe or her considerable number of racehorses, the only negativity shown by the Queen was to scribble an exasperated, 'Oh dear, Mummy!' across them. The £643,000 given to the Queen Mother each year from the Civil List failed to cover the vast amount of debt she accrued, and the Queen was thought to have topped up her mother's allowance by an estimated seven figure sum every twelve months.

Another problem was the Queen Mother's reactionary attitude to moving with the times. She opposed nearly every significant change, from the opening of Buckingham Palace to the public, the Queen having to pay tax, to the scrapping of the Royal Yacht *Britannia* and the disappearance of the royal flight. She even objected to change on the private royal estates of Balmoral, which came under Prince Philip's remit. Even twenty years into the present reign, when Philip decided to re-landscape the approach to Sandringham House, it was made clear that the Queen Mother preferred it as it was – and so that's how it stayed.

One aspect of their relationship the Queen did delight in were the occasions she played second fiddle to her mother, ceding precedence to her on her milestone birthdays. On those days, she and Princess Margaret acted as ladies-in-waiting, trailing after their mother and collecting the bunches of flowers and other gifts lavished on the royal matriarch by an adoring public.

She also kept a protective eye on her increasingly frail mother. The Queen Mother disliked using walking sticks and at first opted for an elegant cane, which simply wasn't adequate for the job. Once it failed to stop her falling as she entered the royal box at Ascot, and the Queen Mother, in her fury with the offending wooden prop, tried to break it over her knee. Eventually, the Queen thought the only way to force her mother to use a typical walking stick was by family bullying. She sent her a special new one with accompanying note, 'Darling Mummy, Your daughters and your nieces would very much like you to TRY this walking stick!'

The Queen Mother died on the afternoon of 30 March 2002 with the Queen by her side and leaving her as the sole survivor of 'we four', the close-knit family unit of the 1930s and 1940s. On the eve of the Queen Mother's funeral, the Queen addressed the nation and spoke of her mother and the 'void she has left in our midst'. She added, 'I thank you also from my heart for the love that you gave her during her life.' Touchingly, she also shared her own feelings on the passing of a mother she had known for seventy-five years. 'I count myself fortunate that my mother was blessed with a long and happy life. She had an infectious zest for living, and this remained with her until the very end.'

34

AND TO CROWN IT ALL

At the age of 27, Elizabeth II was crowned at Westminster Abbey in a ceremony dating back 900 years. She was the sixth queen regnant to be crowned at the abbey, the first being Mary I on 1 October 1553, and the last before Elizabeth was Victoria on 28 June 1838.

Elizabeth's Day

On the morning of the coronation, Bobo MacDonald and her assistants helped the Queen into her coronation dress, designed by Norman Hartnell. The Queen asked that it should

*Detail from the Queen's coronation dress. Norman Hartnell showed
nine designs to the Queen and she selected the eighth, though rather
than an all-silver design she suggested coloured embroidery.
(© Ian Lloyd)*

be made of white satin and should conform to the line of her
wedding dress. She also asked for floral emblems for all the
Commonwealth nations besides those of the four national
emblems Hartnell had shown her.

Cosmetic advice to the Queen had been given to her since
1943 by Thelma Holland, who was the daughter-in-law of Oscar
Wilde, having married his younger son, Vyvyan. It is often presumed Mrs Holland did the make-up for the coronation, but on
the day, Elizabeth chose to do her own. Her hair was styled by
Henri Joerin, the royal hairdresser from 1939 to 1969.

The coronation bouquet was completely white and emblem-
atic – made up of orchids and lilies-of-the-valley from England,
stephanotis from Scotland, orchids from Wales and carnations
from Northern Ireland and the Isle of Man.

One of her attendants said, 'You must be feeling nervous, Ma'am.' To which she replied, 'Yes but I really do think Aureole will win' – a reference to the Derby, to be run four days later.

She journeyed to the abbey with Prince Philip in the Gold State Coach, pulled by eight grey geldings: one of whom was named 'Eisenhower', after the Supreme Allied Commander during the Second World War. The Queen has since recalled the journey in the 4-ton coach as 'horrible', 'not very comfortable' and the coach was 'not meant for travelling in at all'. It was drizzling when they set off from Buckingham Palace and it bucketed down with rain on the return journey, ironically, since one of the reasons 2 June was chosen was because it was statistically the date that had the finest weather.

At the abbey, the Queen was met by her eight maids of honour and the Mistress of the Robes, the Dowager Duchess of Devonshire. As they took up the satin handles on either side of the 18ft-long train, the Queen said, 'Ready, girls?' and they moved off. The 'girls' had previously practised walking with the Queen at rehearsals, with Elizabeth wearing white sheets tied together.

The Queen initially resisted the idea of live television broadcasting of the service but, after several opinion polls showed an overwhelming number of people wanted to see a live broadcast, the Queen agreed, and 27 million people in the UK (out of the 36 million population) watched the ceremony on television and 11 million listened on the radio.

The anointing was the only part of the service the Queen wouldn't allow to be televised. She was anointed with holy oil on the palms of her hands, her forehead and, unlike Victoria, on the breast.

The coronation service took almost three hours – Victoria's lasted five – and began at 11.15 and ended when the Queen left at 2 p.m. During the service, the Queen used three different chairs: the Chair of Estate, which was in front of the Royal Gallery; she then moved to the carved oak Coronation Chair, first used at the coronation of Edward II in 1308; and then finally, the Chair of Estate.

Four-and-a-half-year-old Prince Charles was brought into the abbey to witness the moment of crowning, sitting between the Queen Mother and Princess Margaret. He said, 'Look, it's Mummy!' and the Queen gave him a smile.

Elizabeth was crowned with the solid gold St Edward's Crown, made for Charles II's coronation in 1661. Weighing 4lb 12oz and with 444 precious stones, it is too heavy to wear other than at the moment of crowning. For the return journey to Buckingham Palace, the Queen wore the lighter Imperial State Crown.

Prince Philip was the first lay person to pay homage to the newly crowned sovereign (after the Archbishop of Canterbury had knelt before her first). Then, the Dukes of Gloucester and Kent followed. Philip did have one significant moment – the Queen had insisted he should be by her side for Holy Communion.

Philip's three surviving sisters, Margarita, Theodore and Sophie, lobbied hard to be included in the guest list, having been excluded from the wedding in 1947. They were allowed to attend with their husbands, but just two of their children each and no other German relations could attend. Also banned was the Duke of Windsor, at the suggestion of Elizabeth. According to Archbishop Fisher, 'The Queen would be less willing than anyone to have him there.' A former monarch witnessing the anointing of a new one just didn't sit well.

Coronation Chicken was invented for the foreign guests who were to be entertained after the coronation. It was created by the florist Constance Spry, who suggested a recipe of cold chicken in a cream curry sauce with an accompanying salad of rice, green peas and mixed herbs.

The official coronation photos were taken at Buckingham Palace by Cecil Beaton. Philip would have liked his old Thursday Club pal, Baron Nahum, to take the official photographs, but the Queen Mother lobbied for and succeeded in getting Beaton. Anne Glenconner, one of the maids of honour, recalled, 'Cecil Beaton was in a stew, hopping up and down, and … the Duke of Edinburgh – he was an amateur photographer – kept on saying, "no you've got to be there". Tired of Philip arranging the group, 'in the end Cecil Beaton said, "Look I'm taking the photographs you know, I think I'd better get on with it".

35

FOREVER FAITHFUL: THE QUEEN AND RELIGION

The late Queen Mother may have been somewhat relaxed when it came to her daughters' education, but one thing she was decisive about was their religious instruction. Like her own mother before her, she read her children Bible stories and, later on, the psalms.

For most of her life, the Queen has prayed by kneeling by her bedside with her hands folded. George Carey, the former Archbishop of Canterbury said, 'She comes from a generation in which kneeling by the side of the bed is quite natural.' He also claimed, 'The Queen knows the prayer book backwards.'

Her coronation service reinforced her belief, as her cousin, Margaret Rhodes, explained, 'She wasn't just crowned Queen, she was also anointed.' Mrs Rhodes said this consecration as sovereign 'is why she will never abdicate'. During the service, she was presented with a copy of the Holy Bible as the Archbishop of Canterbury said, 'We present you with this book, the most valuable thing that this world affords.'

The Queen once said, 'The teachings of Christ and my own personal accountability before God provide a framework in which I live my life.' Outside of the clergy, she is probably one of the most regular worshippers at church, attending a Sunday service at the local church, either on or close to each of the royal estates. And no matter where she has been in the world, she has tried to attend a Sunday service, whether at the nearest Anglican church or, if she was at sea, on the Royal Yacht *Britannia.*

She was confirmed at the age of 15, on 28 March 1942, and attends communion three or four times a year, including Christmas and Easter. On Christmas Day, she makes a private visit to St Mary Magdalene Church on the estate, before returning two hours later for the morning service. She's a traditionalist in her beliefs and worship. George Carey said, 'She treasures Anglicanism. She loves the 1662 Book of Common Prayer.' Like her son, Prince Charles, she likes the beauty of the language in the King James version of the Bible.

The Queen appoints archbishops, bishops and deans on the advice of her government and meets the Archbishop of Canterbury for private talks about half a dozen times a year. She personally 'interviews' (usually a relaxed process over a cup of tea) those who are to be appointed as minister of the royal chapels where she worships.

She is not a dry-as-dust worshipper but enjoys a lively sermon with the odd joke. At Sandringham, she enjoyed the minister's crack about the bishop's wife who was handed a brandy snifter and said, 'Oh just half a glass for me!'

At Sandringham she also enjoys when the Sunday School class joins in the service. Once, leaving Flitcham Church on the estate, she was seen to be roaring with laughter. The minister had begun his address to the children by asking, 'Now who knows the name of the headmaster in Harry Potter?' Before him was a sea of blank faces. Safely in the churchyard, the Queen said, 'But I knew the answer – Dumbledore!'

One relative told the author about an occasion at the tiny church of All Saints, next to Royal Lodge, when the guest

The Queen, leaving Flitcham Church in January 2004, reveals she knew who the headmaster in Harry Potter *was. (© Ian Lloyd)*

minister had completely forgotten to turn up. After waiting a while, the Queen looked round at her fellow worshippers and said, 'Well, I am head of the Church of England, perhaps I should take the service!' Thankfully, he turned up before she had to risk it.

36

THE QUEEN AND CHURCHILL

During her Silver Jubilee year, the Queen was asked by a former courtier which prime minister she had enjoyed her audiences with the most. 'Winston of course,' came the instant reply, 'because it was always such fun.' Two jubilees and a posse of PMs later, if asked the question today, her answer, without doubt, would be exactly the same.

Churchill was 78 when Elizabeth became Queen at 25. He had entered Parliament when her great-great-grandmother, Queen Victoria, was alive, and although an imposing figure to the young monarch, he was one she had known all her life. As far back as 1928, he was invited to Balmoral and encountered Elizabeth, aged 2. 'She is a character,' he wrote to his wife, Clementine. 'She had an air of authority and reflectiveness astonishing in an infant.'

During the darkest days of the war the Churchills sent a bouquet to Elizabeth to mark her 15th birthday in April 1941. She sent him a handwritten note offering her sympathy for the 'very worrying time' he'd had of late. Four years later, on VE Day, he was invited to join Elizabeth and Margaret, together with the King and Queen, on the balcony of Buckingham Palace to acknowledge the cheers of a grateful nation.

Like everyone else, he was shocked at the untimely death of George VI at the age of 56. In fact, he was prostrate with grief and unable to write the speech he had to make. With tears pouring down his face, he told his private secretary, John Colville, his concerns at serving the new young monarch. 'I don't know her,' he sobbed. 'She's a mere child. I knew the King so well.' Colville, who had been Elizabeth's private secretary from 1947–49, reassured him. 'You will find her very much the reverse of being a child.'

There was more emotion from the elderly premier at London Airport, the following afternoon, as Elizabeth descended the steps of a BOAC Argonaut. Churchill, once again with tears rolling down his face, was there to greet her with other senior politicians and her uncle, the Duke of Gloucester.

Elizabeth was at first overawed by her prime minister. On his first visit to Balmoral later that year, the mostly young house party were, according to one who was there, 'petrified' at having to entertain the war hero, but the visit was a great success. They soon developed a mutual admiration and Prince Charles would liken it to the strong bond felt by the young Queen Victoria for her first premier, Lord Melbourne.

The new Queen continued George VI's tradition of meeting the prime minister on Tuesday evenings. Churchill would dress in an old-style frock coat and top hat and the meetings, originally scheduled to last thirty minutes, grew and grew to two or three times that length.

When Colville asked him what they talked about, all he was told was an evasive, 'Oh – racing'. His daughter, Mary Soames, later recalled, 'They spent a lot of the audience talking about horses'. Bizarrely, after one meeting Churchill revealed, 'She asked me about my pig-sticking days on the North-West Frontier ...'

But the audiences were more than that and the prime minister was impressed by Elizabeth's conscientiousness and grasp of detail. 'What a *very* attractive and intelligent woman,' he said, after one of their meetings.

He was less euphoric when, once, he failed to read two very important telegrams from the British Ambassador in Iraq during a Middle-East crisis. 'I was extremely interested,' said the Queen, 'in that telegram from Baghdad', and went on to list three or four points that she had elicited from it. The shame-faced PM made sure he read every vital telegram before his audiences after that.

Elizabeth's private secretary, Tommy Lascelles, recorded in his diary:

I could not hear what they talked about, but it was, more often than not, punctuated by peals of laughter, and Winston generally came out wiping his eyes. 'She's *en grande beauté ce soir*,' he said one evening in his school-boy French.

According to biographer Elizabeth Longford, soon after her accession the Queen told a friend, 'I no longer feel anxious or worried. I don't know what it is but I have lost all my timidity somehow becoming the Sovereign and having to receive the Prime Minister.'

Churchill, always a royalist, developed almost an infatuation with the young Queen. Within a year of her accession, he confided in his doctor, Lord Moran, 'All the film people in the world, if they had scoured the globe, could not have found anyone so suited for the part.' Anthony Montague Browne, Colville's successor as private secretary, recalled:

My most vivid memory of the Prime Minister's feelings for the Queen is seeing him gazing with great tenderness at a charming photograph she had given him, with a warm inscription. It showed her laughing and happy as she returned from the State Opening of Parliament. 'Isn't she a winner?' he said.

The Queen returning to Buckingham Palace following her first State Opening of Parliament in 1952. Churchill kept a framed copy of the photograph, which she had signed for him. (© Popperfoto via Getty)

Not that it was all plain sailing between the monarch and the statesman. Asked by a former courtier at the time if Churchill treated her indulgently, the Queen's reply was revealing. 'Not at all. I sometimes find him very obstinate.'

This obstinacy became apparent just twelve days after the death of George VI. Queen Mary had heard that the Duke of Edinburgh's uncle, Lord Mountbatten, was boasting, somewhat chauvinistically, 'that the House of Mountbatten now reigned'. Determined that the House of Windsor, the name of the dynasty chosen by her husband, George V, in 1917, should remain, Mary summoned Churchill's private secretary to see her. The PM and the Cabinet backed the old lady, and the Queen was forced to issue a proclamation that she and her descendants would bear the name of Windsor. Prince Philip was devastated. 'It hurt him; it really hurt him,' said his cousin, Patricia Mountbatten, years later.

Although he was no fan of Philip's, it was Churchill who, in March 1955, first proposed to the Queen that her husband should be given the title of Prince of the United Kingdom, in recognition for his services to the country, a decision that was formalised two years later, long after the PM had retired.

Churchill was also obstinate about where the Queen would reside. Having only moved into the redecorated Clarence House in 1949, she and the Duke were reluctant to leave. Someone suggested they continue to live there and to use Buckingham Palace as an office. 'She was delighted with the idea,' recalled Mike Parker, Philip's private secretary. Churchill had other ideas. For over a century, the palace had been the centre of the empire and at the heart of the monarchy. 'To the palace they must go,' harrumphed the old warhorse. Parker drove with the royal couple on their last commute from Clarence House, 'and I can assure you that there was not a dry eye in that car'.

The Queen was solicitous about Churchill's health. Ten weeks after he had a stroke while still in office, she sent an invitation to the PM and his wife to watch the St Leger race day at Doncaster on 11 September from the royal enclosure, before joining her on the royal train for a break at Balmoral. 'It was a target and a test,' wrote his daughter, Mary Soames. 'Everyone from the Queen and her family downwards made much of them.' The Queen told a friend that the improvement in his health was 'astonishing'.

Elizabeth venerated her first minister in a way she would never repeat during her reign. In 1952, she commissioned sculptor Oscar Nemon to make a bust of Churchill, which is still on display at Windsor Castle. The following year, she made him a Knight of the Garter, the only PM to receive the honour while in office. For his 80th birthday in 1954, she sent him a set of silver wine coasters and some flowers for his 90th.

The Queen was genuinely saddened when Churchill retired in April 1955. On 4 April, he hosted a dinner at No. 10 Downing Street attended by the Queen and Duke. When he visited Buckingham Palace to formally resign the following day, she came out on to the landing to meet him, before escorting him into her study. He left, once again, in tears.

Shortly afterwards, Elizabeth wrote to him from Windsor to say how much she missed him and that none of his successors 'will ever, for me, be able to hold the place of my first Prime Minister, to whom both my husband and I owe so much and for whose wise guidance during the early years of my reign I shall always be so profoundly grateful'.

Winston Churchill suffered a cerebral haemorrhage on 15 January 1965. The Queen, who was staying at Sandringham House for her New Year holiday, asked to be kept informed about his condition. The end finally came on 24 January, and later the same day, the Queen wrote to Lady Churchill to tell her that Winston's death had 'caused inexpressible grief to me and my husband'.

Elizabeth's suggestion of a state funeral had actually been made in 1958 after Churchill suffered a bout of pneumonia.

'It was entirely owing to the Queen that it was a state funeral,' recalled Mary Soames. 'She indicated that to him several years before he died, and he was gratified.'

Shortly before the funeral, the Queen and Duke, accompanied by Princess Margaret and her husband, Lord Snowdon, attended the lying-in-state in Westminster Hall. They stood, dressed in black, before the catafalque for five minutes, unseen by the line of public mourners snaking its way through the hushed building. It was noted that both ladies turned and whispered to their husbands before leaving after five minutes.

The Churchill family was allowed to use some of the Queen's carriages for the funeral procession through the streets of London, with rugs and hot-water bottles thoughtfully added. The Queen broke with precedent before the service by arriving before members of the family – giving them the place of honour. According to Mary Soames, she also instructed them 'not to curtsey or bow as we passed her, because it would have held everything up'.

After the private family committal at Bladon, in Oxfordshire, two wreaths were placed on the grave – one from the statesman's family; the other bore the handwritten message, 'From the Nation and the Commonwealth. In grateful remembrance. Elizabeth R.'

37

DROPPING THE CURTSIES

Just five years into the new Elizabethan era, the young monarch and her court were roundly criticised in the August 1957 edition of *National and English Review.* What made the attack particularly newsworthy was that the author was a peer of the realm. John Edward Poynder Grigg was the 2nd Baron Altrincham. His father, Edward Grigg, had been military secretary to Edward, Prince of Wales, during the royal tours of Canada, Australia and New Zealand, for which service he was knighted by George V.

In his piece, Grigg Junior claimed the household was made up of 'tweedy advisors', the Queen's speeches were 'prim little sermons', her speaking voice was 'a pain in the neck', and the overall impression she radiated was that of 'a priggish schoolgirl, captain of the hockey team, a prefect and a recent candidate for confirmation'.

Needless to say, it caused a sensation, but the Palace took it on the chin. Martin Charteris, assistant private secretary, arranged a meeting with Altrincham through a mutual friend. Thirty years later, at a political meeting at Eton, Charteris told Grigg, 'You did a great service to the monarchy and I'm glad to say so publicly.'

Prince Philip was said to have been intrigued by the piece and speeded up the modernisation of the royal household, which he had been working on since the beginning of the reign. One of the first post-Grigg changes was the axing of the presentation of debutantes at court. Before the war, it was a tradition for aristocratic girls to perform obeisance before the monarch, accompanied by an older female relation who had herself been presented. After the war, the system became discredited as money exchanged hands and seemingly anyone with cash and connections could curtsey before the monarch. Princess Margaret, in full Lady Bracknell mode, memorably said, 'We had to put a stop to it. *Every tart in London* was getting in.'

Rather than limiting access to the Queen to the top echelons of society, Philip wanted to broaden the social stratification of guests so that Elizabeth could meet people from a wider range of backgrounds. In May 1956, he and the Queen hosted an informal lunch at Buckingham Palace. They were to become a fixture on the royal calendar with four or five held every year. Billed as a 'Meet the People' exercise, the guests were limited to the great and good, although they firmly belonged to the meritocracy rather than the aristocracy. The first one included the headmaster of Eton, the chairman of the National Coal Board, the vicar of St Martin's-in-the-Field and the Master of the Queen's Musick. Over the years, the Queen would get to meet hundreds of distinguished British citizens, and the presence of entertainers, writers and those connected to the world of horse racing meant it wasn't always a daunting list of attendees.

By tradition, wives and husbands were not added as a plus one and the invitations went to the recipient's place of work rather than their home. Initially, women were a rarity at the lunches and those who did attend were expected to arrive in a hat and wear it through lunch, even though the Queen, as host, didn't.

Guests assembled in Buckingham Palace's Bow Room at 12.30 p.m. for drinks and a cigarette before the Queen appeared twenty minutes later. The group would then walk through to the 1844 Room, where an oval table had been set up for the seven or eight guests, the Queen and Duke and two members of the household.

Rather than preside at the head of the table, the Queen would sit in the middle, opposite the Duke. During the first two courses, she would talk to the person on her right and during the dessert and cheese courses, she would turn to the person on the left. Formula One driver Lewis Hamilton had this manoeuvre explained to him by his host, as he recalled on *The Graham Norton Show* in 2015:

I got invited to a lunch and was sitting next to the Queen. I was excited and started to talk to her, but she said – pointing to my left – 'No you speak that way first, and I'll speak this way and then I'll come back to you.'

It didn't put him off her. When they did get to speak, he found, 'She is a sweet woman, and we talked about how she spends her weekends, houses and music,' Lewis said, adding, 'She is really cool.'

The Queen is well briefed about her guests. When rugby player Bill Beaumont arrived at Buckingham Palace for his lunch in 1981 'a quivering bundle of nerves', the Queen told him how much she had enjoyed her visit to the Welsh Centenary match. Beaumont said the remark put him at ease and he really enjoyed the next two hours. He was also impressed by how she involved everyone in the conversation. Talking to another guest about the question of management in industry, she asked Beaumont for his opinion, saying he must know something about management as captain of the England rugby team.

For some guests, it's not just meeting the Queen that turns them into nervous wrecks. Butler service also has its terrors. One guest who was placed on the monarch's left side recalled his heart sinking when trays of asparagus were carried in, until he realised that she would automatically be served first, so he could watch how she tackled the buttery vegetable. After she took her portion, the tray loomed into view by his side and the Queen, knowing just what was going through his mind, joked, 'Now it's my turn to see you make a pig of yourself!'

It has not always been meaningless pleasantries around a lunch table. The Queen surprised the distinguished conductor Sir John Barbirolli, asking, 'Sir John, you have been in the public eye for many years. You must have received some adverse criticism from time to time. How do you react to it?'

The musician replied that he'd long ago made up his mind 'not to even notice it. It has no effect whatever'.

The Queen, looking thoughtful, mused, 'I wonder if that can really be possible?'

This sensitive side of the Queen's character was apparent when surgeon David Nott was a lunch guest in October 2014. Nott had recently returned from front-line duties in Syria. When she asked him about his service there, it revived traumatic memories of the horrors he had experienced, and he found himself unable to reply. Speaking on Radio 4's *Desert Island Discs*, he recalled:

> I didn't know what to say. It wasn't that I didn't want to speak to her – I just couldn't. I just could not say anything.
>
> She picked all this up and said, 'Well, shall I help you?'
>
> I thought, 'How on earth can the Queen help me?'
>
> All of a sudden, the courtiers brought the corgis, and the corgis went underneath the table.

The Queen then took a dog biscuit off a silver tray she has ready for her pets and gave one to him, saying, 'OK, why don't you feed the dogs?'

> And so, for 20 minutes during this lunch the Queen and I fed the dogs. She did it because she knew that I was so seriously traumatised. You know the humanity of what she was doing was unbelievable.

The show's host, Kirsty Young, asked if the dogs had helped. Mr Nott said, 'Very much so. Stroking the animals, touching dogs, feeding them … She talked about her dogs and how many she had. She was wonderful and I will never forget it.'

The corgis have been a mixed blessing at the lunches. When they scuttle into view it is a sign the Queen is on her way, and they can be a useful talking point, helping to dissipate any tension among the guests. On the other hand, they can be a distraction. When the poet laureate Cecil Day-Lewis (father of the actor Daniel Day-Lewis) was seated at the lunch table, he put his feet on what he thought was a handily placed footstool, only to find it was a snoozing royal pet.

On another occasion, one of the corgis misbehaved and the Queen snapped, 'Heather!' in its direction, much to the alarm of the opera singer Heather Harper, who was sitting next to Prince Philip.

One of the most memorable corgi-related lunch party stories occurred when Hugh Scanlon, a trade union leader, was seated next to the Queen. Pronging a particularly well-cooked roast potato, he was horrified when it ricocheted off the plate and onto the floor. He hoped Her Majesty hadn't noticed – and she mightn't have, but a stout corgi strolled across to the projectile, sniffed it, kicked it around a bit and then abandoned it in disgust. At which point, the Queen turned to him and said, 'Not your day is it, Mr Scanlon?'

38

TV QUEEN

Five years into her reign the Queen reluctantly decided to embrace the new medium of television. While the 1953 coronation and many of her appearances had been broadcast on TV, she had yet to use it to address the nation. The criticism of the Queen and her Court by Lord Altrincham in August 1957 jolted the Palace old guard into making the monarchy more up to date and accessible. The time was ripe because the broadcasting of the coronation had done much to increase the sales of television sets and, by the end of the decade, three-quarters of the population had them.

Elizabeth would take some persuading. Ahead of her tour of Canada in 1957, during which she would make her first live TV broadcast, she wrote to Anthony Eden, 'Television is the worst of all, but I suppose when one gets used to it, it is not so terrible as at first sight'. She had followed the tradition of broadcasting her Christmas speech live on the radio from the same desk and in the same study that her father and grandfather had used. Like them, she hated the disruption to her Christmas Day festivities and a live television broadcast would, she felt, make it worse. Moreover, she maintained that the vast majority of Commonwealth nations to whom she was addressing did not have TV sets.

It was Prince Philip who was behind the idea. In May 1957, he presented the TV programme *The Duke of Edinburgh's Round the World in 40 Minutes*, a lecture on his recent Commonwealth tour. In his usual inimitable style, he joked that in Papua New Guinea he was known as 'Number One Fella Belong Missus Queen'.

The Queen's television broadcast live from the Governor General's house in Ottawa was to be a dry run for the Christmas speech. She practised beforehand in an improvised studio at Buckingham Palace, using past Christmas messages and coached by Prince Philip.

The Canadian speech was designed to make her appear less stuffy. She began by saying, 'I want to talk to you more personally' and told her audience of 14 million 'how happy I am to be in Canada again'. Afterwards, the *New York Times* wrote that Elizabeth appeared 'shy, a bit bashful and awkward' but that it made her 'so human'.

After the North American tour in October, the royal couple began preparations for the Christmas broadcast. The study was too small for the BBC's necessary equipment, including two cameras and a spare one, so the Prince suggested the Long Library, originally an American-style bowling alley in the days of the pleasure-loving Edward VII.

The Queen later recalled that electricians had to drill holes in the walls to get the cables in, which she claimed let in icy air that caused her to shiver more than her nerves did. Ironically, the theme of her speech was 'I welcome you to the peace of my own home'.

Fearing a technical breakdown on the day, the BBC decided to install duplicate links for the sound and television. This necessitated more power to run it all, so the Eastern Electricity Board had to dig up the Sandringham lawns to run a new power supply, 2–3ft deep, from the main road to the house. Then, the Post Office had to dig another ditch for the vision circuit, so altogether there were 2 miles of ditching through the royal estate. The thinking was that it would be used every Christmas henceforth. In practice, the live television broadcasts only went out for three years running. From 1960 they were pre-recorded, usually at Buckingham Palace or in Windsor Castle.

Having knocked seven bells out of her house, the producers turned their attention to the Queen. The BBC's superintendent of lighting, Harold Mayhew ('Mr Grumps', to his team, for his less than exuberant attitude) bravely told Her Majesty that the dress she had decided to wear wouldn't work that well in black and white, not so much for the colour, but because of the material. In the end, they jointly selected the gold lamé dress she wore on the day, a wise choice as its metallic gleam still shines out from the monochrome fog of a fifties recording.

Much to the Queen's amusement, make-up girls painted bright yellow spots on her forehead, cheekbones, nose and chin to tone down the skin's natural shine. They also had to darken the parting in her hair, which otherwise would have looked like a thick white line across her head.

Meanwhile, she had to pick up a book and read a few lines from John Bunyan's *The Pilgrim's Progress*, which had been printed on a sheet of paper inserted into any old book. Ever the professional, she spotted it wasn't the right one and asked for an actual copy of Bunyan to be brought from her library.

Despite three rehearsals with the BBC producer Anthony Craxton, who went through her speech word for word for fifty-five minutes, and watching an instructional film by the corporation's leading female presenter, Sylvia Peters, Elizabeth was still nervous. 'My husband seems to have found the secret of how to relax on television,' she told a guest at the pre-Christmas staff party at Windsor. 'I have not found the secret yet!'

On the day itself, she later recalled, 'The family looked absolutely horrified at Christmas luncheon and thought I was going to break down with nerves.'

To put her at ease before going on air, Philip told her to 'remember the wailing and gnashing of teeth', a reference to his chasing her along the train corridors during a trip to Canada in 1951 wearing huge false fangs, a joke he repeated at Windsor chasing the children. It was also relaxing watching 9-year-old Charles and 7-year-old Anne clambering all over the set, trying on headphones and sitting where their mother would present the broadcast.

In the end, the broadcast went without a hitch. 'We had a run-through on the day and then went straight into the live broadcast,' recalled Richard Webber, who was in charge of production. 'The Queen was extremely accomplished with the Teleprompter and read the message brilliantly.'

Although the speech seems stilted today, the words she used were less formal than in previous years, reflecting the Palace's aim to learn from the Altrincham criticism. 'I very much hope,' she said, 'that this new medium will make my Christmas message more personal and direct.'

The newspapers felt it had. 'She heeded the Critics' was the headline in the *Daily Herald*. That paper noticed 'her voice was lower and her manner less strained than at previous public appearances', countering Altrincham's criticism that the Queen's speaking voice was 'a pain in the neck' and that she gave 'prim little sermons'. Across the pond, the *New York Times* enthused, 'This was not some remote voice … It was a person speaking personally.'

Afterwards, clearly relaxed, she laughed and joked with the BBC crew before re-joining her family, who had been watching the programme with bated breath in the drawing room.

One souvenir still exists from the day, a Christmas card signed to Harold Mayhew from a grateful monarch on her television debut, 'To Mr Grumps from Elizabeth R'.

39

FOUR-LEGGED FRIENDS

At the age of 12, Princess Elizabeth confided to her riding instructor that she would one day 'like to be a lady living in the country with lots of horses and dogs'. The Queen would remain a countrywoman at heart throughout her long life. Her main passions are outdoor pursuits: riding, walking her corgis, horse racing and working her gun dogs.

The Queen is also an expert on horse breeding, having a detailed knowledge of pedigrees and bloodlines. In over half a century of flat racing, she has won four out of the five English classics – the only one to elude her is the Derby and it remains an unfulfilled ambition to win this legendary race.

This abiding passion for horses began at an early age. Her grandfather, King George V, used to take her around the stud at Sandringham, and in 1931, when she was just 5 years old, he bought her a Shetland pony called 'Peggy'. As a child, she would

The Queen has had a lifelong love of horses and dogs. Here she pats one of her Highland ponies at the 2007 Royal Windsor Horse Show.
(© Ian Lloyd)

ride ponies over the moors at Balmoral and later on, during the war years at Windsor Castle, she learned the basics of stable management and horse care.

In 1938, the royal riding instructor, Horace Smith, was asked to improve her skills and taught her to ride side-saddle, something she would need later on when she came to review troops. He also gave her basic lessons in carriage driving, and in 1943 and 1944 she won first prize at the Royal Windsor Horse Show for driving a cart pulled by one of her own black fell ponies.

In 1946, at the age of 20, she shared the ownership of a steeplechaser called 'Monaveen' with her mother, Queen Elizabeth. The following year, she was given a filly called 'Astrakhan' as a wedding present from the Aga Khan.

Following the death of her father in 1952, the Queen inherited the royal studs, and the next few years were to be a particularly glorious period for the young royal owner. In 1953, 'Aureole' was the favourite to win that year's Derby. The race was the day after the coronation and proved a useful distraction during the build-up to the ceremony. To her disappointment the horse finished second, beaten by 'Pinza'. The following year, however, he went on to win the King George VI and Queen Elizabeth stakes at Ascot as well as the Coronation Cup and the Hardwicke Stakes. Later in the 1950s, the filly 'Almeria' gave the Queen several notable wins and in 1958, 'Pall Mall' won the classic 2,000 Guineas.

The 1970s proved to be the next golden period for the Queen's horses. In 1974, she flew to Chantilly to see 'Highclere' win the prestigious Prix de Diane. Her racing manager, Lord Carnarvon, later recalled the excitement of the French crowd, 'They went bananas, shouting, "*Vive la reine!*" when Highclere won.' Three years later, and the Queen's Silver Jubilee celebrations were capped when 'Dunfermline', another talented filly, won the Oaks and then the St Leger.

One of her most notable wins of recent years was in 2013 when 'Estimate' won the Gold Cup at Royal Ascot. Her grandson, Peter Phillips, told Channel 4, 'It's amazing, this is her passion and her life … To win the big one at Royal Ascot means so much to her. Everyone is just thrilled, it's very close to her heart and today is very special.'

For many years the Queen regularly featured in the Top 20 list of owners, but in 1991 she decided to cut her string of racehorses by a third. This 'rationalisation' was aimed at improving the quality of the bloodstock and thereby ensuring that it paid for itself. The number of horses in training has since increased.

The Queen's bloodstock and racing advisor is John Warren, who is married to Lord Carnarvon's daughter, Carolyn. The royal studs continue to be run from Sandringham and

Wolferton in Norfolk. The stallions, mares and foals are based here, while the weanlings and yearlings are kept at the Polhampton Lodge Stud in Berkshire, which was acquired by the Queen in 1962.

The royal studs are run on a strictly commercial basis and are paid for entirely from the Queen's private funds. At present, the Queen has about thirty horses in training and her trainers include Sir Michael Stoute and John Gosden, both at Newmarket, and Roger Charlton and Richard Hannon, who are both based near Marlborough. A couple more horses are trained by Andrew Balding, brother of the racing commentator Clare Balding.

The Queen's duties often prevent her from seeing her horses in training or racing, so she keeps in day-to-day contact with John Warren as well as the trainers, and video recordings are made of the races she cannot attend.

Horses may mean the world to the Queen, but it is other four-legged animals that are most associated with her in the public's imagination – the corgis. Over the years, no cartoon of the Queen was complete without the addition of a battalion of the sturdy creatures wearing human expressions of bafflement or fear.

The Queen was just 7 years old when, in 1933, her parents were given a Pembrokeshire Corgi called 'Dookie'. He was mated with 'Jane' and the royal corgi line was established. The first one owned exclusively by Princess Elizabeth was 'Susan', who accompanied her owner on her honeymoon in 1947 and whose grave at Sandringham is marked with a small headstone.

As with her horses, the Queen meticulously planned the dogs' breeding programme. However, something seems to have gone awry in the 1960s when one of them mutinied and mated with Princess Margaret's dachshund to produce 'Mr Pipkin' – the first of the royal 'dorgis'.

In 2015 it was reported that the Queen was going to abandon her corgi breeding to allow the dynasty to die out before her death. Her final corgi, 'Willow', died in April 2018, leaving just two dorgis behind. Then in March 2021, with Prince Philip lying seriously ill in hospital, Prince Andrew bought his mother two corgi pups as a useful distraction. She named them 'Muick' and 'Fergus', after the loch on her Balmoral estate and her great uncle, Fergus Bowes-Lyon, who was killed at the Battle of Loos in 1914. Sadly, this namesake died in May and Andrew and his daughters replaced him with another 6-week-old male corgi. Poignantly, they gave the Queen this latest addition on 10 June, which would have been Prince Philip's 100th birthday.

The Queen has always been a hands-on owner, feeding the dogs herself at 4.30 p.m. each afternoon, mixing cooked meat, gravy and dog biscuits before finally having her own tea. This ritual has remained the same throughout her reign, as has the daily walk around the gardens of the royal estates.

The Queen was used to dealing with the occasional fracas between the dogs. Her mother's racing advisor, Sir Michael Oswald, recalled, 'Once there was the most fearful dog fight. And she was far braver than anybody else. She plunged into the middle of this terrible melee and fished out the ringleaders.' If she ever gets bitten, her reaction is a typically stoic, 'It was all my fault'.

The dog fights can be very serious. On one occasion, a bite on the Queen's hand necessitated stitches. A few years ago, the Queen Mother's corgi, 'Ranger', killed one of the Queen's corgis, 'Chipper', and more recently, the family festivities on Christmas Eve 2003 were spoiled when the Princess Royal's English bull terrier mauled 'Pharos', a favourite corgi, which had to be put down as a result.

Apart from her corgis and dorgis, the Queen breeds working Labradors at her kennels on the Sandringham Estate. She became adept at the whistle commands used during shoots to help the dogs locate where the birds have fallen.

Bill Meldrum, the former head keeper at Sandringham, recalled a shoot in the 1970s when she asked him to direct his dog to retrieve a bird. He said that he wouldn't be able to with the dog he had and suggested the Queen might have better luck with her own dog, 'Sherry'. Using whistled commands, the Queen guided 'Sherry' over several hundred yards to the exact spot where the bird lay. The other beaters and the guns stopped to watch her progress and when the dog returned carrying the bird, some forty people applauded the Queen's efforts. 'If I'd known they were watching, I wouldn't have attempted it,' she said later.

That anecdote illustrates why the Queen derives such fulfilment from her relationship with animals. Her Labradors don't perform well because she is the Queen. Her horses don't win the St Leger out of respect and her corgis don't scamper alongside her because she is head of state. They love and respond to her because of who she is, rather than what she is. They allow her to relax in a completely different environment to her working life. More importantly, they are never obsequious or judgemental, and happily none have sold their story to the tabloids – to date.

40

'IT GIVES ME GREAT PLEASURE TO DECLARE OPEN ...'

Owen Falls Dam, 29 April 1954

The Queen pressed a small electric switch which opened the sluice gates, letting the waters of Lake Victoria thunder through in a 100ft-long cascade into the Nile below. Afterwards, she pressed another switch which started one of the hydroelectric generators.

Calder Hall Nuclear Power Station, 7 October 1956

The Queen opened the world's first full-scale nuclear power station at Calder Hall in Cumberland, in 1956. At 12.16 p.m. she pulled the lever which started the process of providing power for the National Grid. The town of Workington, 15 miles (24km) away, became the first town in the world to receive light and heat powered by nuclear energy.

St Lawrence Seaway, 26 June 1959

The Queen and US President Dwight D. Eisenhower opened the 2,300-mile system of locks and canals which links the Atlantic Ocean with the Great Lakes. They were aboard the Royal Yacht *Britannia* and this time it was the bow of the ship that did the opening as it passed the symbolic wooden gates from the obsolete lock of the Lachine Canal.

The Victoria Line, 7 March 1969

The Queen became the first British monarch to use the Underground when she opened the completed Walthamstow to Victoria section's latest development. At 11.00 a.m. she made the one-stop journey from Green Park to Victoria at a cost of 5*d*, returning to Buckingham Palace by Rolls-Royce Phantom IV.

Sydney Opera House, 20 October 1973

It took 10,000 workers fourteen years to build the 185m-long, 235m-tall landmark. 'The Sydney Opera House has captured the imagination of the world, though I understand that its construction has not been totally without problems,' Queen Elizabeth II observed when she opened it, adding, 'The human spirit must sometimes take wings or sails, and create something that is not just utilitarian or commonplace.'

The Barbican Centre, 3 March 1982

Work began in 1971 after seventeen years in the planning and it cost £153 million to build the arts and conference centre, which the Queen said, 'must have some claim as one of the wonders of the modern world'.

The Queen Elizabeth II Conference Centre, 24 June 1986

The QEII Centre, along with Westminster Abbey and the Palace of Westminster, is built on what used to be Thorney Island, formed by rivulets of the River Tyburn which were eventually built over. The centre was designed by Powell, Moya & Partners and can host conferences for up to 2,500 people.

The Channel Tunnel, 6 May 1994

The Queen and the French President François Mitterrand formally declared the £10 billion tunnel open with ceremonies in both France and Britain. The Queen took the high-speed Eurostar train from London's Waterloo, through the tunnel to Calais, where she and Mitterrand cut red, white and blue ribbons. After lunch, the two heads of state took the Queen's Rolls-Royce on Le Shuttle for the thirty-five-minute trip to Folkestone, where a similar ceremony took place.

The Queen Elizabeth II Garden, New York, 6 July 2010

The Queen visited the Ground Zero site to pay tribute to the sixty-seven Britons who were among the 2,750 people killed on 11 September 2001 at the World Trade Center. After laying a wreath, she cut a ribbon, officially opening the British Garden. Two years later, in her Diamond Jubilee year, it was renamed after her.

The Queensferry Crossing, 4 September 2017

Accompanied by Prince Philip, the Queen opened the £1.35 billion road bridge, exactly fifty-three years after she opened the Forth Road Bridge. The Queen said the UK's tallest bridge was a 'breathtaking sight' and one of three 'magnificent structures' across the Forth.

During her reign, the Queen has also opened the Severn Bridge in 1966, carrying the M4 between England and Wales; the Queen Elizabeth II Bridge in Belfast, also in 1966; the Queen Elizabeth II Bridge at Dartford in 1991 and the Flintshire Bridge, over the Dee Estuary, in North Wales, in 1998.

41

PICKING A WINNER: TWO CONTROVERSIAL ELECTIONS

The Queen has to Choose a Leader – Twice

The Queen has tried to remain above politics for all of her seven-decade rule. The resignation of two Conservative prime ministers within six years of each other forced her to use the Royal Prerogative on two occasions to appoint their successors. In each case, the new prime minister wasn't the obvious choice, and it was felt the Palace, and ultimately the Queen, had stayed within the old Etonian 'magical circle'.

The problem was the method used by the Conservative Party for electing a new leader. Unlike the Labour and Liberal Parties, where all their MPs took part in a ballot, the Tories favoured a consultation process in which one or more senior party figures took soundings from Cabinet colleagues, former ministers and the leader of the backbenchers.

When Winston Churchill resigned in 1955, there was really only one choice for the Queen in Anthony Eden, the great man's deputy for the past fifteen years. Two years later, the collapse of Eden's health following his unsuccessful handling of the Suez Crisis necessitated a leadership appointment. This time, there was a choice of two men: Harold Macmillan, Chancellor of the Exchequer, and R.A. 'Rab' Butler, Leader of the House of Commons and, to many, the heir apparent. Butler had deputised for Eden during his recent illness and the outgoing PM told the Queen he would be his choice to succeed him.

Eden suggested that two Tory grandees, the Marquess of Salisbury and Viscount Kilmuir, should ballot senior party members. Kilmuir was Lord Chancellor and is today remembered as Sir David Maxwell Fyffe, who, as Home Secretary, upheld the controversial decision to hang Derek Bentley for the murder of a policeman in 1952. Robert 'Bobbety' Gascoyne-Cecil, 5th Marquess of Salisbury, was a close friend of Elizabeth's parents and regularly attended house parties on the royal estates. As the Queen's biographer, Sally Bedell Smith commented that the monarch 'seemed to have ceded her judgement to a pair of hidebound aristocrats whose soundings were too narrow'.

The two men interviewed the Cabinet colleagues and other senior figures, past and present. Thanks to his speech impediment, Salisbury memorably asked each person if they were for 'Wab or Hawold'. Their deliberations concluded overwhelmingly in favour of Macmillan.

Meanwhile, the Queen also summoned Sir Winston Churchill to Buckingham Palace. As he was leaving, he was heard to mutter to one of the household, 'I said Macmillan. Is that right?', which shows what an unreliable system the Queen had to deal with.

Kilmuir and Salisbury fed back to the Queen that 'an overwhelming majority' of those they had balloted had supported Macmillan, so it was he the Queen sent for to form a government.

It had been a tricky situation for the Queen. In theory, she could have demanded the Tories had balloted a wider number of party members or even had a stop-gap premier, given that the appointment was between elections. This was never likely to happen under Elizabeth II, as the journalist Malcolm Muggeridge pointed out, 'Nothing in her temperament would have induced her to exercise her own judgement'. Although it was her right to have suggested one of the above options, to have done so would have led to criticism from those who opposed the decision she made. The attitude of the Queen's advisors was very much to throw it back to the Conservatives to choose a leader and only then would she act, when she was sure they had decided themselves.

In the autumn of 1963, a similar situation arose. The prime minister, Harold Macmillan, was taken ill with severe prostate trouble. He had already informed the Queen that he would likely resign in the new year, but the rapid decline in his health made the situation more urgent.

This time, there were six names mentioned as possible successors including, once again, 'Rab' Butler. The others were Lord Hailsham (Lord President of the Council), Reginald Maudling (Chancellor of the Exchequer), Iain Macleod (Leader of the House), Edward Heath (Lord Privy Seal) and the Foreign Secretary, Lord Home.

Before resigning, and from his sick bed in the King Edward VII Hospital for Officers, Macmillan interviewed the likely candidates. He also took a poll of the other Cabinet members and found that the majority backed Home.

The Queen visited Macmillan in hospital to accept his resignation on 18 October 1963. To create some sort of formality, Macmillan wore a brown sweater over a white silk shirt and was wheeled in his bed to the boardroom for the ceremony to take place. According to the physician, Sir John Richardson, 'There were in fact tears in her eyes' as she accepted his resignation. She then asked for his advice, and he passed on to her his findings. Rather than invite Home to form a government, she first of all summoned him to Buckingham Palace and asked him if he could form one. He returned the following day and kissed hands as Elizabeth's fourth prime minister.

Home's appointment was widely criticised by the press and some of the rank-and-file Tories. It was felt that the Queen had relied too much on Macmillan's advice, although this is what the Palace had wanted to occur to keep the Queen out of politics as much as possible. Elizabeth's biographer, Ben Pimlott, described it later as the 'biggest political misjudgement of her reign'.

The widespread criticism of the Tory Party selection procedure and the Queen's involvement in it forced the party to change the way it elected a leader. New plans were published in February 1965, bringing the Conservative Party in line with the Labour and Liberal Parties and ensuring Elizabeth was never dragged into choosing a prime minister in such a controversial way again.

42

THE HUMAN SIDE

Former Foreign Secretary Douglas Hurd once commented that the Queen 'has trained the feelings out of herself'. Like her parents and grandparents, she personified the stiff upper lip approach to royal duty, and throughout her long life she has become adept at hiding her real feelings in public.

Occasionally the mask has slipped, most memorably at the decommissioning of the Royal Yacht *Britannia*, when she was photographed with tears in her eyes. It was the only home that she and Philip had created themselves and, as one relative put it, 'it represented freedom to her'.

The sudden and catastrophic loss of life from disasters such as Aberfan or the Dunblane school shooting, both involving the deaths of multiple children, affected her greatly. She is said to have regretted waiting eight days before visiting Aberfan. Her delay was, in part, so as not to hamper rescue work in the immediate aftermath of the mountain of slurry burying the Pantglas Junior School, killing 116 children and 28 adults. She visited Dunblane four days after the shooting dead of sixteen pupils and one teacher. Poignantly, the royal mother visited on Mother's Day and, after laying flowers in tribute, was seen to wipe away a tear.

She was similarly moved during the service at St Paul's Cathedral commemorating the 9/11 atrocities in the United States. She had her own personal grief that week, because her closest male friend and racing manager, the Earl of Carnarvon, known as 'Porchy' to his friends, had collapsed and died of a heart attack on the same day as the Al-Qaeda attacks.

She has sometimes found gatherings of her own generation very moving, particularly when reflecting on the passage of time. She was affected by the D-Day anniversary gathering in France in 2014. In one of her most personal speeches, she declared the day had left her filled 'with sorrow and regret, remembering the loss of so many fine young soldiers, sailors and airmen; with pride, at the sheer courage of the men who stormed those beaches, embodied in the veterans among us; and with thankfulness'. Noting 'the joy of becoming a great-grandmother', the 88-year-old Queen added the poignant words, 'Everything we do, we do for the young'.

At another wartime commemoration, at the Field of Remembrance, outside Westminster Abbey, the Queen was moved to tears by the occasion when veterans always gather to honour their fallen comrades with the planting of wooden crosses. Her tears no doubt welled up because, the year before, it had been her mother officiating at this event, as she had done each November for as long as many could remember.

While the Queen always personified the stiff-upper-lip attitude of the wartime generation, she has on occasions been unable to hide her emotions in public. Here she is clearly moved during the Remembrance Sunday commemorations. (© Ian Lloyd)

One of the most difficult aspects of royal life is that personal sorrow, especially at family funerals, quite often comes under the scrutiny of blanket press coverage. The Queen, trained to hide her sorrow, always remains composed, no matter how much her heart must be breaking. Away from the cameras, it is a different matter. She was moved to tears as the Duchess of Windsor's body was interred with the Duke's in the royal burial ground at Frogmore.

Seven years earlier, she had led the nation's remembrance at the funeral of Earl Mountbatten of Burma, 'Uncle Dickie' to Elizabeth and Philip, following his assassination by the IRA, which also killed three others, including his grandson, Nicholas.

The family mourners took the royal train to Hampshire for a private ceremony at Romsey Abbey. En route, the Queen asked Mountbatten's younger daughter, Lady Pamela Hicks, to join her and to talk about the attack. Later, as they arrived at Broadlands, the Mountbatten official residence, the Queen emerged from her car, very red-eyed. The earl's granddaughter, Joanna Knatchbull, asked, 'Ma'am would you like to go upstairs?' and the Queen replied, 'Yes I think I would.'

When Mountbatten's grandson, Tim Knatchbull, who was badly injured in the IRA explosion, married Isabella Norman at Winchester Cathedral in 1998, the Queen attended with Princess Margaret and Prince Charles. Later, at the reception, Tim spoke movingly about the loss of his twin brother, Nicky, in the IRA attack, and the Queen was seen to have tears in her eyes. Sometimes, it must be a relief not to have to adopt the impenetrable face of composure.

43

ONE'S HAND-ONE-DOWNS

The North Wing of Buckingham Palace houses a treasure trove of queenly couture. A whole floor above the monarch's private suite is given over to carefully storing designer outfits dating from the late 1940s to the present day. Disposing of them, should the need arise, follows a traditional route. Some are donated to charity, but the majority go to trusted outlets – members of the royal household and occasionally to family members. Surprisingly, for a period in the mid-1990s Princess Margaret went through her sister's wardrobe and helped herself to a number of items she thought were too good to go to waste.

Royal author Brian Hoey revealed that the team of dressers working for the Queen's PA, Angela Kelly, have first dibs. 'When she finally tires of [an item of clothing], she will hand it to one of her dressers, who can either wear it or sell it.' There is one proviso, that any labels or anything that might suggest it belongs to the Queen must be removed first. Some of the 'routine' day-to-day items, skirts, blouses and the like, can end up in the donation box. 'One frock found its way to a jumble sale near Sandringham', says Hoey, 'but in spite of its obvious quality, it failed to sell.'

The distribution of clothes to household members is nothing new. Following the death of Queen Victoria in January 1901, much of her underwear was distributed to maids and dressers as keepsakes. From time to time, a pair or two of the Queen-Empress's voluminous 50in plus knickers are star attractions at auction houses. Presumably, she wouldn't have been amused to see occasional publicity shots of two sales staff, side by side, each standing in a leg of her drawers.

Queen Mary discreetly passed on items of clothing to her ladies-in-waiting and other friends. Her mother, Princess Mary Adelaide of Teck, lived at White Lodge in Richmond Park and her close friend was the grandmother of Anthony Blunt, the Soviet spy who was also Surveyor of the Queen's Pictures. Many of Mary's clothes were given to Blunt's Aunt Mabel. His brother, the art teacher and curator Wilfrid Blunt, recalled, 'This was a dead secret and we were never to divulge it.' The dresses were modified or remade, and hats were tweaked with the addition or subtraction of flowers and feathers. Only the royal parasols escaped a makeover. In the end, Mabel became tired of the deception and couldn't be bothered to disguise the clothes. As she had a similar gait, shape and posture to the

Queen, Blunt claims, 'she was often greeted by passers-by with a bow or a curtsey'.

The Queen would have become familiar with the whole hand-me-down process during the war. When Prince Philip's cousin, Princess Alexandra of Greece, met King George and Queen Elizabeth at Windsor prior to her marriage to the King's godson, Peter II of Yugoslavia, the Queen told her that she was having several of her frocks cut down and altered to fit Lilibet. 'Margaret gets all Lilibet's clothes, then,' explained Queen Elizabeth, 'so with the three of us we manage in relays.'

The Queen's childhood friend, Alathea Fitzalan Howard, noted in her diary that Queen Elizabeth had her old Hartnell gowns altered for Princess Elizabeth's first grown-up dances.

In a rare interview in 2016, the Queen's cousin, Princess Alexandra, also recalled these wartime years and their immediate aftermath. 'Because of the clothing coupons, it was quite difficult to get hold of clothes. So they were very kind to me, my cousins – I think it was Princess Elizabeth mainly – they let me have one or two of their dresses.'

Other items went to household staff. When Elizabeth was married and living at Clarence House she gave three gowns to Kathleen Ward, a telephonist on the Buckingham Palace switchboard. Both Elizabeth and Margaret passed items on to their Bowes-Lyon cousins. One of them, Jean Wills, was asked by Margaret to sort them out and either pass them on or burn them. In the 1980s Margaret gave some day dresses from Dior London to her favourite maid, Italian-born Maria Roattino.

Having been the recipient of Elizabeth's hand-me-downs during her childhood, Princess Margaret revived the practice in her mid-60s. She asked Elizabeth if she could look through her collection and selected half a dozen outfits that she liked the look of. She had them altered to fit and then teamed them with completely different hats to the ones the Queen had worn with them, so only a handful of royal watchers would have worked out the link.

It began in June 1994 when Margaret wore a pale-yellow coat when she visited Arromanches in France to mark the 50th anniversary of the D-Day Landings on the Normandy beaches. The outfit was first worn by the Queen at Royal Ascot in 1980.

In 1995, Margaret donned an even older outfit, an orange wool coat, for that year's Trooping the Colour. It was made for her sister in 1977 and worn by the Queen when she addressed both Houses of Parliament during the Silver Jubilee commemorations.

Two other notable sister swaps were also worn during the summer of 1995. Margaret was interviewed about her memories of the war for a BBC programme to mark the 50th anniversary of VE Day. She wore a blue chiffon dress, which she also wore that July at a Holland Park Open Air Theatre performance. It was made for the Queen in 1981 for the christening of Zara Phillips at Windsor, two days before the wedding of Charles and Diana.

Finally in May 1995, Margaret wore an emerald-green Ian Thomas-designed coat when she joined her mother and sister on the balcony of Buckingham Palace to watch a concert in the forecourt as part of the VE Day commemorations. This was originally worn by her sister during her Silver Jubilee visit to Belfast in August 1977.

In the mid 1990s Princess Margaret wore several items from her sister's wardrobe, including these. Left: the blue chiffon gown the Queen wore for Zara Phillips' christening in 1981. Right: the orange wool coat she wore when addressing Parliament in 1977.
(© S.P. Mailer)

Margaret isn't the only close relation to wear the monarch's clothes. In 2020, Princess Beatrice became the first ever royal bride to opt for a second-hand dress to wear at her wedding. The Queen gave her one of her own vintage ivory taffeta gowns, trimmed with ivory duchess satin and encrusted with diamanté details. It was made by Norman Hartnell and was worn by Elizabeth at the 1962 film premiere of *Lawrence of Arabia* and five years later for the State Opening of Parliament. After her wedding, Beatrice tweeted, 'It was an honour to wear my grandmother's beautiful dress on my wedding day.'

The youngest generation of royals have also been spotted in hand-me-downs. In September 2020, Prince Louis wore a blue merino wool top when he met Sir David Attenborough. This was worn by his older brother, Prince George, during the 2016 royal visit to Canada. On that same tour, their sister, Princess Charlotte, was seen wearing a blue Amaia cardigan, which George had worn when he was taken to see his newborn sister at St Mary's Paddington on the day of her birth.

George has also been photographed at Trooping the Colour wearing shorts worn by his father in 1984. Charlotte even wore Prince Harry's 'Mary Jane' shoes, while Louis wore blue shorts at the 2019 Trooping that were made for Uncle Harry in 1986.

One royal lady who doesn't hand-them-down is the Princess Royal, who, amazingly, can still wear clothes she had designed in the 1980s. She once pointed out, 'A good suit goes on for ever. If it is properly made and has a classic look you can go on wearing it *ad infinitum*.' It's obviously the good quality of royal couture that enables coats, day dresses and gowns (though presumably not Victoria's knickers) to be worn time and again, even if it is by friends or other members of the family.

44

THE ADMIRABLE PERKINS

While many of her contemporary heads of state were pro- tected by a ring of steel, for the first twenty years of her reign Elizabeth II was guarded by one officer: Albert Perkins.

Commander Perkins joined the Metropolitan Police Force in 1927, began protecting the future Queen Mother in 1942, and worked his way through the ranks until he ended up in charge of the Queen's security. Loyal, trustworthy and discreet, he was known as 'uncle' to the young Charles and Anne, and was the only one of Elizabeth's security men to be knighted.

Born in 1908 and named Albert Edward after the incumbent king, Perkins was the son of a Warwickshire painter. He joined the Met after leaving Alcester Grammar School and five years later married the Hardyesque-named Mercy Frew.

Perkins became the Queen's personal bodyguard in February 1955, replacing Superintendent Tom Clark. His urbane, unruffled and rather dour character fitted in perfectly with the rigidly formal royal household of the early years of the Queen's reign. If anyone had the temerity to call him 'Perkins', he would take them on one side and inform them that it was 'Mr Perkins'. He once said, 'I don't like reading about myself. I have a tremendously responsible job that I don't talk about and never will' – and he never did.

Then, as now, protection officers were expected to dress the part, whether it was attending a gala at the Royal Opera House or tramping through wet heather at Balmoral. Perkins' usual day wear was a white shirt with a hard collar and a grey tie, and a suit specially designed to cope with carrying a radio transmitter and an Italian Beretta semi-automatic gun. His preferred headwear was a bowler hat for day duty, apart from a top hat for Royal Ascot and a soft trilby for polo.

Perkins was by the Queen's side on all her overseas tours from the mid-1950s until the early 1970s. Each one was a challenge, since the Queen and Duke were global superstars and Prince Philip once said the adulation 'in the early days of the reign was unbelievable'.

Once, in Malaysia, an Indian man burst through the crowd and lunged at the Queen. Perkins and the Duke grabbed him but realised at the last minute that it was a Second World War veteran, wearing his medals, who was trying to garland the monarch with jasmine. Philip apologised and patted him on the back.

The Queen was mobbed time and again. In Chile, crowds broke through the barriers and children were trampled on. In Australia, it was children that mobbed the couple at a playground the royal couple were visiting, and Philip had to help one girl who caught her curls in the buttons of Perkins' jacket. In Venice, in 1961, they were jostled by a crowd of 10,000 in St Mark's Square and the Duke complained that 'everyone seems to want to get in on the act'.

Perkins himself was the victim in Fiji in 1970, when another surge of people went through the police cordon and knocked the protection officer onto his knees.

Nor was it that much easier guarding the Queen in the UK. The crowds were less ecstatic but there were still many awkward incidents. Perkins announced that he would have to review security following a royal visit to Stirling University where drunk students barracked the Queen, shouting obscene remarks and surging round her waving their fists. There was a potentially more serious threat in Belfast in 1966 when Perkins saw a woman about to throw a bottle at the Queen and he helped arrest her. It was on this same visit that a concrete block was thrown at the royal car from a six-storey building, denting the bonnet. The Queen was unfazed by the incident and said, 'At least it's a solid car.'

On a lighter note, he was unimpressed by the film crew following the Queen's appearances for a year for the documentary *Royal Family*. When he once thought they were too close with their boom mike, he performed a karate chop on it. The team ironically dubbed him 'the fastest gun in the west', due to his less-than-lightning reactions.

It wasn't just the Queen he had to come to the aid of. Once, during a service attended by Her Majesty in Binfield Parish Church, an 80-year-old lady seated behind the monarch fainted and Perkins had to carry her out.

It was on the way back from another church service, for the baptism of the Duke and Duchess of Kent's daughter, Lady Helen Windsor, that Perkins was involved in one of Prince Philip's many car accidents. The officer was a passenger, along with the Queen, when the Duke's Rover collided with a Ford Popular driven by learner driver William Henry Cooper. The accident occurred outside the Rising Sun pub near Maidenhead. The Queen was said to 'be pale and shaken by the incident'.

As head of security at Buckingham Palace, he had to investigate a now-famous incident when an underage Prince Charles made front-page news by ordering a cherry brandy in a pub on the Isle of Lewis.

A few years earlier, he also had to try to find out who planted a recording device in the Queen's car at the height of Princess Margaret's romance with Peter Townsend.

Princess Anne once said the royal family had more to fear from unbalanced members of the public than terrorists. Perkins had his fair share of eccentric, but usually harmless, people to investigate. For instance, there was a woman from Lancashire who threw three eggs at the Queen in Glasgow in 1966, believing that she had to end the monarchy as the Queen was very jealous of her.

One night Perkins had to come to the gates of Buckingham Palace to calm a man who explained, 'I've just thrown myself off a bridge in the park for the love of my Queen and now I have come to tell her all about it.'

Of more concern was the phone call he received from a woman who rang Buckingham Palace to say her husband was suffering from a breakdown and had left home to say he was going to join Prince Philip, Prince Charles and Princess Margaret's husband, Lord Snowdon, at a shooting party in Sandringham. Perkins was about to say something along the lines of 'Oh I shouldn't worry about it' when she added '… and he's taken his shotgun with him'. The officer quickly got a network of local police and troops to circle the estate where they found the uninvited marksman.

It wasn't just members of the public who he had to keep a watchful eye on. When he discovered one of his protection team spent his spare time at Communist Party HQ, he was rapidly transferred back to Scotland Yard. Another young detective only lasted a week after he rode his motorbike over the Buckingham Palace lawns and head gardener William 'Nutty' Nutbeam complained to the Queen.

It's hardly surprising one or two dodgy coppers were brought on board, since Perkins seems to have been rather blasé about recruitment. Michael Varney, who became the Prince of Wales's protection officer, was just a Norfolk PC, although one with an ambition. He was told the best way to meet Perkins off duty was to drink in his local pub, The Feathers at Dersingham, near Sandringham. Perkins told him to contact him again in London and, to cut a long story short, Varney claims he was appointed without an interview, an MI5 check, special training or small arms practice.

When it was decided Varney should accompany the Prince to Gordonstoun School, he needed to pass his driving test first. This, he recalled, took place at Balmoral and was 'casual almost beyond belief', with Varney driving a Land Rover with Chief Superintendent Perkins in the back, along with the Queen's head chauffeur, Harry Purvey. His route was the 16-mile loop along the South Deeside Road, through Ballater and back to the castle along the North Deeside Road. Varney recalls never coming out of top gear with 'no traffic, no junctions, not a single wobbly cyclist or even a stray lamb'.

Unsurprisingly, as the risks of bombings, hijacks and kidnappings increased there were calls in the press for Perkins to retire. He was, by 1970, in his early sixties, when the normal retiring age for protection officers was 55. He eventually retired in 1973 and was succeeded by Prince Philip's protection officer, Michael Trestrail.

Perkins retired to a house in Windsor, where he died in May 1977, a year after his wife. He enjoyed the distinction of being one of the most decorated royal protection officers, with honours given to him by Ethiopia, Brazil, France, Yugoslavia and Thailand during royal tours. More significantly, he was knighted by the Queen in 1973 for thirty years of loyal, royal service.

45

MONARCH OF THE GLEN

'I suppose Balmoral is a place one looks forward to very much as the summer goes on,' reflected the Queen in the 1990s. 'You just hibernate; but it's rather nice to hibernate for a bit when one lives such a very movable life.'

Her granddaughter, Princess Eugenie, says, 'It's the most beautiful place on earth. Granny is most happy there.'

Prince Edward's wife, Sophie, thinks, 'It is a magical place. There is a sense of freedom for her.' Elizabeth II herself adds prosaically, 'To be able to sleep in the same bed for six weeks is a nice change.'

For over forty years, her holiday began with a cruise of the Western Isles on the Royal Yacht *Britannia*, which would drop anchor off remote, secluded beaches, where the Queen and her family would picnic.

In recent years, if HM wanted to cruise around the isles, she had to hire the *Hebridean Princess*, a converted car ferry, whose unglamorous shell houses a luxury suite of rooms ideal for the Queen and her family. As a treat to mark her 80th birthday in 2006, they moored by the island of Gigha off the west coast of Kintyre. The Queen wanted to see the famous Achamore Gardens and so Princess Anne cycled to the newsagents run by Russell Town to see if there was a way her mother could be transported around. Mr Town offered to drive them around in his Peugeot people carrier.

Thinking he'd better not speak, he kept mum, until Ma'am herself started up. 'She was a real chatterbox and started asking me lots of questions about my family and about local sights,' said the newsagent. 'When I saw my daughter at the side of the road and pointed her out, the Queen waved at her.'

Latterly, she has flown directly to Aberdeen and based herself at Craigowan Lodge on the Balmoral Estate, where she stays in late July for a couple of weeks while the castle is still open to the public.

On 6 August 2021, she left the lodge and drove round to the main entrance of the castle on the South Deeside Road, where, as usual, she inspected a guard of honour from Balaclava Company, 5th Battalion, the Royal Regiment of Scotland, who remain on ceremonial duty throughout her stay. The Queen takes a motherly interest in the soldiers and inspects the packed lunches they are provided with, visiting the kitchens and sampling the sandwiches to make sure they are up to standard.

The royal routine has remained the same over the past sixty-six years. Immediately she arrives, the Queen changes into a tartan skirt, stout walking shoes with socks, a buttoned-up cardigan and a looser cardie on top. It's the royal equivalent of a relaxing onesie – with pearls.

Mornings are taken over with work on her red government boxes. 'Luckily I'm a quick reader,' she explained in 1991, 'so I can get through a lot of reading in quite a short time, though I do rather begrudge some of the hours that I have to do instead of being outdoors.'

'Outdoors' is given over to daily horse rides, accompanied by a groom, or walking the corgis. In her youth, she enjoyed other country pursuits. 'I taught the Queen to stalk,' Margaret Rhodes once told me. Dressed in mackintosh trousers, they would head to a high ridge where they could look down at the landscape in search of red deer, carrying a canvas bag containing a lunch of cold meat and fruit. 'It was always fun to see a new stalker,' laughed Mrs Rhodes, 'as they suddenly realise just who that person crawling on her stomach with her nose inches from their boots is.'

Her Majesty shot her last stag in 1983 near to the Spittal of Glenmuick, in a spot that is now called the Queen's Corry. Today, hill ponies still bring the deer carcases to a larder for skinning, a place the Queen still visits daily, as those who watched Helen Mirren's performance as Her Majesty in the 2006 movie *The Queen* will recall.

The royal family enjoy picnics and candlelit suppers in log cabins alongside the River Dee. This is very much the Queen's domain. She lays the table and afterwards tidies up, washes the plates and throws the rubbish into plastic sacks. One courtier says it is unnerving sitting there while the Queen does all the work. 'During the meal, she comes behind you and picks up your plate ready for the next course.' On one occasion, he recalled, someone had knotted a black bin liner before everything had been thrown in it. 'Who's done this?' said the Queen irritably, as she untied it. Then as she brushed the floor, a friend made her laugh by saying, 'You could put up a notice: "Queen Elizabeth swept here!".'

The Queen takes her duties as the local laird very seriously. Prince Andrew said, 'She's a part of the community to the people of Ballater, Braemar and Balmoral.' She pops into the local shops, and in the 1969 documentary *Royal Family*, she was filmed buying 4-year-old Edward an ice cream at the local shop. Never carrying money herself, she was obliged to borrow half a crown from one of the film crew (that's around 25p to the under fifties, not something she wore).

Every Sunday, she worships at nearby Crathie Kirk. She also makes an annual appearance at the Braemar Games on the first Saturday in September. Grandson Peter Phillips said, 'It's a sort of world athletics championships of a bygone age. They try and fit an awful lot into a very short space of time and that can lead to some very amusing moments for those watching.'

Each September, the prime minister of the day stays at Balmoral for a weekend. Some, such as Harold Wilson, adored the unpretentiousness of a picnic in a bothy with his wife Mary and the Queen washing up, side by side. Margaret Thatcher, who never changed out of her high heels during her stay, didn't take to country life.

One of the Queen's former prime ministers, Sir Alec Douglas-Home, called the Balmoral stay 'the big rest'. Certainly, it does the Queen the world of good. 'When Her Majesty first arrives at Balmoral, she may look tired and pale,' said a former head stalker. 'But within a few days, spending many hours in her hills, I see the rose and tan come into her cheeks.'

Princes, presidents and prime ministers come and go, but Balmoral remains a constant in the Queen's life. 'I think it has an atmosphere of its own,' she is on record as saying. 'Nothing much has changed. And I think luckily all the children like it. All the grandchildren like it. They sense the freedom.'

46

ROYAL VARIETY – NOT ALWAYS THE SPICE OF LIFE

The Queen has attended thirty-nine *Royal Variety* performances. Her first was just months after VE Day in 1945 and her most recent was on the day before her 65th wedding anniversary in 2012. Prince Philip notched up a similarly impressive twenty-seven visits.

The show was famed for overrunning as performers grabbed more than their allotted fifteen minutes of fame, and it's fair to say members of the royal family at times found it heavy going. Several years ago, the Queen was sitting for a portrait at Buckingham Palace. The anxious young artist apologised for making her keep the same rigid pose for over an hour. 'Don't worry,' said the monarch reassuringly, 'I'm used to it. I've had to sit through the Royal Variety Performance nearly every year.'

The Queen's parents, King George VI and Queen Elizabeth, were both lovers of variety acts and popular radio shows. In 1945, they were joined by Princesses Elizabeth and Margaret. Two years later, the future Queen was accompanied by her fiancé, Lt Philip Mountbatten, and he remained a stalwart, if prickly, supporter of the show. In 1947, it was rumoured that the young lovers had been to see *Oklahoma* time and again and that 'People Will Say We're in Love' was their song. Half a century later, to mark the royal couple's Golden Wedding, legendary Broadway star Barbara Cook was flown over specially to duet the number with Michael Ball. Later, in the line-up of stars, the Duke shook hands with Ball and said, 'You were the chap that sang that special song weren't you? Well, I've never heard it in my life.'

The same evening, Sir Trevor McDonald read out a fulsome and moving tribute to the Queen and Duke from Nelson Mandela. In the royal box, Philip misheard the greeting and asked his wife, 'Who's it from?'

The Queen muttered, *sotto voce*, 'Mandela.'

Turning to the Benevolent Fund executives, he said, 'He could have told us himself. We saw him last Thursday.'

As the real star of the show, it has often been tricky for the Queen to recognise those performing before her, even the odd global superstar. It cost £72,000 to fly Diana Ross over to headline in the 1991 show and the diva was allowed to dominate the whole of the second section of the show. As she walked downstairs to meet the performers, an executive from the Benevolent Fund asked the Queen if she'd enjoyed herself. 'Yes, yes I did,' replied the monarch. 'I thought the girl singer did very well.'

Like her mother, the Queen has always had a soft spot for British comedians and variety acts from the golden age of television: stars who manage to be both cheeky as well as deferential when it comes to dealing with the royals. Tommy Cooper was a particular favourite, and during one backstage meet and greet he asked the Queen, 'Will you be going to the Cup Final next year?'

The Queen thought for a moment before replying, 'No I don't think I am.'

To which Cooper quipped back, 'Well, can I have your tickets?'

Occasionally she was cheeky back to them. After comedian Jimmy Tarbuck had monumentally overrun during one of the shows, the Queen asked him, 'How many Royal Variety shows have you appeared at, Mr Tarbuck?'

He quipped, 'Four more than Your Majesty!'

She retorted, 'It certainly feels like it!'

Lord Delfont once compared producing the show to 'being in a car crash and only suffering from shock'. When it came to the royal guests, two issues were always paramount in his mind: timing and taste. Whenever the shows ran over, polite notes were sent from Buckingham Palace asking him to try and ensure the Queen could leave on time in future. The stars, of course, felt otherwise and the record for overrunning is still held by Ken Dodd, who managed to stretch his twelve-minute slot into forty minutes.

One show lasted until well after midnight. Delfont noticed the Queen glancing at her watch. In less than eleven hours' time she would have to dress in another shimmering gown and more jewels to deliver the Queen's Speech in the House of Lords. Clearly tense, Her Majesty made her way down the line-up of stars without a comment to Delfont, until she reached her limousine. Hitching her Hartnell gown as she bent forward to climb in, she said over her shoulder, 'Thank you, Mr Delfont. Don't be surprised to see me wearing the same dress to open Parliament.'

Taste is even more hazardous for the production team. When the Kwa Zulu African song and dance company were due to appear in the 1975 show, Delfont was unsure whether the women in the company should appear topless as they did in their West End show. He took the precautionary measure of writing to the Palace to check out the royal reaction. 'Don't worry,' came the reply, 'the Queen has seen topless ladies before.'

Her Majesty may have seen topless ladies, but she got more than she bargained for the year *The Full Monty* topped the bill. The idea was for the five actors to strip down until they were just about to whip off their G-strings, at which point the lights would be switched from the stage onto the auditorium and the dazzled audience would be spared any blushes. Unfortunately, the lights failed, and five naked and embarrassed men were left floundering in the footlights. The Queen remained deadpan and, turning to her hosts, said, 'Is that it then?', although they were unclear what exactly she was referring too.

Besides *The Full Monty*, the Queen and her family have collectively had thousands of other acts flash before them since that first programme back in 1912. What do they really think of the show? We'll never know, but the Queen herself recently gave a clue to comedian Roy Hudd. The entertainer was at Buckingham Palace to receive his OBE and poked light-hearted fun at the *Royal Variety Show*. The Queen quipped back, 'Oh yes, we sometimes look forward to that.'

47

A ROOM WITH A VIEW

The Queen as a Sitter

The Queen has sat for over 130 portraits. Artists have usually been offered one or more sittings of ninety minutes. Lucian Freud asked for seventy-two but settled for far fewer. She warned him, 'Don't mention the number of sittings as the others only get two or three.' If needs be, the artist can return to paint her robes or clothes on a lay-model.

The majority of the sittings have taken place when the Queen is in London and are usually held in the Yellow Drawing Room. As you look at the east front of Buckingham Palace, this is located in the left-hand corner. Its tall sash windows provide good natural light. They also provide the Queen with ample opportunity to sit and stare at the comings and goings of tourists below and to provide the artist with a running commentary on all she sees. Normally, she is the person everyone is looking at, whether she's driving past in a car or waving from Buckingham Palace's balcony, and she takes great pleasure when it's the other way round.

The first artist to note this was Dame Laura Knight, who painted the future queen in 1948 for 'Princess Elizabeth opening the New Broadgate, Coventry'. 'This view from the window there delighted the young princess,' said Dame Laura, who recalled her saying, 'I love looking at the crowds gathering when I myself am out of sight.'

It was a similar comment, six years later, which fuelled the imagination of the Italian painter, Pietro Annigoni, and helped him decide the composition of what would become, arguably, the greatest royal painting of the last century. Speaking to the artist in 'informal and warm-hearted' English, and sometimes French, the 28-year-old Queen told him, 'When I was a little child, it always delighted me to look out of the window and see the people and the traffic go by.' She had unwittingly given him the key to how he would portray her; as he recalled in his memoirs, he felt 'a curious sense of excitement, as though the solution to my problem was suddenly very close'. He immediately asked her to change her pose, so she was looking straight ahead out of the window. The result was the iconic image of the young queen at the start of her reign, undeniably royal in her Garter robes – one in ten of her portraits depict her wearing them – but also an ordinary woman in an extraordinary position – 'a prisoner of the palace'. As he explained, 'I began to sense what it means to be Queen in a land where the Queen is loved by millions … I had to try to get into the portrait the feeling of being close to the people, yet very much alone.'

On a less ethereal note, the royal sitter kept Annigoni up to date on what was happening outside. During one sitting, she noticed a car and a taxi collide in the Mall. 'In the meantime,' she joked, 'the clock ticks up and the poor thing in the taxi will have to pay.'

Talking of cars, during a 1974 sitting for the artist Norman Hepple, she reflected on the fact she had not been very lucky with her likenesses. She told him, 'One day when I was driving out of the Palace the car stopped just outside the gate and an old lady came up and peered in at me and said [and she mimicked a cockney voice beautifully], "She ain't very like her pictures is she?"'

People pausing to look through the Buckingham Palace railings have been a constant source of fascination for the sitting monarch. In the 1992 documentary *Elizabeth R*, we see her posing for Andrew Festing and commenting, 'It looks like a few more tourists doesn't it?' before she notices a detachment of guards marching past, which prompts the head of the armed forces to observe, 'There's a very good mixture here. Bearskins and flat hats.'

When Michael Noakes painted her in 1973, standing on a dais and visible to the gawping multitudes, he noted, 'She kept up a very funny running commentary on people's reactions to seeing her. Mostly they looked up in amazement, decided it was her, then it couldn't possibly be and ended up not quite sure whether it was or not.'

During one winter session, the lights were on and the curtains remained undrawn, making her more visible than ever. When a couple stopped and looked up from the pavement below, she mimicked the conversation they were probably having, telling the artist, 'An American has stopped. He has seen us, he has seen us, he has said to his wife, "Gee mam, it can't be!"'

The Queen's non-stop chatter no doubt has an effect on the artists. When she sat for Lucian Freud, she soon cottoned on it was better to remain as silent as possible, 'Because when he talks he stops painting.'

Annigoni wished she would, in the nicest way, keep quiet. Asked by a journalist if she talked while he worked, he answered honestly, 'Well yes, perhaps too much.' Word must have got back to her, because their final four sittings were held in awkward silence. When he returned fifteen years later to paint a second portrait of her, she was back to her talkative best. He recalled, 'At every sitting, the Queen chatted to me in the most natural way and her disarming frankness never failed to surprise and fascinate me, even at those times when, for the purpose of the portrait, it would have been better if she had kept silent.' By the time they reached the final sittings, he 'longed for silence, but the Queen wanted to talk and in the end I gave myself up to conversation.'

This animated discourse leads to another problem: royal fidgeting. John Wonnacott, who painted the royal family in 2000, observed, 'One thing all artists will tell you is that the Queen does not sit still,' inevitably resulting in a third problem – 'And you really cannot say, "Ma'am, will you please bloody well sit still".'

48

AWKWARD CUSTOMERS: THE QUEEN AND IDI AMIN

At one point during the Silver Jubilee thanksgiving service at St Paul's Cathedral, Earl Mountbatten thought the Queen looked 'rather cross and worried'. Afterwards, he asked her if there was a particular reason for her glum expression. She laughed and told him, 'I was just thinking how awful it would be if Amin were to gate-crash the party and arrive after all.' The earl asked what she would have done if he had turned up and she told him she'd decided to use the City's Pearl Sword, which the Lord Mayor had placed before her, and hit him hard over the head with it.

The threat of Ugandan dictator Idi Amin turning up in the middle of the jubilee festivities was just one of many unwelcome problems he created for Elizabeth II and her government. The Queen and Amin met face to face on only one occasion, shortly after he'd ousted his president, Milton Obote, in an army coup.

At the time, Obote's overthrow was not perceived as a great loss by Edward Heath's Conservative Government. He had objected to UK foreign policy in Africa, particularly the resumption of arms sales to South Africa. Although Amin had already begun his atrocious human-rights abuses, when he asked if he could come to London to meet the Queen, Heath, the Commonwealth Secretary General Arnold Smith and the Foreign Office welcomed the idea.

In July 1971, the Queen hosted a lunch party at Buckingham Palace for Amin and Mama Malyam, one of his two wives. Within minutes, she was given an insight into his unhinged personality when she asked him about his plans for Uganda and he told her he was about to declare war on the neighbouring Commonwealth nation of Tanzania. His aim was to cut a corridor of territory through Tanzania to give his landlocked country access to the Indian Ocean. Fortunately, Foreign Secretary Alec Douglas-Home was also present at the lunch and was able to feedback Amin's plans to the PM.

Despite the threatened invasion, the Queen continued the usual diplomatic niceties and added Amin to that year's Christmas card list, although, due to a Palace oversight, it didn't arrive until early January 1972. That same month, the president invited the Queen to visit him later in the year to celebrate a decade of independence from Britain, as usual writing directly to her and bypassing the Foreign Office. He gushed, 'It would do my government a great honour if Your Majesty could grace these celebrations with your presence in the company of your husband and the rest of your family.'

By then, the UK Government had become aware of the massacre of Ugandan citizens, especially Obote supporters in the armed forces, as well as the expulsion of British citizens. The Palace would have preferred to ignore the request but was persuaded by the government that a snub could endanger the lives of British-born residents in Uganda. The Queen, therefore, penned a courteous reply, 'I am very grateful for you asking me to attend the celebrations of the Tenth Anniversary of Ugandan Independence on 9th October 1972. I am most disappointed that my commitments at that time will prevent my accepting your invitation.' She signed off with her customary expression, 'I am your good friend, Elizabeth R.' Amin was mollified, although had he read the Court Circular for 9 October, he might have changed his mind as her only commitment was attending morning service at Crathie Kirk during her annual holiday at Balmoral.

The following summer Amin telegrammed the Queen while she was en route to Canada for the 1973 Commonwealth Conference in Ottawa. He planned to attend and asked her to arrange transport for him from Kampala and back and a bodyguard of Scots Guardsmen. He addressed his cable to 'Your Majesty and my former commander-in-chief', a reference to his time in the King's African Rifles, a British colonial regiment. (Amin's military career, like the rest of his CV was particularly impressive. He served as a cook but ended up a major and eventually became the head of the Ugandan Army in 1965.)

He asked the Queen 'to be so kind as to avail me one of your special aircraft and guards from Scotland for flying to the Commonwealth Conference'. He informed her that he wanted to meet her to 'brief you and your government about matters of mutual interest', including 'how I transformed Uganda into a truly black man's country'. In case she might misinterpret his motives, he helpfully pointed out, 'I am a leader who does not believe in propaganda but only in the truth'. He signed off by assuring 'Your Majesty of my highest esteem and regards'.

The Queen sent a personal message back gently reminding Amin that it was the normal practice for national delegations to make their own travel arrangements to international conferences. She added that she hoped to meet him in audience and at her dinner for the heads of delegations, if he made it. Meanwhile, our man in Kampala, John Stewart, took his life in his hands by personally informing Amin's office that no official plane or regiment was available at such short notice. In the end, the president cabled Arnold Smith to tell him he wouldn't be able to attend 'because of other state preoccupations at home'.

To make sure a similar situation never arose, Amin offered a solution. In April 1975, he cabled the secretary general offering to replace the Queen as head of the Commonwealth. He justified this initiative on the grounds that decolonisation meant that 'the British empire does not now exist'. Secondly, 'the collapse of the British economy has made Britain unable to maintain the position of leadership of the Commonwealth'. The solution was obvious (to him), 'I offer myself to be appointed head of the Commonwealth, in view of the success of my economic revolution in Uganda'. Not only could he run the whole organisation, but he could offer a venue for the 1977 meeting as Kampala 'has now very modern and up-to-date conference facilities'.

The same spring he offered to displace her as head of the Commonwealth, Amin wrote to tell the Queen he would be arriving for a state visit on 4 August. He announced on Ugandan radio that he was advising her ahead of time 'so that you may have ample time to help you arrange all that is required for my comfortable stay in your country'. Referring to Britain's ailing economy, he added, 'I hope there will be at least during my stay a steady and reliable supply of essential commodities', although he failed to specify what 'commodities' he needed.

He also announced that he would be visiting all parts of the British Isles. 'Your Majesty, it is ardently hoped and expected that you will ... arrange for me to visit Scotland, Wales and Northern Ireland.' The reason for his full UK tour was because 'I should like ... to talk to those people who are struggling for self-determination and independence from your political and economic system'. He also wanted to meet the British Asians who 'I booted out of this country in September 1972'.

Having dissed her Union, Amin ended with a chirpier note, wishing the Queen 'a happy and prosperous new year, long life and bright future'. In case she had forgotten which distinguished leader she was dealing with, he signed himself, 'Al-Haji General Idi Amin Dada, VC, DSO, MC, President of Uganda'.

A spokesman for the Foreign Office sniffed, 'It is unlikely that he would be invited to come on a state visit the way things are at the moment', adding for good measure, 'In any case, if he were coming on a state or official visit, he would have to be invited, rather than send a message, informing us he was coming.'

Had he arrived on the 4 August, he would have had a non-royal greeting because the Queen, an authentic colonel-in-chief, had already accepted an invitation to lunch with the Blues and Royals at Combermere Barracks in Windsor and would later be helping her mother celebrate her 75th birthday.

Two years later, she was embroiled in a trickier situation than a threatened state visit. Denis Hills, a British-born teacher, adventurer and traveller, based in Uganda, had released a book entitled *The White Pumpkin*, in which he referred to Amin as a 'black Nero' and a 'village tyrant'. A less-unbalanced head of state might have settled for a public thrashing or expulsion from the country, but Amin condemned Hills to the fate of all his dissenters and ordered execution by firing squad. Before peppering the expat Brit with bullets, Amin realised he might just have another opportunity to involve his favourite monarch. Hills was ordered into his presence and Amin made it clear that he was a good friend of the Queen and, although the writer was to be shot the following day, should the Queen apologise for her subject's behaviour, he might be spared.

The Queen agreed to pen a flattering letter to Amin, recalling their 1971 lunch and appealing for clemency for Denis Hills. Two British military officers dropped her letter personally to the president, having first had to abase themselves by entering Amin's house at Arua in north-west Uganda on their hands and knees. The president was delighted with the royal plea and told them that the Queen 'will not have any problems with him'.

The execution was called off, although Amin enjoyed the power game and vacillated for several weeks about the writer's fate, before the Foreign Secretary, James Callaghan, eventually flew to Kampala to bring Hills home.

During this time, Amin sent another elaborate telegram to the Queen replying to her plea for clemency. In it, he also recalled their earlier meeting and told her 'to be reassured that you have the best friends in Uganda'. He told her:

> [your] message touched my heart very much and because of the love, confidence and respect which I personally, the Defence Council and the Government and entire people of Uganda have for you as the leader of Great Britain and Commonwealth, I decided to postpone the execution of Mr Denis Cecil Hills.

Other critics of the system were not so lucky. A conservative estimate suggests that 300,000 people out of a population of 12 million were murdered. Amin's State Research Bureau, his secret police, favoured executing prisoners in pairs. The victims were forced to fight in gladiatorial combat, clubbing each other with sledgehammers. The victor was 'rewarded' with a swift bullet in the back of the head. Others were thrown from helicopters or over precipices.

Once all British citizens living and working there had had time to sort out their affairs and leave the country, the British Government formally broke off relations with Uganda. Both the Queen and her government were well aware of the Ugandan leader's atrocities and were more than concerned when he announced in February 1977 that he would be attending that summer's Commonwealth Conference. Despite the rift between Britain and Uganda he had, like all the other Commonwealth leaders, been invited by former prime minister Harold Wilson at the 1975 conference.

The dilemma for the Palace and the government was the inevitable involvement of the Queen, because the conference was timed to coincide with her Silver Jubilee celebrations. The highlight was a thanksgiving service at St Paul's Cathedral on 7 June, followed a day later by a banquet at Buckingham Palace for all the heads of governments.

On 3 May, Amin telegraphed the secretary general, suggesting that the role of head of the Commonwealth should rotate each year and not automatically be held by the Queen. Having tried to oust her from a role she had held for a quarter of a century, he also announced that he would be arriving with a party of 250, including tribal pygmy dancers. He liked St Ermin's Hotel in Westminster and would be staying there unless it wasn't 'adequate', in which case 'arrangements should be made for me to stay at Buckingham Palace'.

Fearing Amin was hell bent on attending, the Palace sent an officer from Amin's old regiment, the King's African Rifles, to hopefully dissuade him, but he returned claiming 'it was hopeless'. The 'terrified' PM, Jim Callaghan, consulted Sonny Ramphal, the Commonwealth secretary general, who said simply, 'You cannot turn Amin away.' Ramphal also went to Uganda to try the moral approach, warning Amin that the visit would put the Queen in an embarrassing situation.

Amin made no further announcements and laid low. It was unclear whether or not he might attend the celebrations, hence the Queen ruminating about hitting him on the head with a pearl-studded sword (a medieval-style warrior punishment that Amin himself could have devised).

After a walkabout along Cheapside, the Queen headed for the Guildhall and a celebratory lunch hosted by the Lord Mayor. Hardly had they taken a mouthful of the salmon-trout starter when a press rumour was fed to Home Secretary Merlyn Rees that Amin's plane was in Irish airspace bound for Heathrow. Rees hurriedly passed on the information to his Cabinet colleague. Foreign Secretary David Owen later told the royal historian Robert Hardman, 'We had made plans in case he was crazy enough to fly in so I said: "We will push him to a remote part of the airfield and just not allow him to get off the airplane".' There was, of course, no landing, no jet and no Amin. As with the last two Commonwealth conferences, he had promised a lot, but thankfully never delivered.

There was one final coda from the deranged leader. In February 1978, he announced during a BBC interview that he would shortly be visiting Britain to solve past 'misunderstandings' with the British Government. He also used the interview to claim that allegations of Ugandan atrocities were made by the British, whom he had 'conquered'. He nevertheless felt that the British were his friends and he had a high regard for the Queen.

The Foreign Office was, as always, in the dark about Amin's proposed visit and it never materialised. He would shortly send his troops to invade neighbouring Tanzania and in 1979, Tanzanian forces combined with Ugandan exiles to counter-attack, sending Amin himself into exile.

Although they only met once, Amin played a continual political chess game with the Queen, as well as her advisors, her government and her Commonwealth throughout his eight-year rule. He was second only to Pol Pot as the most murderous dictator of that time and his volatile relationship with Britain involved the Queen in some of the trickiest diplomatic manoeuvres of her reign. Certainly, her personal letters to him, particularly over the Denis Hills case, crafted as they were by her advisors and No. 10 Downing Street, only worked because they were signed by her. He might have disregard for her country and its government, but he never lost respect and even affection for her. Facing him, on the wall of his study, for the whole of his nightmare rule, was a framed photograph of the head of state that he revered the most – Elizabeth II.

49

LIGHTS, CAMERA, ACTION: ROYAL FILM PERFORMANCE

There have been over seventy Royal Film Performances since the Second World War and the Queen has been the most regular of the royal cinemagoers. Besides raising money for the Cinema and Television Benevolent Fund, this red-carpet event is an opportunity for A-list stars and executives to have a rare brush with the greatest and most enduring star of them all, the Queen herself.

The first Royal Film Performance as we know it took place on 1 November 1946 when King George VI and Queen Elizabeth, with the Princesses Elizabeth and Margaret, saw the David Niven movie *A Matter of Life and Death* at the Empire Theatre. An estimated crowd of 40,000 mobbed the royal party and the stars and the King was visibly shaken after his limousine was delayed for over twenty minutes by the dense throng. Other guests arrived with torn dresses and tiaras askew, and over 100 onlookers were carried into the foyer for first-aid treatment.

It is striking, looking back at photographs from the early years, to see the formality of the occasion, with the royal ladies and many of the guests wearing furs, elaborate gowns and every conceivable type of jewellery and many of the men in white tie. At the 1964 performance of *Born Free*, it was noted that the Queen wore the ribbon of the Order of the Garter with the diamond-encrusted Family Orders, as well as a diamond and emerald tiara.

The Queen and Prince Philip take their seats in the Royal Box for the premiere of the film The Guns of Navarone *in April 1961. (Author's collection)*

On 10 December 1962, the royal party travelled through the freezing fog for the premiere of *Lawrence of Arabia*. The premiere very nearly didn't happen as only two copies of the valuable 70mm film were in existence, and the one made for the premier had become scratched. There was a mad dash to London Airport on the day to locate the second copy, which was ready to be flown to the United States. Prince Philip, shaking hands with the film's director before the film was shown, was heard to ask, 'Good flick?'

Another striking factor about the Royal Film Performances is the calibre of A-list stars that have attended the event over the years. At the 1956 premiere of *The Battle of the River Plate*, the Queen was introduced to three of the most famous screen beauties, Joan Crawford, Brigitte Bardot and Marilyn Monroe.

Sadly, the calibre of the films rarely matched the guests. After watching Robert Morley's hammy impersonation of her 'mad' ancestor King George III in the 1954 film *Beau Brummell*, the Queen complained to Prime Minister Winston Churchill, who intervened on her behalf to make sure she was never embarrassed in the same way again.

Having sat through the risqué *Les Girls* in 1957, the Queen decided to put a temporary halt to proceedings and Buckingham Palace issued a statement that she would not be attending a performance the following year 'as Her Majesty does not really want to be tied to going to one particular engagement every year'. For some odd reason, this ruling didn't apply to the Queen Mother, who resumed royal attendance in 1959.

After a gap of five years, the Queen resumed her cinema-going with *West Side Story* in 1962 and has remained faithful to the event for the next half a century. To alleviate the monotony of annual visits, she alternated her attendance, first of all with the Queen Mother and later with the Prince of Wales.

The twenty-first century has witnessed some of the most spectacular premieres. In 2002, the venue for the royal film was
changed to the Royal Albert Hall, which was temporarily transformed into an ice palace for the launch of the James Bond film
Die Another Day. A host of A-list stars turned out for the event
and while the crowd outside became hysterically starstruck, the
Queen seemed endearingly vague when faced with the stellar
cast. Shaking hands with Pierce Brosnan, who was playing 007
at the time, the Queen seemed taken aback, 'But I've just met
two James Bonds downstairs.' Her confusion was understandable, because the last time she'd met Bond he was Sean Connery
at the 1967 premiere of *You Only Live Twice*. She would go on
to see Daniel Craig in *Casino Royale* and memorably play the
ultimate Bond girl alongside him at the opening of the 2012
Olympic Games.

Two years earlier, she was moved to tears by the fantasy film
The Chronicles of Narnia: The Voyage of the Dawn Treader,
which was the 2010 royal film. Simon Pegg, who played
Reepicheep, the leader of the talking mice, was sitting five seats
away from the Queen and recalled, 'She cried a little bit at the
end, too, when my character makes this life-changing decision.'
He revealed she dabbed her eyes with a tissue, unlike Prince
Philip, who turned to the actor and said, 'When did you realise
you had the voice of a mouse?'

While the actors may come and go and, thankfully, so have
some of the films, one attendee remained constant until she
passed on her tickets to the younger generation. These days, it's
William and Catherine who alternate with Charles and Camilla.
It has to be said that, unlike her husband, when it comes to
the Royal Film Performance, Elizabeth II has given her own

Oscar-winning performance in remaining inscrutable about the quality of each film she was attending, as well as resolutely discreet about the horrors she has sat through in the past.

50

REGINA VS CELEBRITIES

When you are the most famous woman in the world, identifying mere A-listers can be a chore, as the Queen has shown time and again.

1 Meeting chanteuse Madonna at the premiere of *Die Another Day* in 2002, it was clear Her Maj. had no idea who Madge was. As the singer laughed nervously, an aide explained the 'Material Girl' star had voiced the title track, to which the Queen replied, 'Oh really, did you?' before moving on. Not that John Cleese, next in line, fared any better. He was asked the perennial royal query, 'And what do you do?'

2 Madonna was not the only world-famous singer the Queen failed to recognise. When she met pop superstars Mick Hucknall and Kate Bush at a Golden Jubilee reception in May 2002, she had to ask, 'And what do you two do?'

Hucknall replied, 'We are singer-songwriters.' It wasn't the flame-haired performer's night, because not only had the Queen forgotten she'd met him two years before at Windsor (and asked him the same questions) but Prince Philip didn't have a clue who he was, even though Hucknall had presented Duke of Edinburgh Awards for the previous two years.

3 Another legend who left the monarch baffled is Eric Clapton, who met her at a Buckingham Palace reception celebrating the country's music industry. The guitar ace shook her hand and told her what he did. The Queen asked, 'Have you been playing a long time?', forcing him to admit, 'It must be forty-five years now.'

4 At the same event, she shook hands with Queen guitarist Brian May, who reminded her that he had played the national anthem from the roof of Buckingham Palace to open the Golden Jubilee concert. To which Her Majesty replied, 'Oh! That was you, was it?'

5 To be fair, it would be invidious for the Queen to recognise some faces and not others, which might account for her blanket failure to recognise many latter-day celebrities. There again, she might just be having a laugh at their expense, as she did in the mid-1970s at a charity fundraiser at the Talk of the Town. Seeing a pink-chiffon-clad figure glide past with bouffant hair and enormous false eyelashes, the Queen asked the impresario Lord Delfont, 'Who's that?' When he replied, 'It's Barbara Cartland', the monarch quipped, 'Oh, I thought it was Danny La Rue!'

6 One famous name she had no problem recognising was film star Marilyn Monroe, who was born just forty-one days after Elizabeth. The two met at the 1956 Royal Film Performance of *The Battle of the River Plate*. Photographs of the occasion are still widely used in biographies of the two women. Monroe, in a low-cut gold lamé gown, is seen shaking hands with an equally beautiful Queen dressed in black velvet and wearing the Grand Duchess Vladimir tiara.

Less well known is what they talked about, which was where they both lived. Monroe was in England to film *The Prince and the Showgirl* and was staying just a few miles from Windsor

Castle. The Queen joked 'we are neighbours' and asked the actress how she was enjoying living in Englefield Green, the home she was renting with her playwright husband Arthur Miller. Monroe replied, 'We love it and, as we have a permit, my husband and I go for bicycle rides and walks in the Great Park.'

Princess Margaret also cracked the 'We are neighbours' joke and then asked her how the filming with Sir Laurence Olivier was going on.

'It's going very well, and it's with regret that we have to leave in about a fortnight's time.'

Anyone who has seen the film *My Week With Marilyn* will know that work on *The Prince and the Showgirl* was a nightmare for all concerned!

7 Like many of us, the Queen is curious to know what celebrities are like in real life. When royal dress designer Stewart Parvin was at a fitting at Buckingham Palace, the Queen asked him, 'What are you up to this week?'

He told her, 'Tomorrow I'm going to be dressing Judy Finnigan, the TV presenter.'

And she said, 'Oh, Richard and Judy?' Then after a pause, 'So you know them?' and after another pause, 'What are they like?'

8 It was the dress rather than the identity that intrigued the Queen when she met cross-dressing ceramicist Grayson Perry at a Buckingham Palace reception honouring the arts. Grayson came dressed as his alter ego Claire in a short red-and-blue floral dress inspired by Dorothy in *The Wizard of Oz*. Like his host, he also carried a black patent leather handbag. Afterwards, he revealed, 'I thought the Queen's eyes were going to pop out of her head when she saw me. I was probably the first t****y at the palace, although one or two may have slipped through unnoticed.' The Queen asked what he did for a living, and he told her he 'made pots'.

9 The Queen is more at home with the homegrown celebrities of yesteryear and would have no problem identifying the likes of Tommy Cooper and Arthur Askey. Each year, variety stars were asked to perform in front of the royals and their staff at a Christmas gala. One year, Eric Sykes decided to sing 'In a Monastery Garden' and after singing the first line, 'When the daylight's softly fading', on cue he began to whistle birdsong, thinking this would bring the house down. He recalled the staff 'standing behind the seated royal party were a frozen tableau' and he left the stage to no applause. He heard later that the Queen remarked, 'He doesn't sing very well does he?'

10 The actress Diana Dors, who was also a cabaret star in her twenties, bounded on to the Windsor Castle stage to sing a cheeky number to another Christmas audience. Having never suffered from a day's nerves in her life, she was shocked to find herself turn into a gibbering wreck as she glimpsed the row of twinkling tiaras just feet in front of her. Afterwards, the Queen came back into the room to seek the star out and tell her, 'Princess Margaret wanted me to tell you she's sorry she can't be here. You're one of her favourites.'

11 Occasionally, stars try to overcompensate when it comes to rubbing shoulders with the Queen. In July 1993, Hollywood actor Richard Gere and his supermodel girlfriend Cindy Crawford, together with Goldie Hawn, were invited to watch the polo at Smith's Lawn, Windsor, from the royal box. They hired two chauffeur-driven vintage Rolls-Royces, which came complete with chintzy curtains at the windows. This was the sight that greeted the Queen as she drove herself into the enclosure in her green Jaguar.

51

LOOKING AFTER
THE PENNIES

Although she's one of the richest women in the world, the Queen is notoriously penny-pinching in her private life. In her personal suite of rooms at Buckingham Palace, the Canaletto paintings, porcelain vases, crystal chandeliers and eighteenth-century carpets sit alongside a utilitarian two-bar electric fire with plastic surrounds.

Her thriftiness is ingrained, as Sir Michael Oswald recalled, 'She deplores any form of extravagance and left to her own devices would live a far simpler life, eating fairly plain, simple food.' He put it down to her ancestry, 'There's a certain amount of Scots blood in the Queen.' If so, she didn't inherit the stereotypical characteristic from her Scottish mother, who enjoyed the lavish lifestyle she felt was her due as a former queen-empress, and who was bankrolled by an obliging Coutts & Co., as well as her eldest daughter.

Neither was the Queen's paternal line particularly thrifty. Her grandmother, Queen Mary, lavished money on her jewellery collection and her great-grandfather, Edward VII, had a rapacious appetite for food, gambling, racing and, of course, women.

George V embraced rationing during the First World War. When one courtier arrived late for breakfast, he rang the bell to ask for a boiled egg. Assistant Private Secretary Frederick Ponsonby recalled, 'If he had ordered a dozen turkeys he could not have made a bigger stir. The King accused him of being a slave to his insides, of unpatriotic behaviour, and even went so far as to hint that we should lose the war on account of his gluttony.' George had, of course, already eaten.

Both he and his consort were similarly inconsistent when it came to alcohol. In March 1915, George informed Downing Street that he and his household had given up the demon drink for the duration of the war. However, according to his eldest son, the royal couple believed cider was non-alcoholic and after dinner, the King would retire to his study 'to attend to a small matter of business', which was, in fact, a large port. Queen Mary was also known to top up her fruit cup with champagne.

There were certain royal relations who remained tight-fisted until the end. Edward's niece, Princess Alice of Athlone, the Queen's Great-Aunt Alice, used to travel to and from her Kensington Palace apartment by bus, and for her annual West Indies vacation, crossed the Atlantic in a banana boat. When the Queen visited Aunt Alice in her sickbed in October 1980, shortly before the old lady's death, the Princess ended the visit with the instruction, 'Turn off the heater as you go out. We only put it on because you were coming.' The monarch duly bent down and unplugged the fire.

Frugality was certainly instilled in the future monarch by her nursery maid, and later dresser, Bobo MacDonald, as well as her governess Marion Crawford. In *The Little Princesses*, Crawfie recalls Princess Elizabeth carefully folding the wrapping paper off her presents so she could use it again.

The trait continued as an adult. Earl Mountbatten used to tell the story about following the Queen's page, Bennett, into her study to ask him to post some letters for him. The earl only had a £5 note and, as the post office was five minutes away and he was about to leave, the Queen offered to help. She opened one of her red government boxes, pulled out an envelope that contained cash, and handed the page £3. Some people would be inclined to say, 'Keep the change', but instead Elizabeth called out, 'Bennett, don't forget, you owe me £3!' As they say, you don't get rich by spending it.

Another page found a scribbled note on the monarch's bedside table asking him to fit one of the new energy-saving lightbulbs, adding, 'but only when this one blows'.

House party guests at a picnic in a Balmoral bothy were amused to be ticked off by the royal laird for trying to throw away half-burned candles. The only thing she allowed them to do was blow them out, insisting they be kept for the next visit – 'There's plenty of light in that one'. One royal cousin was less amused to be handed a packed lunch for her return journey home, only to find she was later invoiced for it.

52

'I NAME THIS SHIP ...'

The Queen is arguably the world's most prolific ship launcher. Beginning in 1944, aged 18, when she named the battleship HMS *Vanguard*, she would smash a variety of wines against cruise liners, an oil tanker, a nuclear-powered submarine and half a dozen lifeboats.

Probably her most historic launching to date was that of the *QE2* on Clydebank in 1967. The name of the new liner had been kept secret until the day, with only the Queen and several Cunard executives being privy to the secret. Ever since the keel of John Brown Job No. 736 was laid in July 1965, speculation had been rife in the press. A total of 15,000 bets were placed at a Glasgow bookmaker's not far from the shipyard with 'Sir Winston Churchill' as the 3–1 favourite. There was a late flurry of bets on 'Princess Margaret', when it was announced she would be joining her sister on the day. Also in the running were 'John F. Kennedy', 'Donald Campbell', 'Queen Victoria' and 'Twiggy'. A royal name seemed unlikely after Cunard director, Basil Smallpeice, announced, 'We shall have to find a name which will reflect this modern age and not recall the days of Henry Hall's band.'

Nevertheless, there was obviously a change of heart and, after wielding the same pair of gold scissors used by her mother and grandmother to cut the ribbon at previous launchings, the Queen declared, 'I name this ship *Queen Elizabeth the Second ...*' Ever since, there has been a debate about if she had named it after herself or her mother, after whom the other *Queen Elizabeth* Cunard liner was named.

North of the border, which was never ruled by Elizabeth I, there was dissent from SNP chairman Angus Donaldson, who harrumphed, 'It could not be a bigger insult to Scotland.' To avoid similar misunderstandings, Smallpeice announced that an Arabic number 2 would be used for the ship's name instead of the Roman numeral II.

53

QUEEN ON SCREEN

Nowadays we're used to seeing the Queen portrayed on screen, with varying success, whether in *The Crown* or in the plethora of Diana films. Portraying Elizabeth II on film must be one of the most challenging roles in an actor's life. It was down to two of our greatest actresses, as well as a comedian, to bring the screen queen to life.

In the early years of her reign, no one would have dared to feature Her Majesty in a film or television show. Fast forward thirty-five years and we saw the Queen lampooned as a *Spitting Image* puppet complete with tiara, headscarf and quilted jacket.

The iconoclast who broke the unwritten rule about daring to imitate the Queen was, ironically, not even a woman, but the Glasgow-born comedian Stanley Baxter. In his 1972 *Stanley Baxter Picture Show*, he gave her Christmas speech thinly disguised as 'The Duchess of Brendagh' – 'Brenda' being the affectionate nickname *Private Eye* magazine gave to the monarch.

Nearly twenty years later, in 1991, one of Britain's greatest character actresses, Prunella Scales, had the daunting task of acting the part of the Queen in the TV adaptation of Alan Bennett's *A Question of Attribution*, having already played the role on stage in the West End. The play focuses on Anthony Blunt, who was exposed as a member of the Cambridge spy ring in the early 1980s and had also once been the Surveyor of the Queen's Pictures.

Having played both Elizabeth I and Victoria, Prunella should have been a dab hand at British queens but appearing as Elizabeth II gave her a completely new challenge. She told the author:

It was terrifying playing the Queen, since everyone watching knows her and can of course check out the performance for themselves.

It helps that she is very well covered, with lots of film and television footage to aid with the characterisation. Of course the play is beautifully written and that was also a terrific help. Another blessing was the fact that I happen to be the same height as the Queen.

As a method actress I had to think, 'Who am I, what do I look like and sound like?'

Getting the voice right proved to be a challenge. 'I listened to as many recordings as I could. Actors are very often not as careful of educated speech as they are of regional dialect. There is such variation in upper-class speech and one has to try and be accurate.'

Anyone portraying the Queen must wonder, at the back of their mind, what the reaction from the Palace is going to be. Prunella need not have worried, 'Princess Margaret came to see the play and I also remember receiving a very nice letter from one of the royal household who told me he'd had to stop himself from getting to his feet when I came on stage, which was very gratifying.'

As for the monarch herself, Prunella, who calls herself 'a socialist royalist', recalled:

> One of my spies at the Palace told me the Queen had watched the play on TV. The following year I went to the Palace to receive a CBE and, as the Queen presented it to me, she said, 'I expect you think you should be doing this!' It was a lovely moment.

In 2006, Elizabeth II celebrated her 80th birthday and Dame Helen Mirren celebrated critical acclaim when she starred in *The Queen*, which won her an Academy Award and scooped another fifty-eight wins and a further fifty-one nominations. The film highlighted the crisis the House of Windsor faced in the days following the death of Princess Diana. For a time, she was so synonymous with the part she was playing that she was introduced to the audience at the Venice Film Festival as 'Her Majesty Helen Mirren'.

Like Prunella Scales, Mirren regularly watched film and video footage of the sovereign and kept photos in her trailer during production. Not for the first time, 'the Queen effect' took hold and by the end of the production, crew members who had been accustomed to slouching or relaxing when they addressed her were standing up straight and respectfully folding their hands behind their backs.

Dame Helen says that she cried when she saw an early news-reel of the future Queen:

> In the footage, she's getting out of one of those enormous black cars. She'd obviously been told you get out and you put your hand out and you are polite to the man who will greet you. But she's doing it with such gravity and grace and dignity as a 12 year old, and it makes me cry every time I look at it. It's beautiful.

In June 2008, Dame Helen was invited to take tea with the Queen during Royal Ascot, a sure sign that the royal household gave the film its blessing. Inscrutable as ever, Her Majesty never revealed her feelings about the Oscar-winning movie. Having said that, when she introduced the actress to the Aga Khan there was something sisterly about the way she said, 'This is Dame Helen Mirren who played me in a film.'

How the Queen feels about having her life portrayed on screen remains a tantalising mystery and, as in nearly every other area of her life, she keeps her thoughts to herself.

54

WE ARE AMUSED: THE QUEEN'S SENSE OF HUMOUR

In the 1969 *Royal Family* documentary, we were treated to a clip of the Queen and Prince Philip having lunch with their two eldest children. The Queen told them, 'It was extremely

Although the Queen has always been dignified in public, she has a terrific sense of humour. When something amuses her, she throws her head back and roars with laughter, as here at the Royal Windsor Horse Show, before swiftly reverting to her usual composed self.
(© Ian Lloyd)

difficult to keep a straight face when the Home Secretary said to me: "There's a gorilla coming in". Her Majesty added, 'So I said: "What an extraordinary remark to make about someone – very unkind". I stood in the middle of the room and pressed the bell and the doors opened and there was a gorilla. He had a short body and long arms.'

It was the first time the world at large had a glimpse of the Queen's delicious sense of humour which, more often than not, is only seen by those closest to her.

Things going wrong are an obvious source of delight. Early on in her reign, she visited Trinity College Cambridge. During luncheon, the Lord Lieutenant, the Earl of Macclesfield, fainted, swiftly followed by his wife who, thinking he'd died, passed out too. Then, to top it all, a waiter tripped and dropped a tray of drinks. Having managed to control her mirth, the Queen thanked her hosts on the way out and said, 'We've had a wonderful lunch. Bodies all over the place!'

People sometimes confuse what she once called her 'Miss Piggy face' with anger. In fact, it is sometimes caused by suppressed mirth. Sir Edward Bridges, in charge of operations during a Privy Council meeting at Balmoral, noticed the Queen was 'blackly furious'. One of the councillors, new to the job, had entered the room, fallen to his knees and shuffled all the way across towards her, knocking a book off a table on his way. Bridges apologised for the odd incident, but the Queen confessed, 'You know, I nearly laughed.'

One of the earliest accounts of her delight in ceremonies going pear-shaped was at a party in February 1946 in Belgravia when she had everyone in fits of laughter by telling them about a guardsman who lost his bearskin while presenting arms.

The Queen uses humour to ease the inevitable tension that goes with meeting royalty. When one of Charles's earlier girlfriends arrived at Windsor Castle for the first time, the Queen asked, tongue in cheek, 'Did you find us alright?'

A few years later, the Dutch Ambassador told her he was thinking of retiring to England and she asked him, 'Whereabouts?' He replied, 'South Gloucestershire.' Thinking of all the members of her family with estates there – Charles, Anne and, at the time, Prince Michael of Kent – she quipped, 'How common!'

Then there was the nervous guest at Sandringham who, when being served coffee, managed to flick the sugar spoon in a cartwheel, spraying sugar on the table. The Queen, aware of his discomfort, said kindly, 'See if you can do that again.'

She is also happy to joke about herself, revealing a few years ago that she almost ruined her James Bond cameo by laughing.

During a visit to Stirling Castle, which was undergoing extensive repairs at the time, she asked the foreman, 'When will all this be complete?' to be told bluntly, 'It won't be in your time, Ma'am', which really tickled her.

Thankfully, she can see the funny side of growing old. When Irish First Minister Martin McGuinness asked her, 'Are you well?', the Queen replied, 'Well I'm still alive.' Similarly, when Justin Trudeau lavished praise on the Queen for her years of service to the Commonwealth, she started her own speech with the words, 'Thank you, Mr Prime Minister of Canada, for making me feel so old.'

When the Polish President Lech Walesa came on a state visit, the Queen told an aide, 'He only knows two words', and after a slight pause, she added, 'They are quite interesting words.'

Her humour can occasionally verge on the ribald. Former royal correspondent Simon McCoy once mentioned to her a welcoming dance of scantily clad locals, saying, 'That was a remarkable ceremony with all the native costumes, Ma'am.'

She replied, 'There's one country where all they have is a feather … and I do worry when it's cold.'

Apparently, she was a fan of the risqué humour of Sir Donald Gosling, the founder of National Car Parks (NCP), who always had a fresh supply of jokes, but his sense of humour was pretty salty. He once told her a naughty joke involving a horse trainer giving Viagra to a runner in the 2.30 at Newton Abbot. The

Defence Minister hurriedly interjected to stop the punchline before HM berated the minister and got Sir Don to repeat the joke, complete with the ending, which had something to do with winning against stiff competition.

On another occasion, during a visit to the Milk Marketing Board, the Queen was shown a plastic 3D model and enquired, 'What is that?'

The chairman, Sir Richard Trehane replied, 'It's a cow's vagina, Ma'am.'

Without batting an eyelid, she replied, 'Ask a silly question ...'

Once, at an art exhibition, she was trying to avoid being photographed next to a huge Lucian Freud painting which showed, in his uncompromising style, a female nude splayed out with sagging breasts and rolls of flesh. Her host reminded her that she too had been painted by the legendary artist. 'Yes,' she replied, 'but not like that.'

Occasionally, her humour is at the expense of her family, with Prince Philip usually top of the list. During a 1954 review on Horse Guards Parade, a low and rather wet flag hanging over the dais was whipped up by a breeze and slapped his cheek. A smile was seen to cross the Queen's face. On another occasion, Philip, who liked to assume an alpha-male role with the barbecue at Balmoral picnics, was grilling steaks with Princess Anne when black smoke started to appear. Turning to a guest and laughing her head off, the Queen said, 'Made a complete hash of it, haven't they?'

Her humour is deadpan. Take, for instance, the anecdote about her having dinner with her sister and mother at Kensington

Palace with all three women in evening gowns. Margaret's butler slipped and dropped some of the flambé dessert on the hem of the Princess's dress. While he hurriedly tried to clear up the mess, the three royal ladies, trained not to react to anything amiss, ignored the drama until the Queen leant across and said, 'Do look, Mummy, Margot's on fire.'

One aspect of her humour is widely reported but never seen in public: her gift for mimicry. She is adept at imitating accents – cockney and Australian are two specialities. Nearer home, she can do a spot-on impersonation of her personal assistant Angela Kelly's scouse accent, and apparently also imitated Princess Margaret, who grew increasingly plummy in her delivery the older she got, while the Queen went the other way and spoke with less received pronunciation.

Her gift for mimicry once backfired when a Commonwealth diplomat arrived at Buckingham Palace to present his credentials. After he bowed and the Queen thought he'd gone, she began an impersonation only to find he was still standing by the door. Fortunately, he took it in good part, telling her, 'Not bad, Ma'am, not bad.'

One former master of the household claims she can 'mimic anyone and anything'. Her hit-list over the years has included Boris Yeltsin, Neil Kinnock and Ian Paisley. The latter heard about it and said, 'The Queen is a great mimicker of me when she has her friends round so I suppose that's a form of flattery' (giving her the benefit of the doubt).

Former Dean of Windsor, the late Michael Mann, has also left us with a fascinating glimpse of Elizabeth the entertainer, 'The Queen imitating Concorde landing is one of the funniest things you could see.'

55

DAUGHTERS-IN-LAW

In theory, Diana Spencer and Sarah Ferguson were the ideal choices to marry Charles and Andrew, the heir and spare to the throne.

Born at Park House on the Sandringham Estate in July 1961, Diana had grown up on the periphery of royal life. Her father, Johnny Spencer, was an aristocrat – Viscount Althorp, later Earl Spencer – a former equerry to the Queen, who accompanied Elizabeth and Philip on their mammoth 1953–54 coronation tour of the Commonwealth. Diana's grandmothers were both ladies-in-waiting and close friends of the Queen Mother.

Sarah's family also mixed in royal circles. Her father, Ronald 'Major Ron' Ferguson, was a first-rate polo-playing chum of Philip's, who appointed him to run Guard's Club, the royal polo venue at Smith's Lawn in Windsor Great Park. It was here that the young Sarah and Andrew, born four months apart, got to know each other, watching their fathers play in countless matches.

Like Diana and Camilla Parker Bowles, 'Fergie' (as she was inevitably dubbed by the tabloids) has royal Stuart blood flowing through her veins. All three are descended from that friskiest of monarchs, Charles II, albeit via the wrong side of the sheets. The Merry Monarch's liaison with his French-born mistress, Louise de Kérouaille, produced his seventh and youngest illegitimate son, Charles Lennox, 1st Duke of Richmond, the ancestor of all three royal women.

Diana was not only stunningly beautiful but had a shy, insecure personality with a self-deprecating sense of humour which the world fell in love with. Sarah, initially, delighted everyone with her overenthusiastic zest for life, the mischievous glint in her eye and her clear adoration of the good-looking Prince, still basking in his post-Falklands hero status.

The Queen and Duke welcomed both women into the family in their own, no-nonsense way. Elizabeth, however, struggled to find much in common with the new Princess of Wales and admitted she couldn't understand her personality. Prince Philip, on the other hand, was one member of 'The Firm' who made a concerted effort to help Diana adjust to life as a princess, mindful of his own uncomfortable welcome from courtiers and family friends, both before and after marrying Princess Elizabeth. At one full family gathering, he helped her overcome her insecurity by playfully waltzing her into dinner when she appeared nervous.

Diana was used to the traditional hunting, shooting, fishing lifestyle of the royal family from her own upbringing, but she much preferred life in the city and in the later stages of her marriage would leave family gatherings at Balmoral and Sandringham and head back to London. As a child, she had fallen off a horse and broken her arm and, while she once or twice rode one of the Queen's ponies, she was never happy in the saddle.

Fergie, on the other hand, was an adept rider who accompanied her mother-in-law on horseback, which was an opportunity to bond with her. The two even had the occasional night on the town, once going to see Maggie Smith in the Peter Shaffer comedy *Lettice and Lovage*.

Andrew's parents found the new Duchess of York far more straightforward to deal with than the emotionally complicated Princess of Wales. She also shared the irreverential royal sense of humour and the family's fondness for practical jokes. The older royal couple were delighted when Sarah learned how to fly light aircraft and helicopters. All in all, she was on the same wavelength as her in-laws.

Both Diana's and Sarah's marriages started to show signs of strain after just a few years. By the mid-1980s, Charles had resumed his relationship with Camilla Parker Bowles and Diana had embarked on an affair with former cavalry officer James Hewitt. Although she professed being 'terrified' of her mother-in-law, Diana took to calling on the Queen unannounced to pour out her heart to her. Sometimes, the Queen's schedule meant the Princess had to wait. One footman later reported to the Queen, 'The Princess cried three times in a half hour while waiting to see you.' The Queen replied, 'I had her for half an hour and she cried non-stop.'

Diana and the Queen attend the Queen Mother's 87th birthday lunch. The Princess was in awe of her mother-in-law and the two women failed to come to terms with each other's personalities.
(© Ian Lloyd)

For Fergie, the problem was the separation from her husband, whose naval duties included a six-month tour in the Far East and another lengthy deployment to the North Atlantic. Neither the Queen nor Prince Philip, for whom such duties were second nature, were sympathetic. Philip told Sarah, 'Well the Mountbattens managed, and so can you.'

At the same time, her honeymoon period with the press barely outlasted the Yorks' actual honeymoon cruise around the Azores islands on the Royal Yacht *Britannia*. By the late 1980s, the tabloids moved into overdrive and started to lambast her for everything from weight gain, fashion misses (who can forget the orange wrap, likened to a duvet, that she wore to the film premiere of *White Mischief*), her many holidays and that sheer exuberance everyone had adored back in 1986 but which now seemed graceless. When she waved and called out the first name of a butler before a Windsor Castle dinner, Philip 'looked at me askance and said, "Surely you have outgrown flirting with the staff?"'. The Queen's former private secretary, Lord Charteris, memorably referred to her as 'vulgar, vulgar, vulgar'. (He also dismissed Diana as someone who didn't know how to behave in front of servants.)

Both marriages ended with separation in 1992 with Andrew and Sarah splitting in March and Charles and Diana in December. The Queen tried her best to support both estranged daughters-in-law. After the Yorks split, the monarch and duchess were seen talking intently in a Land Rover at the Royal Windsor Horse Show in full view of dozens of photographers.

Diana acknowledged the support she had received from Charles's parents when she memorably announced her resignation from public duties in her 'Time and Space' speech at a Headway charity lunch at London's Hilton Hotel. She told the rapt audience, 'I would also like to add that this decision has been reached with the full understanding of the Queen and the Duke of Edinburgh, who have always shown me kindness and support.'

That 'kindness and support' evaporated two years later, when Diana made her extraordinary *Panorama* interview (which we now know she was manipulated into giving by reporter Martin Bashir). Besides her comments that 'there were three of us in this marriage, so it was a bit crowded' and 'I'd like to be a queen of people's hearts', she dropped in the real bombshell statement that, in her opinion, Charles wasn't cut out for the 'suffocating' role of king.

Philip found it frustrating that the behaviour of Charles, who had admitted adultery in his own jaw-dropping interview the previous year, and now Diana, was undermining the respect he and the Queen had generated for the monarchy over the previous four decades. The Duke of Edinburgh told his wife there was no alternative to divorce for the Prince and Princess of Wales and the Queen wrote firm letters to both of them instructing them to end their acrimonious marriage.

Charles and Diana divorced on 28 August 1996. The final meeting between the Queen and Diana came the following spring when, on 9 March, they both attended Prince William's confirmation at Windsor, where three generations of the royal family put on a united front for the sake of 14-year-old William, as well as for the monarchy. No one could have predicted that just a matter of months later, the Prince and his brother would lose their mother in a car crash, or that the failure of the Queen and her advisors to respond to the outpouring of grief from a bereft nation would, for a time, seriously damage the monarch's reputation.

Sarah, Duchess of York, was ostracised from the royal family following her divorce. Prince Philip, in particular, felt she had let the side down when topless photographs of her appeared in a tabloid newspaper. He never really warmed to her again. The

Queen, on the other hand, visited her at Christmas when the duchess was forced to spend the festive season at Wood Farm on the Sandringham Estate while her two daughters and ex-husband were with his family in 'the Big House'. Sarah was also invited to stay at Balmoral many times while the Queen was on her annual summer break, though she beat a carefully choreographed exit before the Duke of Edinburgh flew north.

In recent years the wedding of her daughter Eugenie saw Sarah back on centre stage with the royal family and while scandal-hit Prince Andrew has been forced to all but abandon a public life, his former wife has stood by him. For the Queen, that is one very small consolation.

56

COO, WHAT A HOBBY!

Along with whippets and flat caps, they were once synonymous with working-class northern men, but rearing homing pigeons has always been a passion for the Queen and her blue-blooded relations. The first feather load were a gift from King Leopold II of the Belgians, who gave them to the future Edward VII as a gift in 1886. 'Bertie' built a small loft for them near to Sandringham House, Norfolk, where they were joined by more Belgian birds, a few years later.

Edward wasn't as adept at naming royal animals as Elizabeth II has been and so it was pigeon '189' that won the National Flying Club's Grand National from Lerwick to Sandringham in 1899.

Royal pigeon-fancying really took off under Edward's heir, the future George V. In 1895, as Duke of York, he agreed to be a member of the Central Counties Pigeon Flying Club. At the same time, he built a pigeon loft near to his York Cottage residence on the Sandringham Estate. According to one journalist, it was 'a pretty, two storeyed building, capitally fitted up'.

The royal birds have been used as gifts by their compassionate owners. In 1938, George VI, hearing that pigeon owners in Cambridgeshire had lost 900 birds when a railway truck caught fire in a siding, sent four birds as a gift. In 2011, the Queen sent some birds to a young offenders' institution so inmates could learn a new hobby. Five years later, she came to the aid of tearful schoolchildren who had lost their own flock to a local cat. Pupils of Longshaw School in Blackburn, Lancashire, were left heartbroken by the feline felon and when the Queen was informed about it, she agreed they could visit the Royal Loft at Sandringham and receive one of her own birds. Like the others in her ownership, it had a ring on its leg bearing her 'ER' cypher.

Given she's a whizz at modern methods of communication, especially email and text, as well as video conferencing, it's unlikely the Queen uses pigeons to carry personal messages, but her grandparents memorably did on one occasion. Visiting Lincoln in April 1914, they sent a message to their third son, Prince Henry, who was due to return to Sandringham that day for the Easter holiday. If proof were ever needed of their emotional coldness regarding their children, the pigeon message could be used as evidence. 'Hope you arrived safely. Give messages to all our friends at Sandringham – PARENTS.' Meghan Markle would have had a lot to say to the Great War equivalent of Oprah.

Having said that they weren't used for messaging, in January 1953 Elizabeth II did receive a New Year greeting by pigeon flight from the trawler *Cape Spartel* at the mouth of the River Humber en route to the Arctic. 'The trawlermen of Britain send their heartiest loyal good wishes to Your Majesty on this happy coronation year and pray for a long and successful reign – Skipper J.H. Woodell – bound for Bear Island.' We'll never know if alcohol prompted the seamen to tie the messages to three Norfolk-based pigeons on New Year's Eve and point them towards Sandringham, but they did arrive home and were taken round to the Big House by a Sheringham man.

For thirty years, the Sandringham birds were reared and trained by Norfolk men at their own homes. In 1962, Len Rush, a self-employed carpenter and joiner, became Manager of the Royal Lofts from his home in King's Lynn. He was succeeded in 1983 by Alan Pearse, a farm lorry driver, from Weasenham St Peter, near Sandringham. Both men received visits from the Queen, who is patron of the Royal Pigeon Racing Association, eager to see her birds when she was holidaying on the estate each New Year.

In 1992, the Queen appointed retired boxer Carlo Neapolitano as Manager of the Royal Lofts and she also gave him some decent lofts to manage, having a deluxe unit built on the Sandringham Estate at Wolferton, housing around 200 birds. The Queen has been a frequent visitor to the lofts, a mile or two from Sandringham House. 'The Queen is very keen,' the late Mr Napolitano explained. 'Her Majesty is interested in breeding and racing, and often drops round here, sometimes at very short notice.'

She was no doubt touched when her own birds took part in a commemorative fly past to mark the passing of the Duke of Edinburgh. Birds from the royal lofts at Sandringham and Windsor were released at midday on the day of his funeral. The Royal Pigeon Racing Association released ten birds – one for each decade of the Duke's life – from sixty-five cities and towns, as a winged tribute to Prince Philip, who, like the Queen, was a great fan. It's safe to say the old boy would have been chuffed.

57

JAM AND JERUSALEM: THE QUEEN AND THE WI

On a midweek afternoon each January, the Queen can be found sitting around a card table in a village hall pouring tea for three other women of a certain age. She's there as the President of the Sandringham branch of the Women's Institute (WI) and the first meeting of the year is one of the annual fixtures on her calendar. She's following in the footsteps of her mother and grandmother.

Queen Mary founded the branch in 1919 for the local community, mostly the wives and daughters of Sandringham Estate workers. From 1937 to 1953 she shared the presidency with her daughter-in-law, Queen Elizabeth, who had first attended a meeting as far back as 1924. Following the death of George VI in 1952, the present Queen asked her mother to carry on as president until her death, half a century later.

Elizabeth II is now the branch president, having been a member since February 1943 when she accompanied her mother and sister to the WI. They listened to Mrs Sam Peel give a talk called 'Post-war Planning' and looked at the entries in the 'Something new, from something old' competition. As Princess Elizabeth and later as monarch, Elizabeth has paid her subscription fee, starting at a shilling a year.

A more useful financial aid came from her annual raffle prize. Each year, the vice president would write separate letters to Elizabeth and her mother asking if they would care to donate something. They always sent something of quality – a cut-glass decanter, barometer, clock or a set of silver spoons. The lucky winner not only received a gift from Sandringham House but an accompanying card proclaiming, 'given by the Queen'. This helpfully added to the provenance and each year ticket sales went through the roof.

The meetings are usually held at West Newton Village Hall, a two-minute limousine drive from Sandringham House. There was one notable exception in January 1974. Edward Heath's government had rationed electricity following an industrial dispute with coal miners which would eventually bring about the downfall of his ministry. With no power at the village hall, the institute relocated to the nearby Sandringham Club, a bigger venue that would provide more natural light. With an average age of 80, the members had enough trouble putting out chairs and tables without also clearing the front of the club where a healthy supply of empty beer barrels and bottles in crates neatly framed the entrance. The Queen and her mother took one look and roared with laughter. Turning to the photographers, the younger Elizabeth joked, 'I hope you're not taking pictures of us standing by the empties', which, needless to say, they of course were.

The Queen leaving West Newton Village Hall in January 1994 having attended the Sandringham WI meeting. Her Majesty had broken her left wrist having fallen from her horse during the Christmas holidays. (© Ian Lloyd)

In 2018, there was another power cut. The committee contacted the house to inform the Queen's private secretary and he reported that if the meeting was able to go ahead, Her Majesty would still attend. Once again, she took it in good spirit and told the members she couldn't really see them in the dark and that there was less light inside the hall than outside in the car park. King's Lynn police came up trumps by providing urns of hot water so at least the traditional tea could go ahead.

Each of the royal meetings follows a traditional format. Following the national anthem, the Queen will listen to the minutes of the last meeting and sign them off. She will present various prizes to competition winners and there may also be a group photograph if it's an anniversary year. And then the fun starts. The non-royal members usually perform a play, throwing themselves with great gusto into 'Cinderella' or 'Dick Turpin', or something cobbled together by the ladies themselves.

The Queen Mother gives us an inkling of the royal guests' delight in these performances in a wartime letter to her brother-in-law, the Duke of Kent. The institute put on a special patriotic tableaux. 'If only you could see them,' she wrote. 'Dear Mrs Way, as Neptune, glaring furiously through a tangle of grey hair and seaweed, and Miss Burroughs (the Verger's daughter) as Britannia were HEAVEN. The words were spoken by Mrs Fuller's cook, who was draped in the Union Jack, and it was all perfect.'

Then there is a talk given by a visitor. Many of the early ones verged on the esoteric and there is no record of the Queen's reaction to Mrs Waddington's talk on herbs, Mrs Forman's forty minutes on 'Haunted East Anglia', Mrs Thompson on members of her family who had become well-known artists and writers, or Les Kershaw's account of his struggles to become an actor, which ended when he got a bit part in a West End show in 1938. She did react positively to the talk by Mrs Love from Spalding on 'how to make ornamental birds, lamps and jewellery out of shells'. Apparently, on her way out, she admired the latter's Cutty Sark made out of crustaceans, and after a demonstration of 'simple embroidery' by Mrs Fell, she said she'd found the machine embroidery 'most exciting' and surely easier than the hand-done version.

In recent years, the committee has upped its game and invited household names who would be a safe pair of hands in such an intimate setting. Newsreader Robert Dougall was an early offering in 1970. Then there was celebrity gardener Alan Titchmarsh, who spoke before the Queen in 1999 and when they met again a few months later, when she presented him with his MBE, she recalled, 'You've given a lot of ladies a lot of pleasure', which he's often said he'd like on his gravestone.

In 2017, royal historian Lucy Worsley gave a talk on Jane Austen to mark the bicentenary of the author's death. She later commented that she was going to begin her speech by saying that Austen was the first woman to be portrayed on a modern banknote, until she suddenly remembered that Austen was the second woman and the first would be sitting on the front row.

Two years later, the Queen took part in a live game based on the TV quiz show *Pointless* when its presenter Alexander Armstrong visited the Sandringham branch. The ladies were divided into two teams with Her Majesty captaining one, and Vice President Yvonne Brown heading the other. The royal team won three out of five games and Armstrong later said the Queen answered some of the questions herself and had 'some deft, silky Pointless skills'. He also claimed she was a fan of the programme – 'our most distinguished viewer'.

Without a doubt, the most popular speaker is the Queen herself who, every few years, gives a talk on a subject close to her heart, usually the Commonwealth. In 1974, the Queen spoke about her forthcoming visit to the Commonwealth Games in New Zealand and in January 1983, she told the group about her recent visit to Australia, Papua New Guinea and Fiji.

In 2018, her WI address was released by Buckingham Palace. The Queen told her fellow members:

> Of course, every generation faces fresh challenges and opportunities. As we look for new answers in the modern age, I for one prefer the tried and tested recipes, like speaking well of each other and respecting different points of view; coming together to seek out the common ground; and never losing sight of the bigger picture.

Her words were seen as a veiled reference to the Brexit debate which was becoming increasingly toxic. Her timing was significant, because it was just over a week since MPs in the House of Commons had voted 432 to 202 against Theresa May's draft withdrawal agreement. It was regarded as no coincidence that the Queen's words, ostensibly about the WI movement, but relevant to the wider picture of Britain as a whole, were made public.

Towards the end of the meeting the ladies enjoy a tea party. They sit in groups of four around card tables. The Queen presides at hers and pours the tea and hands round the cakes for the other three ladies. There is usually ginger cake – a favourite of the Queen – profiteroles, cheese scones, fruit cakes and meringues.

The teatime chat is an opportunity for her to find out what is happening in the local community, all the births, marriages and deaths, who is having a golden wedding, another grandchild, a hip replacement or all three. The Queen tells them what is happening in her own family. For instance, in January 1994, she had arrived wearing a plaster cast on her left arm having fractured a bone in her wrist when she fell from her horse over the Christmas holiday. She told one member, 'I threw myself over the horse's neck to prevent it getting up' while they waited for help. The ladies expressed concern that a young man had fired blanks from a starting pistol at Prince Charles in Australia and the Queen told them, 'Yes, he rang me later to tell me all about it and to say he's alright.'

Younger members of the family have also followed in the Queen's WI footsteps. Camilla is a member of Tetbury WI, Sophie Wessex is a member of Bagshot WI and Princess Anne is an associate member. Catherine, Duchess of Cambridge, has been invited to join the Anmer branch, just down the road from Sandringham.

58

THE ROYAL STAMP OF APPROVAL

Deep in the vaults of St James's Palace lies the most valuable stamp collection in existence. Estimated to be worth over £100 million, it's the private property of Elizabeth II and makes up a sizeable chunk of her personal wealth. Having said that, it's considered inalienable, and along with much of her jewel and art collections is part of the Royal Collection.

The stamp collection dates back to 1864 when Queen Victoria's second son, 20-year-old Prince Alfred, Duke of Edinburgh, began it as a hobby. He sold it to his older brother, the future Edward VII, though it really came into its own under Edward's son, the future George V.

George instructed his philatelist John Tilleard, 'Remember, I wish to have the best collection and not one of the best collections.' He is thought to have acquired the stamp collection of the Tsarevich Alexei of Russia, who was murdered with his family in 1918. It was bought from a soldier who had smuggled it out of the country in an empty tomato tin.

He made his most famous purchase in 1905, when he was Prince of Wales, paying the staggering sum of £1,450 for a Mauritian two-pence blue, said to be the finest of the twenty-seven blues in existence. This led to a memorable exchange between the King and one of his courtiers who, knowing of George's interest, said he had heard 'that some damned fool had paid as much as £1,400 for one stamp'. 'Yes', replied George. 'I was that damned fool!'

When the Queen inherited the collection, any new acquisitions were mounted in green leather volumes known as the 'Green Collection'. Stamps bought or given during the reign of her father form the 'Blue Collection', while the bulk of the Royal Stamp Collection are in the 328 volumes in the 'Red Collection' from the reign of George V.

Elizabeth was keen to share her collection. In October 1965, she held an exhibition of her key stamps in the recently opened Queen's Gallery. This slightly backfired in January 1966 when a thief stole three penny blacks that were joined together and were able to be slipped out from the bottom of the glass. Red-faced Buckingham Palace curators later claimed they were not a major loss and only worth £100.

It was a break-in of a more sensational type that brought the stamp collection to international prominence. When, in 1982, Michael Fagan broke into Buckingham Palace and managed to find his way to the Queen's bedroom, he first of all climbed through an unlocked window into the room where the collection is kept. He not only tripped off an alarm but failed to get any further as the interior doors were locked so he had to climb back out.

In 2001, she ordered a 'programme of enhancement' under the new Keeper of the Stamp Collection, Charles Goodwyn. He decided to sell off duplicate sets in order to finance the purchase, at £250,000, of a first-day cover of ten penny black stamps dated 6 May 1840, the date Britain introduced the Penny Post.

59

HANDBAGS AT DAWN: THE QUEEN AND MRS THATCHER

The relationship between the Queen and her eighth prime minister has been a continual source of fascination to journalists, biographers and, latterly, TV producers. Born six months apart, they both began public life in the early post-war years when women were largely regarded as submissive and inferior beings in a male-dominated world. Both had young children and supportive husbands who were used to playing second fiddle to their wives, and both had immaculately coiffed hair, pearls, handbags and well-tailored suits.

When it came to dealings with the Queen, Thatcher was a scrupulously deferential minister, who, long after she left office, kept on display in her bedroom a photograph of herself posing with the Queen and Queen Mother. 'Her curtsey almost reached Australia,' recalled her policy advisor, Lord Charles Powell. She did try to bond with the monarch – once sending her a pair of rubber gloves for Christmas upon seeing her wash the dishes after a Balmoral picnic without using any.

The Queen could also be warm to the PM. Hearing Mrs T was to visit Saudi Arabia, which she had visited herself, and where visiting women were expected to wear head coverings and floor-length dresses, she briefed her on the etiquette.

Nevertheless, as the Queen's biographer Ben Pimlott noted, between the two women, 'there was a rigidity that never softened'. This 'rigidity' is evident in an oft-quoted anecdote about Mrs Thatcher turning up at an event wearing a similar outfit to the Queen's. The ever-practical premier contacted the Palace to ask if there was any way she could find out the royal colour choice ahead of an event. The Palace replied, 'Do not worry. The Queen does not notice what other people are wearing.' Nelson Mandela, hearing about it thousands of miles away in South Africa, said later, 'I thought that was beautiful.'

Although Thatcher was fiercely patriotic and wanted what she believed was best for Britain, hers was the business of bringing about change, whereas the Queen, by the very nature of her role, was conservative with a small 'c' and keen to maintain the traditions of the past. Elizabeth has always been a country-woman at heart and once said, regarding the time spent reading official documents each day, 'I do rather begrudge some of the hours that I have to do instead of being outdoors.' To Mrs T, the thought of relaxing – indoors or out – was totally anathema.

Another character difference was humour. The Queen has a dry wit, while Thatcher had next to none, as her chauffeur Denis Oliver recalled at the time of her death. 'I don't think she knew what humour was. You'd try telling her a joke, usually a political one, but you'd get these questions at the end – "But why did he ...?" – and it would kill the whole thing.'

A royal issue was part of the agenda on Mrs Thatcher's debut as Tory leader in the House of Commons in February 1975. The Civil List Act of 1972 allowed the Treasury to review the payments made to finance the monarchy from the public purse every ten years. Three years on, and with the expenditure of the royal household exceeding the amount voted by Parliament, the Palace had to go cap-in-hand to the government seeking an increase. Prime Minister Harold Wilson raised the issue in the Commons and Thatcher's opposition party backed the Civil List (Increase of Financial Provisions) Order.

Wilson, who defined his working relationship with the Queen as 'relaxed intimacy', was delighted when the monarch confided in him that Thatcher had felt faint during a visit to Buckingham

Palace. 'She doesn't like her,' the PM confided to Joe Haines, his press secretary. Over the years, the Tory leader fainted or felt dizzy several times in the Queen's presence, suggesting she was overwhelmed by her visits. During one reception, she was forced to ask for a chair to sit on, and the Queen, whose own health was consistently robust, joked to Archbishop Robert Runcie, 'She's keeled over again!'

As prime minister, Thatcher found her weekly audiences with the Queen an ordeal. Journalist Anthony Sampson commented, 'The weekly meetings ... are dreaded by at least one of them.' Mrs T would arrive far too early for each appointment, although the Queen would always make her wait until the allotted time. One former private secretary recalled that, rather than having a relaxed, informal discussion with the monarch, the PM would have a written agenda in her handbag which she would go through without giving the Queen the opportunity to answer. Thatcher's official biographer, Charles Moore, claimed the list 'was usually an anodyne recitation of current business' and 'the audiences were rarely productive because Mrs Thatcher was nervous'. Certainly, there is no account of her staying on afterwards for drinks as Harold Wilson was occasionally asked to do.

Three months into Thatcher's first administration, the issue of the Commonwealth showed that the two women were certainly not singing from the same hymn sheet. As head of the Commonwealth, the Queen has dozens of prime ministers reporting to her in this loose association of a billion people. One of her lasting legacies is how she has overseen its transference from a small close-knit group of former colonies to the vast international organisation it is today.

In August 1979, the Commonwealth Heads of Government Meeting (CHOGM) was due to meet in Lusaka, Zambia. The main topic on the agenda was the thorny problem of Rhodesia. Fourteen years after its unilateral declaration of independence from Britain, Rhodesia was experiencing an ongoing civil war between Ian Smith's white-minority-led government and two armed groups. There was a feeling among Asian and African Commonwealth countries that Britain was not doing enough to end the rebellion.

For Margaret Thatcher, three months into her premiership and keen to sort out the industrial chaos she had inherited from the Labour Party's handling of the Winter of Discontent, it was an unnecessary distraction. She was reluctant to attend and also made it clear she might block the Queen's attendance on the spurious grounds of security.

In the end, the Queen did attend and so did Thatcher. Sonny Ramphal, Commonwealth secretary general at the time, claimed Elizabeth 'brought to Lusaka a healing touch of rather special significance'. At a reception for the various representatives, she was overheard telling three African leaders, 'I've known you all longer than you've known each other, and isn't it better to talk about it?'

In brief, the mood of the conference became more positive, Mrs Thatcher became involved and the discussions in Lusaka led to the Lancaster House Meeting in London, which proposed a new constitution for Rhodesia – henceforth to be known as Zimbabwe – which led to the end of that country's civil war.

Relations between monarch and prime minister reached their lowest point in the summer of 1986. On 20 June, the *Sunday Times* claimed the Queen felt Thatcher's approach to the domestic issues such as the Miner's Strike was 'uncaring, confrontational and socially divisive' and as head of the Commonwealth, she was at odds with Thatcher's reluctance to impose sanctions against South Africa's white-led government.

The source of the story was the Queen's press secretary, Michael Shea, whose indiscretion put the Queen in an awkward situation. After consulting with her private secretary, Elizabeth rang Mrs Thatcher to express her dismay at the press coverage and, according to one former aide, the two women commiserated with each other.

It was noted that at her next audience, two days after the story broke, the prime minister stayed for two hours instead of her customary one. When Elizabeth's former private secretary, John Colville, met with the Queen later in the year, he asked her if the *Sunday Times* story was true and she replied, 'Not at all, absolutely wrong.' When he asked her if she got along with the PM, she was at first very put out – 'you do ask the most impertinent questions' – but later conceded, 'I get on with her alright but like all prime ministers she won't listen.'

One place the two women didn't get on alright in was Balmoral. It is a long-established tradition that the prime minister of the day spends a weekend on the royal estate during the summer months. For Mrs Thatcher, the annual stay was, according to one aide, 'purgatory'. She would always set off far too early and end up having to pull up her chauffeur-driven limo in the middle of the Highlands, where mystified locals stared at the unmistakeable figure of the PM pacing up and down the road in her high heels.

The late Woodrow Wyatt, for many years chairman of the state betting organisation, the Tote, and a close friend of the Queen Mother's, recorded in his journal a dinner conversation with the Queen's cousin, Lady Mary Colman. She apparently told him that she had been among the house party staying at Balmoral when Thatcher came for the annual stay and everyone had been beastly to her. Some asked her silly questions about what she was going to do about unemployment and the PM gave her stock answers. At one point, the conversation turned to the topic of the Falklands and the Queen said sharply, 'I don't agree with you at all', which made Mrs Thatcher appear very uncomfortable and flushed.

Nevertheless, it appears the Queen was genuinely moved when Thatcher was forced to resign. She honoured her with membership of the Order of Merit, an award founded by Edward VII for those who have 'rendered exceptionally meritorious service in Our Crown Services'. Limited to twenty-four members, it is given at the monarch's discretion. In 1992, Mrs Thatcher was given a life peerage and, three years later, made a Lady of the Garter, honouring Britain's first female prime minister, who had won three consecutive elections and was the longest-serving head of government during Elizabeth's reign.

60

THE ROYAL FAMILY ON THE QUEEN

Prince Philip

The main lesson that we have learned is that tolerance is the one essential ingredient of any happy marriage. It may not be quite so important when things are going well, but it is absolutely vital when things get difficult — you can take it from me that the Queen has the quality of tolerance in abundance.

Prince Charles

There is no doubt that the world in which my mother grew up, indeed in which she became Queen, has changed beyond recognition. She has shown remarkable fortitude remaining a figure of reassuring calm and dependability, an example for so many, of service, duty and devotion.

Princess Anne

Her greatest strength as a mother was her consistency and the way we were all treated the same. That's not always easy to achieve, especially if, like her, you're not always around as much as you would like.

Prince Andrew

She has a special touch, and that touch can change a person's life. We've been privileged to be a part of the family and to see it on a more regular basis than other people. It is not something that is put on, it is not something that is acted. That is it, that is the way she is.

Prince Edward

The Queen has provided a huge stability and wealth of experience for those who want to tap into it and she is simply the greatest mother in the world.

Prince William

She is an incredible role model. I would like to take all her experiences, all of her knowledge and put it in a small box and constantly refer to it. She's been one of the greats.

Sophie, Countess of Wessex, Princess Beatrice, Prince Andrew, Princess Eugenie, Queen Elizabeth II, Prince Philip, Duke of Edinburgh, Prince Harry, Princess Anne and Prince Charles, Prince of Wales, on the balcony of Buckingham Palace. (© Anwar Hussein/Alamy)

She's led the way and long may that continue. She is also an extremely caring grandmother to me.

Prince Harry

She is a very normal grandmother and takes a huge interest in her children as well as her grandchildren. But it is only in the last ten years that I've really learned to understand the huge deal that she is around the world and especially in the UK.

Princess Beatrice

She is the most amazing woman anyone could ever meet. So wise, so kind, and I love her to bits.

Princess Eugenie

She just adores having all of us around.

Prince George (According to the Duchess of Cambridge)

George calls her 'Gan-Gan'. She always leaves a little gift or something in their room when we go and stay and that just shows her love for her family.

61

TWO AWKWARD STATE VISITS

Besides Idi Amin, mentioned in Chapter 48, during her seven-decade rule, Elizabeth II has met more than her fair share of despotic, tyrannical or plain barmy heads of state.

Nicolae Ceaușescu

Her most difficult incoming state visit was that of Romanian dictator, Nicolae Ceaușescu, and his hatchet-faced wife, Elena. Prime Minister James Callaghan hoped the visit would be a success for economic reasons. Ceaușescu agreed to sign a £200 million trade deal for British Aerospace to build eighty-two BAC 1-11 aircraft on Romanian soil as well as to pay a further £100 million for Rolls-Royce engines to put in them.

The Queen was under no illusions about her soon-to-be guest. The French President Valéry Giscard d'Estaing had telephoned to tell her that during their recent state visit to France the Ceaușescus had trashed their guest suite. They had made off with vases, lamps, ashtrays, bathroom fittings and anything else not secured. To top it off, their security team had bashed holes into the walls looking for bugging devices. The Queen ordered her household to make sure the contents of the Belgian Suite at Buckingham Palace, where VIPs usually stayed, should be pared back to the bare minimum.

She had also read Foreign Office telegrams about the Romanian leader's abuse of power. 'They've blood on their hands!' she warned her staff.

Another problem ahead of the visit was Elena Ceaușescu's desire to be awarded an honorary degree. She rather fancied herself as an academic in the field of polymer chemistry and wanted to add a citation from a top British university to her very dubious CV. The Foreign Office worked through a list of academic institutions, from Oxbridge downwards, with no take-up whatsoever. Eventually, the Polytechnic of Central London agreed to bestow one and the word from Bucharest was that their First Lady was delighted.

The Ceaușescus were met at London's Victoria Station by the Queen and Prince Philip with Charles and Anne, and received the usual carriage procession through the capital. At Buckingham Palace there was an exchange of gifts. The Queen gave Nicolae the hunting rifle he had requested, adding his name and her 'E II R' cypher to the leather case, while Elena was given a gold brooch. The Queen received two handmade rugs in return.

The Romanian duo were paranoid about being bugged and their luggage arrived sealed so that the palace staff were not able to unpack it as they normally did for guests. Their security staff checked for recording devices behind light fittings and gold panelling but weren't as heavy handed as they had been in Paris.

Fear of being overheard meant Ceaușescu and his team pre-ferred discussing business affairs outside in the open air. This led to a near miss with the Queen, who was giving her corgis their daily constitutional around the garden when she saw the Romanian contingent bearing down on her. Quick as a flash, she and her dogs hid in the undergrowth until her muttering guests had passed by.

The state visit of a Communist head of state had clearly been one to remember. After Ceaușescu's fall, he was stripped of his KCB (Knight Grand Cross of the Order of the Bath), that had been personally bestowed by the Queen. Only eight of the BAC jets were ever produced and no one seems to know what hap-pened to the two Romanian rugs. It's never been revealed what the Queen felt on hearing of the abhorrent couple's eventual fate at the hands of a firing squad, but she has been known to refer to Ceaușescu as 'that frightful little man'.

Hassan II

Two years after the Romanian state visit, Elizabeth II trav-elled to Morocco as guest of another paranoid autocrat, King Hassan II. Princess Margaret, who had made an official visit to Morocco in 1976, reportedly warned her sister, 'Going to Morocco is rather like being kidnapped, you never know where you are going or when.'

The visit is today recalled for Hassan's total disregard for timing. The Queen is punctual to the dot and was, according to one of her household, 'absolutely livid' when the king wanted to cancel three events on the first day, including a 'Welcome to Morocco' lunch, and was still undecided about whether to hold the state banquet. It did go ahead, but when the Queen and her entourage arrived at the palatial venue there was no sign of life, and she was obliged to sit and wait in all her finery in her limousine. The Duke of Edinburgh's private secretary managed to find a dry Martini, which he handed to the Queen through the car window.

On the second day, Hassan kept the Queen waiting outside in the heat for several hours while he kept disappearing into an air-conditioned caravan where, his spokesman said, he was supervising the lunch arrangements. After much toe-tapping and looking thoroughly disgruntled, the Queen finally received her lunch and, more to her taste, a gift of four Arab stallions.

Part of the reason for Hassan's capricious nature and his inability to adhere to timetables was his paranoia about security. He had survived two assassination attempts. During one of them, nine years before Elizabeth's visit, nearly 100 people had been killed during an army coup which was quelled by loyalist troops.

Hassan wanted to change the time of the return banquet, hosted by the Queen on the Royal Yacht *Britannia*. Unsure what he should reply to the Moroccan court, Foreign Secretary Douglas Hurd consulted the Queen, who refused point-blank to postpone it. 'Of course I can't change it,' she retorted sharply. 'People have been invited for such and such an hour and there's no way of reaching them all and saying it's an hour late.' She did however have a perfect compromise. 'Please tell the chamberlain that I will quite understand if His Majesty is delayed.' According to Hurd, Hassan arrived in a terrible temper, but he was totally courteous to the Queen, 'I think he was rather frightened of her.'

He was certainly not frightened of the foreign secretary and hissed to him in French that he was 'not being treated like a gentleman' and that the next day's meeting with a trade delegation was off. Again, Hurd consulted the royal couple and Prince Philip advised, 'do absolutely nothing.' The next day, it was all smiles. The Queen and Hassan exchanged gifts and pleasantries, the delegation got to meet the King and a relieved

Elizabeth knighted her worn-out Ambassador to Morocco on the deck of *Britannia*.

62

DEATH OF A PRINCESS

On 31 August 1997, the Queen, like nearly everybody else, was shocked to the core when Princess Diana was killed in a car crash in Paris.

The Queen's first thoughts were for their grandsons, William and Harry, who were also staying at the castle. Their grandparents counselled Charles to let them sleep on and to take the radios out of their room and the TV out of what was still known as the nursery. The Queen and Duke thought the best thing for their grandsons was to carry on with the normal activities of the day, hoping they would find some comfort in the familiar routines of life on the estate while suffering the reeling shock of what had happened to them.

'The boys were very calm,' recalled one who was present. 'They simply busied themselves helping Prince Philip get the food for the usual barbecue picnic. They ate a very good supper.' Had the British public been made aware of this, there might have been less criticism of the Queen's decision to remain with her grandsons at Balmoral in the aftermath of their mother's death.

Those close to the Queen have (and had) no doubt that her decision to stay with William and Harry, rather than to hotfoot it to London to console sobbing members of the public, who, for the most part, had never known the Princess, was definitely the right one.

For Margaret Rhodes, it was an obvious choice:

The Queen's priority was for her two grandsons. Of course she wanted to be close to them and to make sure they were alright. I mean what else was she to do? I think all the criticism hurt her terribly. Balmoral was the ideal place for them all to be as a family. It's private and secluded and peaceful, and I know William and Harry adore the Queen and Prince Philip, and would have wanted to have been with them.

Criticism grew during the week, fanned by negative newspaper headlines. 'The media were circling, looking to blame someone other than themselves,' recalled one of the Queen's advisors.

By Thursday, the negative press coverage reached a crescendo, with headlines screaming, 'SHOW US YOU CARE!', 'WHERE IS OUR QUEEN?', 'SPEAK TO US MA'AM.'

Plans for the Queen and Duke to travel to London on the royal train on Saturday morning were abandoned. Urgent damage limitation meant they needed to fly down on Friday afternoon and be seen to be reacting to the distraught crowds in the capital. Being forced to yield to pressure was, in Philip's mind, the Queen's greatest public humiliation.

By coincidence, I interviewed Mrs Rhodes at her home in Windsor Great Park shortly after Diana's death to talk about the Queen and Philip's forthcoming golden wedding anniversary. Before discussing the latter, Mrs Rhodes unexpectedly went off-piste, 'Look, what on earth's happening? Whatever is going on in London? I've never seen anything like it in my life. Why are people behaving like this?' She was due to drive up to Balmoral in September to join the Queen and Duke, and it was clear just how baffled those close to the couple were about the near hysterical mood of the country and how much they wanted to try and offer some shred of comfort to the royal couple.

Returning to London, Philip was by the Queen's side during the tense walkabout outside Buckingham Palace, where there was an almost tangible sigh of relief from courtiers when the brooding crowd treated the couple with respect rather than abuse. Neither the Queen nor the Duke like to parade their emotions in public, and there was a moment of exasperation from the Prince when a woman in the crowd urged the monarch 'to take care of the boys, Ma'am!'

'That's what we've been doing,' Philip interjected, repeating, 'That's what we've been doing!'

Inside Buckingham Palace, press officer Mary Francis noted the Queen and Philip 'spent a long time talking about what the mood was, and what was on people's minds, wanting to understand but not quite being able to be just out there and mingle and hear as private individuals'.

The monarch's electrifying speech, broadcast live from Buckingham Palace and deliberately filmed through an open window at the front to show the grieving people outside, was one of the most significant of her reign. Had she failed to speak for the nation or to convey her admiration for Diana, who knows what might have happened. As it was, she spoke genuinely and with sincerity on the eve of the funeral to diffuse much of the tension that had been palpable over the previous days.

63

HER GODCHILDREN

The Queen has thirty godchildren. The first four were born in 1945, when Princess Elizabeth was only 19: Guy Nevill was the son of Lady Camilla Nevill, a childhood friend of Elizabeth's and a member of the 1st Buckingham Palace Company of Guides; Alexander, Crown Prince of Yugoslavia, was the son of the exiled King Peter II; Charles Strachey, 4th Baron O'Hagan, was the son of the Princess's first lady-in-waiting, Lady Mary Strachey; and Julian Hardinge, 4th Baron Hardinge of Penshurst, was the grandson of the Queen Mother's life-long friend, Helen Gascoyne-Cecil, who married Alexander Hardinge, private secretary to George VI.

The Queen is godmother to three paternal relations: David, 8th Earl of Harewood, the son of her cousin, George Lascelles; Princess Margaret's son, David, 2nd Earl of Snowdon; and Princess Alexandra's son, James Ogilvy.

From her mother's side of the family, she is godmother to Victoria Rhodes, daughter of Margaret Rhodes, and to Rosemary Elphinstone, whose father Andrew was Mrs Rhodes's older brother. Finally, Fergus Leveson-Gower, Earl Granville, is the son of the Queen's cousin, the late James, 5th Earl Granville.

She is also godmother to three of Philip's relations: Princess Friederike of Hanover, daughter of his sister, Sophie; Michael-John Knatchbull, second son of his cousin, Patricia Knatchbull, who was the elder daughter of Earl Mountbatten of Burma; and to Edwina Hicks, elder daughter of Patricia's sister, Lady Pamela Hicks.

Two of the godchildren have links with the late Princess of Wales: her brother, Charles, Earl Spencer and her second cousin, Lavinia King.

Her youngest godchild is Princess Theodora of Greece, born in 1983, daughter of the exiled King Constantine II and Queen Anne-Marie.

64

HOW THE QUEEN
WAS HOAXED

In 1995, the Queen was sensationally hoaxed when the impressionist Pierre Brassard rang Buckingham Palace, pretending to be Jean Chretien, the Prime Minister of Canada, and managed to have a seventeen-minute conversation with her. Brassard was, at the time, one of the presenters of *Le Bleu Poudre*, a satirical programme broadcast by CKOI FM in Montreal. He taped the conversation at 5 p.m. London time on Thursday, 26 October and broadcast it several hours later.

The hoaxer managed to elicit a promise from the Queen that she would consider broadcasting a message ahead of Quebec's referendum on whether the province should break away from Canada. The timing was perfect for the ruse, because the referendum was due to be held on 30 October and Chretien was fighting to keep the country unified. He could conceivably have contacted the Queen, Canada's head of state, to see if she might agree to deliver such a television address.

The Queen's pro-unity stance was no secret since, in a 1992 speech marking the 125th anniversary of the Confederation of Canada, she made a plea for it to remain one country.

Brassard/Chretien began the conversation, 'Your Majesty, I am really stressed out these days.'

'I'm sure you are,' replied Elizabeth.

'We deeply believe,' Brassard said, 'that should Your Majesty have the kindness to make a public intervention, we think that your word could give back to the citizens of Quebec the pride of being members of a united country.'

'The situation is very critical,' he told her. 'Our latest polls show the separatists are going to win the referendum for independence.'

The Queen replied, 'Well, it sounds like the referendum might be going the wrong way.'

We could hear the Queen discussing it with an advisor, whom she called 'Robert' (presumably her private secretary, Robert Fellowes). She then asked Brassard, 'Do you think you could give me a text of what you would like me to say? ... I will probably be able to do something for you.'

Brassard said he would send a statement to the queen by fax.

She replied, saying, 'I will probably be able to do something for you.'

And so it went on. At one point, the Queen asked, 'It would have to be *moitié-moitié*, wouldn't it? It would have to be half-English, half-French.'

'OK,' Brassard said. 'Half and half.'

The conversation then switched to French after Brassard told the Queen, 'Your Majesty, I am very nervous. It is possible to talk in French?'

'*Allez*,' she said. 'Go on.'

'I am more at ease in French, Your Majesty,' Brassard said.

From that point, the conversation switched from French to English and back to French, and started to get ridiculous when he asked Elizabeth about her plans for Halloween. 'You are not going so far as to wear a costume?'

'Oh no,' she said, laughing, 'that's for the children.'

Brassard told her, 'You just have to wear a nice hat on your head and you have a costume', which made her laugh.

Afterwards, Brassard did send his fax to the Queen which, rather than a transcript for her proposed speech, instead told her, 'Sorry, Your Majesty. We are a radio station, and we will be broadcasting our conversation with you.'

The Palace didn't quite see it as a joke and told journalists, 'We think it's annoying. We think it's irritating. We think it's a waste of the Queen's time,' although they did concede 'Mr Brassard said he never intended to make the person of the Queen look ridiculous'.

In a sense, the Palace was partly to blame since, Brassard told the author, they rang the number the hoaxers left to confirm Chretien wanted to talk to the Queen. However, it was actually one of the telephone numbers of the studio and the team had to man it night and day in the off chance the Queen's advisors rang.

Not every official was put out by the prank. Royce Frith, the Canadian High Commissioner in London, said, 'I thought the Queen was terrific. I don't think it embarrasses the relationship between the two countries or between the Queen and her subjects, particularly considering how well she did.'

Indeed, the Queen came out of it rather well. As Pierre Brassard said, 'That kind of conversation is a good thing because we see the human side of the person. She is a person like you and me.' He added, 'She has a great sense of humour and laughed a lot.'

The radio station claimed the hoax had boosted the Queen's popularity in Canada, 'We have been deluged with listeners. Everyone is talking about how approachable she is.' It gave the world a glimpse of how the Queen operates with her ministers, how willing she is to help with political situations if need be, how she run things past her private secretary and also how well she speaks French.

The Queen saw the funny side. At her next meeting with the actual Jean Chretien, she joked, 'I didn't think you sounded quite like yourself. But I thought, given all the duress you were under, you might have been drunk!'

65

ELIZABETH AND THE OTHER WINDSORS

According to Marion Crawford, the future Edward VIII, known as 'David' to his family, was Princess Elizabeth's favourite uncle. Press photos from the period show him sharing a carriage with Elizabeth on the way to morning worship at Crathie Kirk on the Balmoral Estate and posing for photos in the garden at Birkhall with his arms on Princess Margaret's shoulders. Crawfie tells us that 'handsome golden-haired Uncle David', then Prince of Wales, would often drop in for romps with his two small nieces.

Such a romp made front-page news in July 2015 when stills from a family video showed Elizabeth imitating a Nazi salute with her mother, egged on by her uncle. David, like Elizabeth's father Bertie, derived as much pleasure from these family larks as the girls did. It was a marked contrast to their own fraught childhood with the authoritarian George V and his emotionally constrained consort. It was little wonder, then, that in his abdication address to the nation, David mentioned the 'matchless blessing, enjoyed' by his brother of 'a happy home with his wife and children'.

While Queen Mary gave her granddaughters birthday gifts of 'improving' literature such as Jane Austen or Rudyard Kipling, David bought them well-received presents of A.A. Milne's *Winnie the Pooh* and *When We Were Very Young*. His god-daughter Princess Margaret was devoted to her glamorous uncle, but another god-child, Patricia Mountbatten, told the author 'he wasn't a particularly good god-father. He never remembered my birthday or sent me presents'.

The arrival of the divorced American socialite Wallis Simpson on the scene inevitably affected Edward's relationship with his York nieces. Crawfie recalled the 'rumours and whispers' about the scandalous liaison. As his obsessive infatuation grew and grew, 'there were fewer occasions when he dropped in for a romp with his nieces'.

Isolated in the schoolroom at No. 145 Piccadilly, the governess and her charges were aware that something wasn't right: 'It was impossible not to notice the change in Uncle David. He had been so youthful and gay. Now he looked distraught and seemed not to be listening to what was said to him. He made plans with the children and then forgot them.'

Halfway through Edward VIII's 326-day reign, the princesses had their only childhood meeting with Wallis Simpson when David brought her over to the Royal Lodge to show off his new American station wagon to the Yorks in the summer of 1936. In her memoirs, written twenty years later, Wallis recalled having tea in the Yorks' drawing room. 'The two little princesses joined us. Princess Elizabeth ... was then ten and Princess Margaret Rose was nearly six. They were both so blonde, so beautifully mannered, so brightly scrubbed, that they might have stepped straight from the pages of a picture book.'

During the fifteen years of her father's reign, Princess Elizabeth never saw her uncle and she grew up avoiding the mention of his name. Unsurprisingly, given this ostracism, the Windsors were omitted from the guest list for Elizabeth and Philip's wedding in 1947.

The Duke's exclusion was also apparent when George VI died unexpectedly in his sleep on 6 February 1952. David was the only senior member of the family not to be told the news by the Palace. He and the Duchess were staying at the Waldorf Astoria at the time and the news was broken by reporters eager to find out his reaction.

Before leaving New York on the *Queen Mary* to attend his brother's funeral, the Duke read a statement to reporters, telling the world, 'Our hearts go out to the widowed Queen Mother and her two daughters in their grief. The eldest, Elizabeth, has by God's will been called upon to succeed her father. His well-known attributes will I am sure descend to the young princess.' With the death of her father, Uncle David was, of course, the only member of the family who had any idea of the challenge facing the young Elizabeth. 'I was 41 when I succeeded my family and many considered that young. But Queen Elizabeth is only 25 – how young to assume the responsibilities of a great throne in these precarious times.' In private, the Windsors were far less respectful, referring to the new Queen as 'Shirley Temple', suggesting Elizabeth had a squeaky clean, curly-haired image.

Despite the tragic family circumstances, the Duke told his wife he was pursuing the question of his allowance and other issues 'relentlessly but tactfully'. He had lunch with Elizabeth and Philip at Clarence House, a reunion that at least made it into the Court Circular. According to Edward VIII's official biography, the former king was 'not left with the feeling that his niece, the new Queen, would be likely to start her reign by defying what she knew to be the deeply felt convictions of her grandmother and mother'.

This intransigence became apparent that autumn when it became clear the Windsors wouldn't be invited to the new Queen's coronation, scheduled for the following June. Once again, the Duke had harboured the naïve hope that Wallis would be included in a major royal event, but the Palace feared such a move would overshadow the occasion.

On a positive note, in a letter to his cousin, Princess Arthur of Connaught, following the coronation, he wrote that he had found it very moving and 'we thought Lilibet conducted herself superbly throughout the long and trying ceremony'.

If he was hoping for a thawing of relations during the new reign, he was initially disappointed. The Queen appointed John Wheeler-Bennett to write an official life of her father, but the author was prevented by the Palace from sending the sections relating to the Duke for his comment and approval. Incensed, he wrote to his solicitor, 'Unless my niece has the common courtesy to give me an opportunity to read then no mention of me whatever shall appear therein'. According to his official biographer, it was 'the only time he voiced any criticism of the Queen'. In the event, she relented, and David was allowed to check through the relevant chapters and pointed out several inaccuracies, which were corrected.

The Palace was more co-operative when the Duke began work on his second book, *A Family Album*. King George VI had refused his brother access to the Royal Archives to research *A King's Story* but for this latest book the ghost writer, Lord Kinross, was allowed access to family papers at Windsor.

At the same time, in the summer of 1959, the Duke came over to tour the castle while the Queen was at Balmoral. He discovered the dust-sheeted room from where he made his abdication broadcast in 1936. He also visited Frogmore House, where he was reunited with the caretaker, Bertha, who had been looking after his uniforms there since he left for France.

Clearly touched by the poignant tour, the Duke wrote to ask the Queen if he and Wallis could be buried in the Royal Burial Ground at Frogmore. In December 1960, Lord Tryon, Keeper of the Privy Purse, wrote to the Windsors informing them the Queen agreed to the proposal.

It was the Duke's declining health in the mid-1960s that led to a thawing of the frosty relations between the two sides. In December, he underwent open-heart surgery in Texas and the Queen sent a bouquet of flowers. The following February, the Duke was admitted to the London Clinic for an operation to correct a detached retina in his left eye.

This time, the Queen sent wine and foie gras, but perhaps feeling sorry for her uncle after he underwent two more minor procedures on the same eye, she decided to visit in person. It would be the first time she had seen her uncle since Queen Mary's funeral and, more significantly, her first meeting with the Duchess since the Royal Lodge tea party of 1936. The Queen visited on the evening of Monday, 15 March, arriving shortly before 6.30 p.m. and staying, according to journalists outside who timed the visit, for thirty-four minutes.

A less formal meeting between the two was captured by paparazzo Ray Bellisario on 30 March. Perched at a vantage point in a Park Lane hotel, Bellisario snatched a photo of the Queen, wearing a headscarf, and the Duke of Windsor walking together in the grounds of Buckingham Palace.

Two years later, the Duke finally got his wish when Wallis was included in a public royal meeting when the Queen unveiled a plaque to mark the 100th anniversary of Queen Mary's birth. The ceremony lasted a mere ten minutes, but it was enough time for cameras to capture the Queen shaking hands with her uncle and aunt and the Queen Mother kissing her brother-in-law.

While the Duke never made much headway in advancing his and Wallis's public association with the royal family, he received a series of concessions from the Queen on personal issues. She agreed to her uncle's request that the Duchess should receive half his allowance following his death, and the £5,000 grant was duly made from 1972–86.

In a letter to David, she also mentioned the investiture of the Prince of Wales at Carnarvon Castle the following year. 'I have hesitated to enquire whether you would like an invitation considering the circumstances,' began Her Majesty cautiously, 'but if you would reply to this indirect form of invitation in whatever way you feel, I shall quite understand.' While it was more cordial than the blunt coronation invitation of 1952, it was hardly killing the fatted calf. David took the hint and replied, 'As I do not believe that the presence of his aged great uncle would add much to the colourful proceedings centred upon Charles, I do not feel that I should accept. At the same time, I do appreciate your nice thought.'

There was a poignant, final meeting between uncle and niece in May 1972, during the Queen's state visit to France. On the day of the visit, the Duke, smart to the last, was dressed in a blue jacket and trousers, which helped to disguise his clear weight loss as well as the intravenous drip under his shirt. Due to his incapacitation, it was left to the Duchess to greet the royal party. She sat beneath her portrait in the drawing room and poured tea for the Queen, Prince Philip and Prince Charles. She was so nervous her own teacup clattered in its saucer. Afterwards, she escorted the Queen upstairs to the Duke's bedroom where, to the alarm of his doctor, he unexpectedly rose to greet his niece, gave a courtly neck bow and said, 'My dear', before kissing her on both cheeks. The Queen bade him to sit down and asked how he was feeling. 'Not too bad,' he replied.

Ten days later, on 28 May 1972, Edward VIII, the man who renounced a throne and an empire for love, died during the night. According to his valet, Sydney Johnson, just before he died, the Duke, who had dismissed his mother as 'a hard woman' to Prince Charles, poignantly uttered four words, 'Mama, Mama, Mama, Mama'.

As with the death of Diana, a quarter of a century later, the Queen had the dilemma of how to treat a 'former' member of the royal family. Her then private secretary, Martin Charteris, recalled, 'He had been a threat. The Queen wanted to play things down.'

Although the widowed Duchess stayed at Buckingham Palace prior to the funeral, 'The Queen didn't want to have much to do with Wallis', remembered one member of the household. 'A stiff and awkward' dinner was given in the Chinese Room rather than in the monarch's private suite. 'There was certainly no outpouring of love between the Queen and the Duchess of Windsor, or vice versa.'

There may have been no love lost between them, but at the Duke's funeral a few days later, the Queen sat next to a heavily sedated Wallis and reassured the clearly bewildered old lady. Clarissa Eden, wife of the former prime minister, Anthony Eden, noted Elizabeth 'showed a motherly and nanny-like tenderness and kept putting her hand on the Duchess's arm and glove'.

The Duchess would live on for another fourteen years. For the last ten, she remained bedridden at their Paris mansion in the Bois de Bologne, a pathetic figure, fed intravenously and zealously guarded by her formidable lawyer, Maître Suzanne Blum.

In April 1986, she died in her 90th year and, following the Duke's wishes, her funeral also took place at St George's Chapel, Windsor, and was attended by all the senior royals including the Princess of Wales. Afterwards, her body was taken to the Royal Burial Ground, where she lies beside the Duke and near to his brothers, the Dukes of Kent and Gloucester, and their wives.

During the short interment ceremony, the Queen was seen to momentarily break down and weep. Perhaps she was thinking, had it not been for this much vilified woman who had captured the heart of a king, how very different her own life may have been.

66

TECHNO-QUEEN

One of the few benefits of lockdown for the Queen was that she was able to 'meet' people from all walks of life from the comfort of her own study using video conferencing. It's a far cry from 5 December 1958 when the Queen launched trunk dialling by telephone. She travelled to the Bristol Telephone Exchange and dialled the Lord Provost of Edinburgh, more than 300 miles (482km) away.

When it comes to advances in technology, and latterly social media, the Queen and her household have moved with the times.

1976: The Queen sent her first email from an army base.

2001: Prince Andrew bought his mother a Siemens C35i phone when she was 75 and he stored the family's numbers in it for her.

2003: She texted Prince Harry after the 2003 Rugby World Cup and asked him to pass on her congratulations to the England team. Two years later, she texted granddaughter Zara Phillips after she won the European three-day eventing championship.

2005: She told Bill Gates, co-founder of the Microsoft Corporation, that she still hadn't got a computer, although Prince Philip had had one for twenty years. Also in 2005, Prince William bought her a 6-gigabyte mini iPod and reportedly stored *Last Night of the Proms* on it for her.

2007: The Queen met *Vanity Fair* editor Elizabeth Saltzman at a reception for the Household Cavalry and revealed she had an email address. An astonished Saltzman blurted out, 'Good Lord, you use email!' to which the Queen replied, 'Oh yes, but I don't actually write them – I dictate them all, of course.'
Dec 2007: The royal household put a Royal Channel on YouTube. Beforehand, she asked her granddaughters Beatrice and Eugenie to explain the whole concept to her.

October 2008: The Queen visited Google HQ in London and met some fellow members of the YouTube community, including someone with the user name 'Geriatric1927'.

November 2008: The Queen and Duke visited the headquarters of Vodafone near Newbury, Berkshire, to see the latest developments in mobile phone technology. During the visit, they witnessed a video link-up between Vodafone employees in Newbury and Mumbai, India. A Palace spokesperson said, 'The Queen likes to embrace new technology and change.'

2009: The Queen's official gift from Barack Obama and his wife, Michelle, was an MP3 player featuring footage of her 2007 visit to the United States, as well as numerous Broadway songs, and came with a songbook for the *King and I* signed by composer Richard Rodgers.

2016: She admitted her grandchildren help her with technology and, like many of her generation, lamented the amount of time they spent on their phones. The Queen was speaking to Barbara Wilkins, 82, who runs eight preschools, at a Buckingham Palace garden party. 'The Queen was talking to me about young children and asked me if they had changed a lot,' said Ms Wilkins, adding:

> She didn't say exactly what her grandchildren did for her but she did say she gets them to help her out and to do things for her … but she didn't like them to be on their phones and computers all the time. She says they need social skills. She was like any other grandmother really.

July 2020: The Queen took part in her first public video call, during lockdown to support the nation's carers, with the Princess Royal joining in the conversation. Anne is shown helping her mother to get used to the Zoom call. The Princess is heard saying, 'Can you see everybody? You should have six people on your screen.'
The Queen replies, 'Yes, well I can see four anyway.'
To which Anne replies, 'Actually, you don't need me. You know what I look like!'

67

MY HUSBAND AND I

Theirs was the longest royal marriage in British history. As we have seen, Elizabeth fell in love with her dashing, distant cousin, Prince Philip of Greece as long ago as 1939. She overcame opposition from her family, their friends and some in the royal household, who objected to Philip as a maverick and an outsider. She, who had never rebelled in her life, held firm and resolutely stood by her man. He, in turn, gave up a promising career in the Royal Navy and, after Elizabeth succeeded to the throne in 1952, gave sixty-five years of constant service to queen and country.

Their love was a slow-burning one that had developed through letter writing over six years of wartime separation, and then more frequent meetings as the conflict subsided and Philip returned from sea. What he lacked was a home and the stability of family life. What she needed was stimulation, a link with the outside world, someone to broaden her horizons and to give her a glimpse of life outside the rarefied atmosphere of court life.

When their relationship finally blossomed during the summer of 1946, the couple gave few clues away, even to those close to them. Peter Ashmore, the King's equerry, recalled Philip's three-week stay at Balmoral, when the couple came to what Philip called 'an understanding'. Ashmore noted, 'They certainly did not drool over each other ... They scarcely held hands.' It was hardly a surprise, since Philip had never been shown much affection from his parents.

Mike Parker recalled trying to encourage Philip to show some kind of public affection to his wife. 'He doesn't wear his heart on his sleeve', Parker commented in a 1992 interview:

The newly created Duke and Duchess of Edinburgh on honeymoon at Broadlands, the Mountbatten family estate in Hampshire. For their diamond wedding anniversary in 2007 the couple would recreate the shot in the same setting and with the Queen wearing the same sapphire chrysanthemum brooch. (© PA Images/Alamy)

I always wanted to see him put his arms around the Queen and show her how much he adored her. What you'd do for any wife. But he always sort of stood to attention. I mentioned it to him a couple of times. But he just gave me a hell of a look.

Love and marriage did help both of them to evolve. Elizabeth was emotionally controlled and the fact he wasn't all over her was something she quite liked. What Philip gave her was excitement and a huge contrast with the deferential royal household and those chinless aristocrats who had followed the traditional Eton College, Guards officer path.

Philip's childhood traumas had given him almost impenetrable defence barriers. He was unable to cope with intimacy and warmth, but as Lady Mountbatten reflected, 'Philip had a capacity for love which was waiting to be unlocked and Elizabeth unlocked it.' His passion was clear in a letter to his new mother-in-law, written shortly after the wedding, 'Cherish Lilibet? I wonder if that word is enough to express what is in me?'

All this changed with the death of the King on 6 February 1952. Within twelve months, Philip had to cope with leaving the navy, being ostracised by courtiers and politicians who would only deal with the young Queen and the almighty snub of not being able to pass on his Mountbatten surname to his children.

Lady Mountbatten's husband John Brabourne noticed that following his marriage Philip's 'life changed completely. He gave up everything.' His strategy henceforth was to carve a niche for himself. He became obsessed, in his own words, with making 'a sensible contribution'. In the decades ahead, he would take on almost 800 patronages and very much ran the private estates of Balmoral and Sandringham as well as being Ranger of Windsor Great Park. Elizabeth also ensured that while she was head of the country, he was head of the family, making key decisions about the children's futures. The Queen grew resigned to his determination to excel in his own areas, joking in their late forties, 'I gave up trying to stop him years ago.'

Philip's frustration with his subordinate role and his annoyance that, in the early days of her reign, his dutiful wife slavishly followed the wishes of the Palace old guard and Winston Churchill, led him to occasional bursts of temper. These were witnessed by courtiers, friends and relations. 'He could be brutal,' recalled a former member of staff who heard him berate the Queen with 'Don't talk such rubbish!' or 'You're completely wrong!'

Margaret Rhodes recalled Philip's awkward habit of jumping down people's throats. 'He was like that with the Queen. He'd say, 'why the bloody hell?' 'what the bloody hell?' I think she did find it disconcerting.'

Philip's uncle, Earl Mountbatten, who liked to think of himself as Elizabeth's knight in shining armour, also witnessed a Philip outburst against his wife. He was a back-seat passenger when Philip was driving the three of them around Cowdrey Park at breakneck speed. As he approached each bend at full throttle the Queen kept giving a sharp intake of breath. Philip shouted, 'If you do that once more, I'll put you out of the car!' When they were safely on terra firma, Mountbatten asked Elizabeth why she let his nephew talk to her like that. 'But you heard what he said,' explained the Queen, 'And he meant it.' Lady Pamela Hicks later commented to the author, laughingly, 'My father couldn't believe what he'd heard.'

Deep down, the Prince was aware he could occasionally make hurtful comments. To a family friend, he once made the revealing comment, 'I don't seem able to say nice things to people, though I'd like to. Why is that?'

In the early days, the Queen, aware of the huge sacrifice Philip had made, tolerated his outbursts. After all, he had not only given up a promising naval career but also turned his back on a life lived without press intrusion and the restrictions of Court life. 'She would clam up and wouldn't fight back,' recalled a close friend. 'It was very much like that in the first ten or fifteen years of their married life.'

What he did give the Queen, right from the beginning, was his total support. Mike Parker recalled, 'He told me the first day he offered me a job, that his job, first, second and last, was never to let her down.'

The Duke always knew that, unlike her mother, the Queen was not a natural performer in public, and on hundreds of walkabouts while Elizabeth made polite chitchat with the crowds, it was Philip who always bantered with them. When he spotted a small child clutching flowers for the monarch, he often lifted the youngster over the crush barriers himself and direct them to the Queen. He was known to shout, 'Back off!' (and other four-letter instructions) to photographers getting too close to her and he eased tension with the odd joke or two.

In private, he was notably deferential to the Queen. Guests at Balmoral Castle noted how he poured a drink for the Queen, handing it to her with a 'Here you are, darling'. Once he was unavoidably detained and arrived for dinner after her. An equerry was astonished to see him formally bow and apologise, 'I'm very sorry I'm late.'

The artist Michael Noakes noticed the Duke would also step in if he thought the Queen was flagging slightly. He said, 'Prince Philip would latch on to this and take over and he would say that he would have people laughing in 15 seconds.'

The arrival of Elizabeth and Philip's 'second family' – Andrew in 1960 and Edward in 1964 – heralded a new phase in the marriage. The Queen was now a decade into her role as head of state. She was more confident in her approach to dealing with ministers and private secretaries, and the authoritarian Alan Lascelles and Winston Churchill had long since left office.

On 8 February 1960, eleven days before the birth of Prince Andrew, the Queen issued an Order-in-Council stating that she and her family would be known as the House of Windsor but that her descendants would take the name Mountbatten-Windsor. It corrected what Philip had felt to be the huge personal snub from eight years before, when she confirmed she and her descendants would be known as the House of Windsor, thereby stopping Philip from giving his surname to his own children and eventual grandchildren. Prime Minister Harold Macmillan noted, 'The Queen only wishes (properly enough) to do something to please her husband – with whom she is desperately in love.' Deeply suspicious of Philip and his uncle, the PM added, 'What upsets me … is the Prince's almost brutal attitude to the Queen over all this.' He added cryptically, 'I shall never forget what she said to me that Sunday night at Sandringham.'

Philip himself inadvertently gave a clue to their intimacy when he fact-checked a manuscript by biographer Tim Heald. The author wrote, 'It was generally known that at the Palace the royal couple had separate bedrooms.' In the margin the Prince scrawled, 'wrongly'.

A surprisingly frank admission from one of Earl Mountbatten's household came to light when reported in the *Daily Mail* in 2016. Chief Petty Officer William Evans recalled the Queen, then in her mid-thirties, screaming with laughter and shouting, 'Stop it! Philip, stop it, stop it, stop it!' as Philip ran after her, pinching her bottom repeatedly and growling, 'Get up there, girl, get up there!'

By then, the Queen was beginning to answer her husband back more. Former private secretary Martin Charteris later commented, 'Prince Philip is the only man in the world who treats the Queen simply as another human being. And, of course, it's not unknown for the Queen to tell Prince Philip to shut up. Because she's the Queen, that's not something she can easily say to anybody else.'

As with many couples, they agreed on the big things but squabbled on the minor ones. One former courtier told biographer Graham Turner, 'He and the Queen have phenomenal rows' but they soon blow over, 'There's a terrific mutual tongue-lashing and then they end up the best of friends.'

In the tight-knit Buckingham Palace environment, some of these rows inevitably happened in front of members of the household. Martin Charteris recalled one on the Royal Yacht *Britannia* when the Queen declared, 'I'm not going to come out of my cabin until he's in a better temper. I'm going to sit here on my bed until he's better.'

On other occasions, her technique was to throw up a smoke-screen when he was in a mood. By changing the subject or talking in riddles, she confused him and threw him off guard, as he preferred straightforward arguing to such a cryptic approach.

Among those they trust, the Queen was often able to poke fun at her husband, whether he was there or not. Susan Crosland, wife of Foreign Secretary Anthony Crosland, later wrote about accompanying the Queen and Duke on the royal yacht during their 1976 state visit to the United States. *Britannia* was caught in a storm off the American coast and the Queen joked, 'I have *never* seen so many grey and grim faces round a dinner table. Philip was not at all well.' She paused, before adding, 'I'm glad to say', and started giggling. Susan Crosland realised, 'I'd forgotten her consort is an Admiral of the Fleet.'

In November 2017 they marked their platinum wedding anniversary. The same year, the Duke retired from public duties and based himself at Wood Farm on the Sandringham Estate, while the Queen carried on her usual round of engagements. Philip once said the secret of a happy married life was for each partner to pursue their own interests. Having said that, they remained a rock-solid team until the end and, as Lady Pamela Hicks commented, 'What is so lovely is that they are still so much in love with each other.'

The Queen lit up when he was around, when he walked into a room or when he paid her a compliment. Once, her dress designer, the late Ian Thomas, was making some adjustments to the hemline of her dress when Philip happened to walk past the open door and he said, 'Hmm, nice dress.' Thomas said the Queen 'flushed scarlet' at the compliment. They never completely softened with old age. 'They are not a sweet "Darby and Joan",' says Lady Pamela, 'They're both *very* strong characters.'

In the two decades since the deaths of her mother and sister in the spring of 2002, Elizabeth was to rely on him even more as the touchstone for the values she grew up with: duty, self-sacrifice, service to Queen and country. They spoke every day on the telephone from wherever they happened to be. During the lockdown spring of 2020, Philip left Wood Farm and joined the Queen at Windsor and over the summer at Balmoral. It was the longest the two had been together, apart from their early tours and their time in Malta as a young naval couple, and was no doubt a consolation to her following his death just twelve months later.

Neither of them was ever comfortable wearing their hearts on their sleeves but on the day they celebrated their Golden Wedding in November 1997, the Queen paid a rare public tribute to her husband:

> He is someone who doesn't take easily to compliments but he has, quite simply, been my strength and stay all these years, and I, and his whole family, and this and many other countries, owe him a debt greater than he would ever claim, or we shall ever know.

The Queen paid a more tangible tribute to her husband to mark his 90th birthday. She gave him the title of Lord High Admiral, a position only ever held by the sovereign. For the man who had given up his own promising career to help support her for the rest of his life, it was a touching gesture and one that apparently moved him close to tears.

It was clear that the little girl who had fallen in love with her naval cadet cousin, all those years before, had chosen wisely.

68

ANNI HORRIBILES

'1992 is not a year on which I shall look back with undiluted pleasure' was the Queen's understated reaction to what should have been, for her, a joyous fortieth anniversary year as monarch. Speaking at a luncheon at London's Guildhall in the November of that year, she added, 'In the words of one of my more sympathetic correspondents, it has turned out to be an *annus horribilis*.'

The 'sympathetic correspondent' was her former assistant private secretary, Sir Edward Ford. The use of the Latin phrase, meaning 'terrible year', is thought to have been an ironic adaptation of '*annus mirabilis*' – the title of a poem by John Dryden – meaning 'The Year of Wonders'.

There was no sign of anything '*horribilis*' at the dawn of 1992. The main royal story in the headlines was of the new landmark documentary, *Elizabeth R*, which had, like its 1969 predecessor, *Royal Family*, filmed members of the House of Windsor over twelve months. This time, the focus was very much on the work of the monarch herself, partly to redress the balance of the tabloid media's obsession with the lives of the younger royals.

At the end of the year, royal commentators looked back through their tapes to see if there had been any clues as to what was to unfold in coming months. Tellingly, the Queen, in a voice-over for the programme, suggested the next generation sometimes found the royal round quite a challenge. 'I think that this is what the younger members find difficult – the regimented side,' she said.

One of the most criticised 'younger members' of the family was Sarah, Duchess of York. In January 1992, she once more hit the headlines when photos of her were taken on holiday in Morocco with Texan businessman Steve Wyatt, and more crucially, without her husband. Prince Andrew was said to be furious and, on 19 March, it was announced that the Yorks would separate less than six years after they had married in Westminster Abbey. An off-the-record Palace briefing resulted in a BBC report that 'the knives are out for Fergie'.

There had been rumours for several years that the marriage of Charles and Diana was far from harmonious. In June 1992, the publication of Andrew Morton's biography *Diana: Her True Story* revealed Charles's relationship with Camilla Parker Bowles, Diana's struggles with bulimia and her attempt at suicide.

It was difficult to imagine the summer could get any worse for the Queen. However, on 20 August, shocking photos of the Duchess of York topless and being kissed on her feet by her friend and 'financial advisor' John Bryan were published in the *Daily Mirror*. In February 1993, Sir Angus Ogilvy, Princess Alexandra's husband, told Woodrow Wyatt over dinner that when the Queen saw the papers first thing in the morning, she spread them all around the breakfast table so Fergie had no choice but to see them when she came down to eat. Ogilvy claimed the Queen was 'distressed', and Sarah herself admitted the monarch was 'furious' and she felt obliged to beat a hasty retreat to London by the next flight. One senior courtier, who was part of the Balmoral house party, recalled, 'The Queen was grey and ashen and completely flat. She looked so awful, I felt like crying.'

Another personal blow for the Queen was the massive fire at Windsor Castle, which broke out on 20 November, the forty-fifth anniversary of Her Majesty's wedding. The blaze began at 11.33 a.m. in the Private Chapel in the north-east wing, when a powerful spotlight was left switched on too near a curtain. Flames quickly swept through the neighbouring Brunswick Tower and St George's Hall. The structural damage was estimated at £36.5 million.

Sympathy was felt four days after the fire when the Queen, clearly looking tired and suffering from a heavy cold, made the '*annus horribilis*' speech at the Guildhall. In a voice hoarse from the effects of her cold and the smoke she had ingested from the Windsor fire, Her Majesty reflected on the events of 1992. 'I sometimes wonder how future generations will judge the events of this tumultuous year. I dare say that history will take a slightly more moderate view than that of some contemporary commentators.'

On 9 December, the prime minister announced to the House of Commons that the Prince and Princess of Wales were to separate.

The events of 1992 had an impact on the whole royal family. The Queen's cousin, Princess Alexandra, at the dinner with Woodrow Wyatt mentioned previously, nervously asked her host if he thought the monarchy would survive. 'They are all very rattled', he noted in his journal.

The following few years would continue to be a low point for the monarchy, with the argument over taxing the royal finances, the continuing 'war of the Waleses' and the tragic death in 1997 of the Princess of Wales. It would take a new millennium, rather than a new year, to fully restore the House of Windsor to its former popularity.

2021

Like the '*annus horribilis*' of 1992, the year 2021 began uneventfully for the Queen, with a quiet Christmas with Prince Philip at Windsor where they had mostly been shielding throughout the lockdown during the coronavirus pandemic. In the first week of January, they both received vaccinations administered by the household doctor.

On 17 February, the Duke was admitted to the King Edward VII Hospital, Marylebone, on the advice of his doctors. The statement issued by the Palace was reassuring.

The admission came after the Duke felt 'unwell', it was 'a precautionary measure' and he was expected to remain in hospital for a few days of 'observation and rest'.

Concern began to grow as 'a few days' stretched into a few weeks and at one point he was transferred to the Royal Brompton Hospital for treatment on his heart. The Duke left hospital on 16 March, looking frail and gaunt.

After his return from hospital, the Duke was never again seen in public. During his final few weeks, he became increasingly confined to his room overlooking the castle's East Terrace. He spent his days resting and was often asleep, though occasionally he was taken outside in a wheelchair to enjoy the spring sunshine.

In a family tribute screened in September, the Prince of Wales recalled speaking to his father on the eve of his death and telling him, 'We're talking about your birthday.'

Philip gave a typically blunt reply, 'Well, I've got to be alive for it, haven't I?'

Charles said, 'I knew you'd say that!'

The Prince had been well enough to see Princess Eugenie, who had taken her newborn son to meet his great-grandfather. 'I brought little August to come and meet him,' she revealed. 'I told him that we'd named him after him. [August Philip] It was such a lovely moment. We were very lucky to do that.'

Shortly after noon on 9 April 2021, a statement issued by the Palace declared:

It is with deep sorrow that Her Majesty The Queen has announced the death of her beloved husband, His Royal Highness The Prince Philip, Duke of Edinburgh. His Royal Highness passed away peacefully this morning at Windsor Castle.

The end came peacefully. The Duke had remained lucid until the day before his death when he began to noticeably deteriorate.

He died early on a Friday morning, just as he wished, in his own bed, with the Queen nearby and the minimum of fuss. He was just two months away from his 100th birthday.

As Sophie, Countess of Wessex, revealed to a well-wisher, 'It was so gentle. It was like someone took him by the hand and off he went. Very, very peaceful ...'

On the day of the Duke's funeral, there was a moving moment as his family were returning on foot to the state apartments, when William and Harry cast aside their recent differences and walked side by side and deep in conversation. It came just over a month after Harry and Meghan's astonishing interview with Oprah Winfrey, the most devastating knife in the back to the House of Windsor since Diana's *Panorama* exchange with Martin Bashir.

Happier times: along with William and Catherine, Harry represented the future of the monarchy when he appeared with the Queen on the Buckingham Palace balcony following the Diamond Jubilee Thanksgiving Service in 2012. (© Ian Lloyd)

Their public chat at Windsor was a temporary show of unity by the two brothers. Another would come in July when they met again for the unveiling of the statue of their mother in the private gardens outside Kensington Palace.

Since Harry and his wife Meghan opted to move to the United States, the two brothers have followed two very different paths. Their grandmother has been torn between her affection for Prince Harry, with whom she has always been close, and her need to maintain the monarchy's strength and relevance. Her close rapport with her grandson has been evident time and again in public. One only has to think of the footage of them side by side on a sofa recording the hilarious video message in response to one from Barack and Michelle Obama, promoting the Invictus Games.

In the couple's engagement interview Meghan referred to Harry's 'honour and respect for [the Queen] as a monarch' as well as 'the love that he has for her as a grandmother'.

As early as 2019, it was reported that when Harry announced he wanted to marry Meghan after less than a year dating, Prince William had cautioned him that things were moving too quickly, leaving Harry angry and hurt. Had she been consulted, the Queen herself would almost certainly have agreed with William's point of view. She had, after all, seen the marriages of Charles, Andrew and Anne end in divorce. The common denominator was that each HRH had only dated their partners for less than a year.

Royal protocol in the 1970s and 1980s meant that, during their courtships, the couples couldn't be seen to sleep under the same roof together, take part in royal family events until the engagement was announced, or undertake royal engagements before their betrothal. In other words, it was not clear until after they were married whether Diana Spencer, Sarah Ferguson or Mark Phillips could cope with life in the royal family.

Prince Edward broke the royal mould by dating Sophie Rhys-Jones for almost six years before they married, while William and

Catherine Middleton dated for even longer, having met at the University of St Andrews some eight years before they became engaged. During this time, Kate was able to live with William and to join in royal events, both public as well as private.

Harry and Meghan's situation was, of course, slightly different. When they met on a blind date in July 2016, she was a few weeks short of her 35th birthday and as the couple both wanted children, they couldn't afford to spend several years courting. There were also the problems of maintaining a relationship across the Atlantic Ocean, given they both had commitments – she in Canada and he in the UK. Finally, Harry had been longing for a relationship ever since splitting with his last girlfriend, Cressida Bonas, and he looked on enviously at his brother's close relationship with his wife and their growing family.

While Harry and Meghan may have alienated Charles, William and Kate with their comments and criticisms, they have been careful never to voice anything negative about the Queen, who is revered by many and beyond censure, even for an often-cynical media. Indeed, Meghan has gone out of her way to praise Harry's grandmother. In her incendiary interview with Oprah Winfrey, she revealed meeting the monarch for the first time was 'lovely and easy'. After going on to praise Harry's grandmother for having 'always been wonderful to me', she also revealed she will occasionally 'just pick up the phone and call the Queen just to check in'.

By the time of the Oprah interview, Harry and Meghan had 'checked in' in ways no one could have foreseen at the time of their engagement. Shortly before the wedding the couple were, some claim, very offhand with the Queen's dresser and trusted aide Angela Kelly over selecting the tiara Meghan would wear at the wedding. Angela produced a selection sanctioned by the monarch, but the bride-to-be is said to have wanted a different one. This wasn't allowed and Harry was reportedly furious. The Queen would always back Angela and she didn't give way.

It's difficult to imagine the Queen relishing every moment of the couple's wedding at St George's Chapel in May 2018. From having the Quire dotted with A-Listers, one or two of whom, like the Clooneys, were allegedly unsure why they'd been invited, to Bishop Michael Curry and his ceaseless sermon, it was not a usual royal wedding. Being a traditionalist, she may have raised an eyebrow at Meghan's pure white gown and virginally veiled arrival in the chapel. Nevertheless, she would no doubt have been impressed by the calm dignity of Doria Ragland, Meghan's mother, the sole representative from the bride's side, sitting opposite a Who's Who of the House of Windsor.

What would have saddened the Queen most about the newly ennobled Duke and Duchess of Sussex was their announcement in January 2020 that they intended to step back from their roles as working royals after spending Christmas in Canada. Harry later denied that he had 'blindsided' his grandmother with the bombshell statement about moving away from royal life, and said he believed the report probably could have come from 'within the institution'.

The Queen called a family meeting at Sandringham attended by Charles, William and Harry. Prince Philip, no doubt disillusioned with his grandson's actions, was seen driving away shortly before Harry arrived and William refused to attend the lunch, only the meeting.

The Queen was said to be keen for a swift resolution to the crisis and a few days later issued a statement which was a master stroke in negotiation, managing to be both affectionate and uncompromising. She emphasised, 'Harry, Meghan and Archie will always be much-loved members of my family', and said she was 'particularly proud of how Meghan has so quickly become one of the family'. Having reassured the couple of her continued support and affection, the accompanying statement 'from Buckingham Palace' cut to the chase and made it clear the couple would stand back from royal duties, including military appointments, would not be allowed to use their HRH titles and would repay the Sovereign Grant expenditure for the restoration of Frogmore Cottage (their home at Windsor). In addition, it was made clear that the cost of their security would not be funded by the public purse.

The Queen also said that the agreement would be reviewed after a year, implying it could be amended or even cancelled if the couple returned to the UK and undertook full-time royal duties. In the event, the Sussexes confirmed they would be staying on in the United States, and they and the Palace issued statements on 19 February 2021 announcing the news.

The Queen made it clear Harry and Meghan would not be able to hold royal patronages, and Harry's military appointments would also have to be returned. It concluded, 'While all are saddened by their decision, the Duke and Duchess remain much-loved members of the family.' The Sussexes statement confirmed their decision and ended with a dig at the royal family, 'We can all live a life of service. Service is universal.'

In making both statements, the Queen had to walk a tightrope: on the one hand, trying not to alienate the very thin-skinned Harry and Meghan in the hope they wouldn't break off all links with the family and become a rival court in the way the Duke and Duchess of Windsor had; on the other, she had, once again, to ensure the survival of the monarchy by removing the Prince's royal patronages, military positions, money from the Crown and security, which, had they remained would have caused widespread criticism from taxpayers and the media.

Then, in early March 2021 came the Oprah Winfrey interview watched live by over 17 million people in the United States and by 12.4 million, about a fifth of the population, in the UK. There was much criticism in the press about the timing of the broadcast, with the Duke of Edinburgh so ill in hospital, though the scheduling would have been out of the hands of the Sussexes.

Their bombshell revelations ranged from Meghan's suicidal thoughts – 'I just didn't want to live any more' – to an unnamed member of the royal family raising 'concerns and conversations about how dark their baby's skin might be when he's born'.

What would have also wounded the Queen was Harry's insistence that he felt 'really let down' by his father, 'because he's been through something similar, he knows what pain feels like, [and] Archie's his grandson'.

The Cambridges also came in for a bruising. Harry repeated an earlier assertion that he and William were 'on different paths'. Meghan put a different spin on the rumour that she had made Kate cry during a fitting for Charlotte's bridesmaid's dress. She insisted it was the other way round and that she had cried and her sister-in-law 'owned it and apologised' and sent flowers.

Ironically, Harry said he had been 'trapped within the system, like the rest of my family are', although his critics could point out that he himself is also 'trapped within the system', since the main reason the Sussexes are so high profile in the United States is due to the fact that he is Elizabeth II's grandson and the child of the still much-adored Diana.

In another masterly response, the Palace statement included 'recollections may vary', which became the headline in several of the following day's newspapers. They also highlighted the Queen's insistence that allegations of racism by the couple would be 'dealt with personally by the family', which was clearly a slap on the wrist for the Sussexes' very public airing of dirty linen.

Harry and Meghan continued to make headlines throughout the summer of 2021. Discussing his mental health on the podcast *Armchair Expert* with Dax Shepard, Prince Harry suggested Charles's parenting left him with 'genetic pain and suffering'.

Then, on 4 June, Meghan gave birth to a daughter at the Santa Barbara Cottage Hospital in California. Two days later, the couple announced they were naming their second born

Lilibet after the Queen, which raised some eyebrows as it is not the monarch's actual name but the private one she was given by her family as a baby when she was unable to pronounce Elizabeth. A spokesperson for the Sussexes quashed rumours that the Queen wasn't consulted about the name of her great-grandchild by stating:

> The Duke spoke with his family in advance of the announcement – in fact his grandmother was the first family member he called. During that conversation, he shared their hope of naming their daughter Lilibet in her honour. Had she not been supportive, they would not have used the name.

It was another case of 'recollections may vary', and the BBC reported that an unnamed member of the household told the corporation that the Queen hadn't been consulted.

A final blow to the Queen over the summer of 2021 was the news that Penguin Random House are set to publish Prince Harry's memoirs in the autumn of 2022. He is expected to focus on his royal service, his time in the military and his marriage, but it is unclear how much detail will be given over to family matters that his great-grandmother would prefer to remain private. Ominously, it has been suggested that it is a multi-volume deal, and one book will only be published when the Queen's reign is over. The Queen and his UK family will no doubt be hoping he keeps to his word and produces 'a first-hand account of my life that's accurate and wholly truthful'.

Another family crisis contributing to the second '*annus horribilis*' was the continuing fallout from Prince Andrew's association with the convicted paedophile Jeffrey Epstein.

In August 2021, a civil lawsuit was filed against the Prince by Virginia Roberts Giuffre, who alleged that she had been trafficked to and forced to have sex with the Duke of York three times when she was 17. The lawsuit accused him of 'sexual assault and intentional infliction of emotional distress', and sought unspecified damages.

Following his car-crash interview with the BBC's Emily Maitlis, which resulted in enormous criticism from press and public alike, Andrew had no choice but to voluntarily resign from royal duties. As with Harry and 'Megxit', it is presumed Charles and William were involved in the damage-limitation exercise. In a personal statement, the Duke of York said that he had asked for permission from the Queen to 'step back from public duties for the foreseeable future', as his association with Epstein had become a 'major disruption' to his family as well as the many organisations he was patron or president of. In the immediate aftermath of the statement, many of these organisations dropped their association with the Prince.

Just as the Queen acted decisively in stripping Prince Harry of his military appointments and insisting that neither he nor his wife should use the style of 'HRH' as they no longer carry out public duties, so too the Queen ended Andrew's military affiliations and patronages, and made it clear that he, like his nephew, could no longer be referred to as 'HRH' in any official capacity.

The Andrew case has no doubt been awkward for the Queen. Once again, as the head of The Firm, her overriding concern is to preserve as much dignity and relevance for the monarchy, going into the next reign, as is possible. On the other hand, as a mother, it must concern her that her second son is in such a no-win situation.

The Queen has always been close to her second son. In a surviving letter to her second cousin, Lady Mary Cambridge, she described the newborn Prince as 'adorable' and she lavished more time and attention on her two younger sons than she had been able to on Charles and Anne, a decade earlier. As with Harry, she was proud he readily agreed to front-line service, serving in the Falklands conflict, flying decoy helicopters to draw the fire of Argentine Exocet missiles – probably his finest hour.

With the retirement of the Duke of Edinburgh in 2017, Andrew occasionally escorted the Queen to royal events. In March 2019, he was by her side when she arrived at Westminster Abbey for that year's Commonwealth Day service. A more telling demonstration came just two months after the *Newsnight* interview when the Prince accompanied his mother to Sunday worship at St Mary's Church, Hillington, in Norfolk, during her stay at Sandringham.

In August 2021, when Ms Giuffre's lawyers tried to serve legal documents to the Prince, he made it virtually impossible by staying with the Queen on the secluded Balmoral Estate, giving rise to criticism that he was hiding behind his mother's skirt, so to speak. Meanwhile, she instructed her solicitors to warn British media outlets not to take or publish paparazzi photos of the royals or their guests on the estate, though photos of an irate-looking Andrew did appear.

Later that summer, it was reported that the Queen would privately fund Andrew's defence case against the allegations of sexual abuse, although most of it was paid by Andrew from the sale of his £17 million Swiss ski chalet.

The Queen's unconditional affection for her second son and her solidarity for him is understandable. While it must have been a relief to her when, in February 2022, the Prince made an out-of-court settlement with Virginia Giuffre, the fact that he knowingly associated himself with a convicted paedophile has caused irreparable damage to his reputation and that of the monarchy. That would undoubtedly have broken the Queen's heart and will cast a blight on the final phase of her long reign.

69

ON BEING QUEEN, IN HER OWN WORDS

On Being a Monarch …

'It's a question of maturing into something that one's got used to doing, and accepting the fact that here you are and it's your fate; because I think that continuity is very important. It is a job for life.'

It's Not a 9–5 Job …

'Most people have a job and then they go home and in this existence the job and the life go on together because you can't really divide it up. The boxes and communications just keep on coming and of course with modern communications they come even quicker.'

On How She Is Briefed …

'Audiences are my way of meeting people without anyone else listening, and that gives one a very broad picture of what is actually going on either in the government or the civil service.'

On the Many Letters She Receives …

'But I've always had this feeling that letters are written to *me*, and I want to see what people want to write to me. I think in a way one feels that there is a sort of "the buck stops here" so to speak.'

The Importance of 'Away Days' ...

'I have to be seen to be believed ...'

On State Visits ...

'I think, in a way, it's quite an old-fashioned idea that you do put out the red carpet for a guest. I think people don't really realise this, you know. I do tell the guests we do put on our best clothes and everybody dresses up and that the best china, and the glass, and the gold plate comes out. But sometimes it's worth explaining that we put it on especially – and that we don't actually live like this all the time.'

Always Go for Closed Rather than Open Questions ...

'One mustn't have a long conversation obviously because you'd never finish. The question you ask is the one you hope is going to get the answer you want. This doesn't always happen!'

On Her Prime Ministers ...

'I have had quite a lot of prime ministers, starting with Winston and some stay longer than others. They unburden themselves or they tell me what's going on or if they have any problems.'

A Job for Life ...

'If you live this sort of life, which people don't very much, you live very much by tradition and continuity. I find that's one of the sad things – that people don't take on jobs for life. They try different things all the time.'

On Leadership ...

'I know of no single formula for success, but over the years I have observed that some attributes of leadership are universal and are often about finding ways of encouraging people to combine their efforts, their talents, their insights, their enthusiasm and their inspiration to work together.'

70

A CREDIT TO THE NATION

Elizabeth II has been the most consistent of monarchs. Although often compared to Queen Victoria for having the same grave dignity, she has never mirrored that monarch's youthful impetuosity or her later protracted withdrawal from public life following the death of the Prince Consort. The present Queen set out to emulate her father, the steadfast and virtuous George VI. Although only 25 when she succeeded him as monarch, she immediately adapted to a life of unending duty with a rigid self-discipline that has never deserted her. If a time traveller observing the Queen at work in her mid-90s were to be transported back to the Britain of 1952, they would find the young Elizabeth performing engagements, from attending the

Happy and glorious: the Queen attends a service for the Order of the Bath at Westminster Abbey in May 2014. She is wearing 'Granny's Tiara', a wedding present to her from Queen Mary, who was given it as a gift for her own wedding in 1893. (© Ian Lloyd)

Maundy Service to holding a Buckingham Palace investiture, with the same professionalism.

At the same time, she has adapted the monarchy in the face of criticism, whether it was from Lord Altrincham and the like in the late 1950s, or from the press and public in the aftermath of the death of Diana. To become a less-remote figure, she embraced modern technological developments in communication, from television through to social media. She took part in landmark documentaries and agreed to the walkabout, both of which brought her closer to the people.

While the Princess of Wales made headlines for embracing a variety of worthy causes, from AIDS to landmines, it is often overlooked that the Queen also highlighted organisations supporting the less fortunate. In 1956, she visited a leper colony in Nigeria and on New Year's Eve 1999, she visited the Crisis cold weather shelter for the homeless in Southwark before opening the Millennium Dome.

What makes her contribution to national life all the more creditable is that she isn't a touchy-feely person or a natural performer like her mother was. Yet, she has never shirked her duty.

As a photographer in the 1980s, the author once followed her around an exhibition promoting the WI. She looked at many of the stalls and displays with polite interest and the occasional frown. Then, in the final section, she met a choir in fancy dress portraying highwaymen and she roared with laughter and remained wreathed in smiles for the rest of her visit. What wouldn't have escaped her notice was the illuminated 'EXIT' sign at the end of the final corridor. As the press officer organising the visit said, 'She's home and dry.' Many of us that day realised what a challenge an event like that, where she was the centre of attention and watched by hundreds of onlookers, could be for a fundamentally shy person.

So, how has the Queen been able to find the strength to continue this inexorable programme of duties, year in, year out? According to Margaret Rhodes, 'She has the ability to compartmentalise her life, and gives everything her full attention at the time, whether it's a public engagement or discussing with her groom what university accommodation would suit his child.'

Hers has been a job for life, a public role for almost three-quarters of a century. Many of her European royal counterparts have abdicated – and Benedict XVI proved that even popes can retire – but for Elizabeth II, it is anathema. When her own primate, George Carey, 103rd Archbishop of Canterbury, told her he was planning to step down in 2003, she replied, 'Oh that's something I can't do. I am going to carry on to the end.'

BIBLIOGRAPHY

Books

Berg, A. Scott, *Lindbergh* (Berkley Books, 1988).

Blair, Tony, *A Journey: My Political Life* (Alfred A. Knopf, 2010).

Bloch, Michael, *The Secret File of the Duke of Windsor* (Bantam Press, 1988).

Blunt, Wilfrid, *Married to a Single Life: An Autobiography 1901–1938* (Michael Russell, 1983).

Boothroyd, Basil, *Prince Philip: An Informal Biography* (McCall, 1971).

Bradford, Sarah, *George VI* (Weidenfeld & Nicolson, 1989).

Bradford, Sarah, *Elizabeth* (William Heinemann, 1996).

Bradford, Sarah, *Diana* (Viking, 2006).

Brandreth, Gyles, *Philip & Elizabeth: Portrait of a Marriage* (Century, 2004).

Brown, Craig, *The Book of Royal Lists* (Simon & Schuster, 1983).

Buckle, G.E., *The Letters of Queen Victoria: Series III, Vol III* (John Murray, 1932).

Castle, Barbara, *The Castle Diaries, 1964–70* (Weidenfeld & Nicolson, 1984).

Catterall, Peter (ed.), *The Macmillan Diaries, Vol. I: The Cabinet Years 1950–1957* (Macmillan, 2003).

Catterall, Peter (ed.), *The Macmillan Diaries, Vol II: Prime Minister and After: 1957–1966* (Macmillan, 2011).

Crawford, Marion, *The Little Princesses* (Duckworth, 1993).

Curtis, Sarah (ed.), *The Journals of Woodrow Wyatt: Volume One* (Macmillan, 1998).

Curtis, Sarah (ed.), *The Journals of Woodrow Wyatt: Volume Two* (Macmillan, 1999).

Curtis, Sarah (ed.), *The Journals of Woodrow Wyatt: Volume Three* (Macmillan, 2000).

Dean, John, *HRH Prince Philip, Duke of Edinburgh* (Robert Hale, 1954).

Dimbleby, Jonathan, *The Prince of Wales: A Biography* (Little, Brown and Company, 1994).

Duncan, Andrew, *The Reality of Monarchy* (Heinemann, 1970).

Eade, Philip, *Young Prince Philip: His Turbulent Early Life* (Harper Press, 2012).

Ellis, Jennifer (ed.), *Thatched With Gold: The Memoir of Mabell, Countess of Airlie* (Hutchinson, 1962).

Farrow, Mia, *What Falls Away: A Memoir* (Bantam Books, 1998).

Field, Leslie, *The Queen's Jewels* (Weidenfeld & Nicolson, 1987).

Forster, Margaret, *Daphne Du Maurier: The Secret Life of the Renowned Storyteller* (Doubleday, 1993).

George, Don, *Sweet Man: The Real Duke Ellington* (G.P. Putnam's Sons, 1981).

Goldsmith, Annabel, *Annabel: An Unconventional Life: The Memoirs of Lady Annabel Goldsmith* (Orion, 2004).

Hardman, Robert, *Queen of the World* (Century, 2018).

Harewood, Earl of, *The Tongs and the Bones* (Weidenfeld and Nicolson, 1981).

Heald, Tim, *The Duke: A Portrait of Prince Philip* (Hodder & Stoughton, 1991).

Heald, Tim, *Princess Margaret: A Life Unravelled* (Weidenfeld & Nicolson, 2007).

Hibbert, Christopher, *The Court of St James's* (Weidenfeld & Nicolson, 1979).

Higham, Charles and Roy Moseley, *Princess Merle: The Romantic Life of Merle Oberon* (Coward-McCann, 1983).

Hoey, Brian, *Anne, The Princess Royal* (Grafton, 1989).

Hoey, Brian, *Not in Front of the Corgis: Secrets of Life Behind the Royal Curtains* (Robson Press, 2011).

Howard, Alathea Fitzalan, *The Windsor Diaries: 1940–45* (Hodder & Stoughton, 2020).

James, Robert Rhodes, *Chips: The Diaries of Sir Henry Channon* (Penguin, 1970).

Jebb, Miles, *The Diaries of Cynthia Gladwyn* (Constable, 1995).

Knatchbull, Timothy, *From a Clear Blue Sky: Surviving the Mountbatten Bomb* (Hutchinson, 2009).

Lacey, Robert, *Majesty* (Hutchinson, 1977).

Lacey, Robert, *Royal: Her Majesty Queen Elizabeth II* (Little, Brown, 2002).

Lacey, Robert, *Battle of Brothers* (William Collins, 2020).

Lloyd, Ian, *The Duke: 100 Chapters in the Life of Prince Philip* (The History Press, 2021).

Longford, Elizabeth, *Elizabeth R: A Biography* (Weidenfeld and Nicolson, 1983).

Longford, Elizabeth (ed.), *The Oxford Book of Royal Anecdotes* (Oxford University Press, 1990).

Mayer, Catherine, *Born to Be King: Prince Charles on Planet Windsor* (Henry Holt & Co., 2015).

Menkes, Suzy, *The Royal Jewels* (Grafton Books, 1985).

Menkes, Suzy, *The Windsor Style* (Salem House Publishers, 1988).

Morgan, Janet, *Edwina Mountbatten: A Life of Her Own* (Fontana, 1992).

Parker, Eileen, *Step Aside For Royalty* (Bachman & Turner, 1982).

Paxman, Jeremy, *On Royalty* (Penguin, 2007).

Pimlott, Ben, *The Queen* (HarperCollins, 2001).

Rhodes, Margaret, *The Final Curtsey* (Umbria Press, 2001).

Rogers, Malcolm, *Elizabeth II: Portraits of Sixty Years* (National Portrait Gallery, 1986).

Shawcross, William, *Queen and Country* (McClelland & Stewart Inc., 2002).

Shawcross, William, *Queen Elizabeth, the Queen Mother: The Official Biography* (Macmillan, 2009).

Shew, Betty Spencer, *Royal Wedding* (MacDonald & Co., 1947).

Smith, Sally Beddell, *Elizabeth the Queen* (Random House, 2012).

Strober, Deborah and Gerald, *The Monarchy: An Oral History of Elizabeth II* (Hutchinson, 2002).

Tharoor, Shashi, (Arcade Publishing Inc., 2003).

Thatcher, Carol, *QE2: Forty Years Famous* (Simon & Schuster Ltd, 2007).

Townsend, Peter, *Time And Chance: An Autobiography* (Collins, 1978).

Turner, Graham, *Elizabeth: The Woman and the Queen* (Macmillan, 2002).
Vidal, Gore, *Palimpsest: A Memoir* (Random House, 1995).
Warwick, Christopher, *Princess Margaret: A Life of Contrasts* (Andre Deutsch, 2000).
Wheeler-Bennett, John W., *George VI: His Life & Reign* (St Martin's Press, 1958).
Whistler, Laurence, *The Laughter and the Urn: The Life of Rex Whistler* (Weidenfeld & Nicolson, 1985).
Windsor, The Duchess of, *The Heart has its Reasons* (David McKay Co. Inc., 1956).
York, Sarah, Duchess of, *My Story* (Simon & Schuster, 1996).
Yugoslavia, HM Queen Alexandra of, *Prince Philip: A Family Portrait* (Hodder & Stoughton, 1960).
Ziegler, Philip (ed.), *From Shore to Shore: The Final Years. The Diaries of Earl Mountbatten of Burma, 1953–1979* (Collins, 1989).
Ziegler, Philip, *King Edward VIII: The Official Biography* (Fontana, 1991).

Magazines

Mail on Sunday, 'The Royal Rich Report'.
Majesty Magazine.

Newspapers

Daily Express.
Daily Mail.
Daily Mirror.
Edinburgh Evening News.
New York Post.
Sunday Post.
The Telegraph.
The Times.
Yorkshire Post.

TV Documentaries

An Intimate Portrait of the Queen at 80, Andrew Marr, BBC (2006).
Anne: the Princess Royal at 70, ITV (2020).
Crawfie: The Royal Nanny Who Wouldn't Stay Mum, Channel 4 (2000).
Elizabeth R: A Year in the Life of the Queen, BBC (1992).
HRH the Princess Margaret: Memories of VE Day, BBC (1995).
Prince Philip: The Plot to Make a King, Channel 4 (2015).
The Duke: A Portrait of Prince Philip, ITV (2008).
The Queen's Coronation: Behind Palace Doors, Channel 4 (2008).
The Queen's Mother-in-Law, Channel 4 (2012).

INDEX

You may also enjoy ...

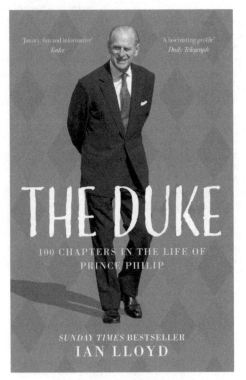

978 0 7509 9846 8

'A fascinating account of Prince Philip as seen from every conceivable angle. Ian Lloyd demonstrates that there is much we didn't know about this much-loved – and at times controversial – royal consort.'

Joe Little, *Majesty* magazine